CONTENTS

S0-BTC-793

CHAPTER 14   THE FAMILY   *421*

CHAPTER 15   PEERS, MEDIA, AND SCHOOLING   *455*

PREFACE

As you embark on the fascinating journey of studying the development of children and adolescents, it is our hope that this Study Guide will help you master the material in your text, *Child Development*, by Laura E. Berk. Our intention in preparing the Study Guide is to provide you with active practice in learning the content in your textbook and thought-provoking questions that help you clarify your own thinking. Each chapter in the Study Guide is organized into the following six sections.

CHAPTER SUMMARY

We begin with a brief summary of the material, mentioning major topics covered and general principles emphasized in text discussion. Each text chapter includes two additional summaries: an informal one at the beginning of the chapter, and a structured summary at the end of the chapter. Thus, the summary in the Study Guide will be your third review of the information covered in each chapter. It is intended to remind you of major points in the text before you embark on the remaining activities in the Guide.

LEARNING OBJECTIVES

We have organized the main points in each chapter into a series of objectives that indicate what you should be able to do once you have mastered the material. We suggest that you look over these objectives before you read each chapter. You may find it useful to take notes on information pertaining to objectives as you read. When you finish a chapter, try to answer the objectives in a few sentences or a short paragraph. Then check your answers against the text and revise your responses accordingly. Once you have completed this exercise, you will have generated your own review of chapter content. Because it is written in your own words, it should serve as an especially useful chapter overview that can be referred to when you prepare for examinations.

STUDY QUESTIONS

The main body of each chapter consists of study questions, organized according to major headings in the textbook, that assist you in identifying main points and grasping concepts and principles. Text pages on which answers can be found are indicated next to each entry. The study question section can be used in a number of different ways. You may find it helpful to answer each question as you read the chapter. Alternatively, try reading one or more sections and then testing yourself by answering the relevant study questions. Finally, use the study question section as a device to review for examinations. If you work through it methodically, your retention of chapter material will be greatly enhanced.

ASK YOURSELF . . .

In each chapter, critical thinking questions that appear at the end of each section of material in your textbook are listed, with space to answer each of them. Answering these questions will help you analyze important theoretical concepts and research findings. Many questions require you to apply what you have learned to problematic situations faced by parents, teachers, and children. In this way, they will help you think more deeply about the material and inspire new insights. Each question is page-referenced to chapter material that will help you formulate a response. Model answers to each question can be found on the text's website.

PUZZLES

To help you master the central vocabulary of the field, we have provided crossword puzzles that test your knowledge of important terms and concepts. Answers can be found at the back of the Study Guide. If you cannot think of the term that matches a clue in the puzzles, your knowledge of information related to the term may be insecure. Reread the material in the text chapter related to each item that you miss. Also, try a more demanding approach to term mastery: After you have completed each puzzle, cover the clues and write your own definitions of each term.

PRACTICE TESTS

Once you have thoroughly studied each chapter, find out how well you know the material by taking the 25-item multiple choice practice test. Then check your answers using the key at the back of the Study Guide. Each item is page-referenced to chapter content so you can look up answers to questions that you missed. If you answered more than a few items incorrectly, spend extra time rereading the chapter, writing responses to chapter objectives, and reviewing the study questions of this guide.

Now that you understand how the Study Guide is organized, you are ready to begin using it to master *Child Development*. We wish you a rewarding and enjoyable course of study.

JoDe Paladino
Laura E. Berk

CHAPTER 1
HISTORY, THEORY, AND APPLIED DIRECTIONS

BRIEF CHAPTER SUMMARY

Child development is the study of all aspects of human constancy and change from conception through adolescence. It is part of a larger discipline known as developmental psychology, or human development, which includes the entire lifespan. Child development is an interdisciplinary, scientific, and applied field of study. Researchers often divide the subject of development into three broad domains—physical, cognitive, and emotional and social—through five periods of development from conception through adolescence. Theories provide organizing frameworks that guide and give meaning to the scientific study of children. Major theories can be organized according to the stand that they take on three basic issues: (1) Is the course of development continuous or discontinuous? (2) Is there one general course of development that characterizes all children, or are there many possible courses? (3) Is development primarily determined by nature or nurture, and is it stable or open to change? Some theories, especially the more recent ones, take a balanced point of view and recognize the merits of both sides of these issues.

Contemporary theories of child development have roots extending far into the past. Those theories that are major forces in child development research vary in their focus on different domains of development, in their view of development, and in their strengths and weaknesses.

In recent years, the field of child development has become increasingly concerned with applying its vast knowledge base to the solution of pressing social problems. Public policy, laws, and government programs designed to improve current conditions are essential for protecting children's development. In addition, collaboration between researchers and communities in the design, implementation, and evaluation of policy-relevant interventions holds promising outcomes for the improvement of the well-being of children and their families.

LEARNING OBJECTIVES

After reading this chapter, you should be able to:

1.1   Explain the importance of the terms *interdisciplinary* and *applied* as they help to define the field of child development. (p. 4)

1.2   Cite major domains and periods of development that help make the study of human change more convenient and manageable. (pp. 5–6)

1.3 Explain the role of theories in understanding child development, and describe three basic issues on which major theories take a stand. (pp. 6–9)

1.4 Trace historical influences on modern theories of child development from medieval times through the early twentieth century. (pp. 11–14)

1.5 Describe the theoretical perspectives that influenced child development research in the mid-twentieth century, and cite the contributions and limitations of each. (pp. 16–22)

1.6 Describe five recent theoretical perspectives on child development, noting the contributions of major theorists. (pp. 22–31)

1.7 Describe the methods commonly used to study children, and cite the strengths and limitations of each. (p. 31)

1.8 Discuss factors that affect public policies serving children and families, noting their impact on the status of American children relative to children in other industrialized nations. (pp. 31–38)

STUDY QUESTIONS

1. Child development is the study of human constancy and change from
   _____ through _____. (p. 4)

2. Child development is part of a larger discipline known as _____
   psychology, which includes all of the changes we experience throughout the lifespan. (p. 4)

Child Development as a Scientific, Applied, and Interdisciplinary Field

1. Child development is an *interdisciplinary* field. Explain what this means. (p. 4)

   _____

   _____

   _____

Domains of Development

1. List and describe the three broad domains of development. (p. 5)

   A. _____

B. _____

C. _____

1. List the five periods of development used to segment the first two decades of life, noting the corresponding ages for the latter four. (pp. 5–6)

    A. _____

    B. _____

    Age Span: _____

    C. _____

    Age Span: _____

    D. _____

    Age Span: _____

    E. _____

    Age Span: _____

Basic Issues

1. What is a *theory*? (p. 6)

    _____

    _____

2. Cite two reasons that theories are important to the study of child development. (p. 6)

    A. _____

    B. _____

3. True or False: Theories differ from opinion and belief in that they are subject to scientific verification. (p. 6)

4. Match each theoretical approach with the appropriate description: (pp. 6–9)

_____ Considers development to be universal across children and across cultures	1. Multiple courses of development
_____ Views development as a process of gradually building on preexisting skills	2. Single course of development
_____ Regards the environment as the most important influence on development	3. Continuous
_____ Considers child development in light of distinct contexts	4. Discontinuous
_____ Views development as a progression through a series of qualitatively distinct stages	5. Nature
_____ Views heredity as the most important influence on development	6. Nurture

5. True or False: Most modern theories of development take a strong position on controversial issues such as the nature-nurture debate. (p. 9)

Biology and Environment: Resilient Children

1. What is *resiliency*? (p. 10)

_____

_____

2. Briefly list and describe three broad factors that appear to offer protection from the damaging effects of stressful life events. (p. 10)

A. _____

_____

B. _____

_____

C. _____

_____

Medieval Times

1. Explain the concept of *preformationism*. (p. 11)

   _____

   _____

The Reformation

1. True or False: Puritan doctrine stressed the innate goodness of all children. Briefly explain your response. (p. 11)

   _____

   _____

   _____

2. True or False: The Puritans placed a high value on the development of reasoning in children. (p. 11)

Philosophies of the Enlightenment

1. During the Enlightenment, the British philosopher John Locke regarded the child as a *tabula rasa,* which means _____. Briefly explain his view. (pp. 11–12)

   _____

   _____

   _____

2. Jean Jacques Rousseau, a French philosopher during the Enlightenment, introduced the notion of children as *noble savages*. Explain what he meant by this term. (p. 12)

   _____

   _____

   _____

3. Describe some of the key differences in the theories put forth by John Locke and Jean Jacques Rousseau. (p. 12)

   _____

_____

_____

Darwin: Forefather of Scientific Child Study

1. Describe Darwin's theory of evolution, making sure to cite the two related principles emphasized in his theory. (p. 12)

_____

_____

_____

_____

_____

Scientific Beginnings

1. What technique did scientists in the late nineteenth and early twentieth centuries use to develop the baby biographies, and what are the limitations of using this technique to study child development? (p. 13)

   Technique: _____

   _____

   _____

   Limitations: _____

   _____

   _____

   _____

2. Who is generally regarded as the founder of the child study movement? (p. 13)

   _____

3. The _____ *approach* to child development uses age-related averages to represent typical development. (p. 13)

4. Who constructed the first successful intelligence test? (p. 14)

   _____

5. Why did this test succeed, while previous efforts to create a useful intelligence test had failed? (p. 14)

_____

_____

6. A translated version of this test was developed for use with American children. What is the name of this instrument? (p. 14)

_____

7. True or False: James Mark Baldwin regarded nature and nurture as distinct, opposing forces, only one of which could control development. (p. 14)

From Research to Practice: Social Change and the Popular Literature on Parenting

1. Discuss themes presented in the popular parenting literature throughout the past few decades. (p. 15)

Prior to the 1970's: _____

_____

1980's: _____

_____

Mid-1990's-today: _____

_____

_____

_____

Mid-Twentieth-Century Theories

The Psychoanalytic Perspective

1. Explain the *psychoanalytic perspective* of personality development. (p. 16)

_____

_____

_____

_____

2. Freud's theory of development is known as _____ *theory*. It emphasizes that how parents manage their child's _____ and _____ drives in the first few years of life is crucial for healthy personality development. (p. 16)

3. Name and briefly describe the three components of personality outlined in Freud's theory. (p. 16)

    A. _____

    _____

    B. _____

    _____

    C. _____

    _____

4. Match each of the following stages of psychosexual development with the appropriate description: (p. 17)

    _____ Stage in which sexual instincts die down and the superego develops further

    _____ Stage marked by the onset of puberty

    _____ Stage in which the infant desires sucking activities

    _____ Stage in which the Oedipal / Electra conflict occurs and the superego is formed

    _____ Stage in which toilet training becomes a major issue between parent and child

    1. Oral
    2. Anal
    3. Phallic
    4. Latency
    5. Genital

5. True or False: According to Freud, the relations established between the id, ego, and superego during the adolescent years determine the individual's basic personality. (p. 17)

6. Cite three criticisms of Freud's theory. (p. 17)

    A. _____

    _____

    B. _____

    _____

C. _____

_____

7. In what ways did Erikson build on and improve Freud's theory? (p. 17)

_____

_____

_____

_____

8. Match each of Erikson's stages with the appropriate description: (p. 18)

_____ Successful resolution of this stage depends on the adult's success at caring for other people and productive work

_____ The primary task of this stage is the development of a sense of self and a sense of one's place in society

_____ Successful resolution of this stage depends on a warm, loving relationship with the caregiver

_____ In this stage, children experiment with adult roles through make-believe play

_____ Successful resolution of this stage depends on whether the parents grant the child reasonable opportunities for free choice

_____ In this stage, successful resolution involves reflecting on one's life accomplishments

_____ The development of close relationships with others helps ensure successful resolution of this stage

_____ Children who develop the capacity for cooperation and productive work resolve this stage successfully

1. Basic trust vs. mistrust
2. Autonomy vs. shame and doubt
3. Initiative vs. guilt
4. Industry vs. inferiority
5. Identity vs. identity diffusion
6. Intimacy vs. isolation
7. Generativity vs. stagnation
8. Integrity vs. despair

9. Discuss two contributions and two limitations of psychoanalytic theory. (p. 18)

Contributions: _____

_____

Limitations: _____

_____

Behaviorism and Social Learning Theory

1. True or False: Behaviorism focuses on the inner workings of the mind. (p. 18)

2. Watson's study of little Albert, a 9-month-old baby who was taught to fear a white rat by associating it with a loud noise, supported Pavlov's concept of _____ *conditioning*. (p. 19)

3. Distinguish between primary drives and secondary drives, as discussed in Clark Hull's Drive Reduction Theory. (p. 19)

    Primary drives: _____

    _____

    Secondary drives: _____

    _____

4. Summarize B. F. Skinner's *operant conditioning theory*. (p. 19)

    _____

    _____

    _____

    _____

5. Bandura's social learning theory suggests that _____, otherwise known as *imitation* or *observational learning*, is an important basis for children's behavior. (p. 19)

6. Describe Bandura's most recent revision of his social learning theory. (pp. 19–20)

    _____

    _____

    _____

    _____

7. The term _____ refers to an individual's beliefs about his/her own abilities and characteristics that guide responses in particular situations. (p. 20)

8. Explain what is meant by the term *behavior modification*. (p. 20)

    _____

    _____

9. Discuss two limitations of behaviorism and social learning theory. (p. 20)

A. _____
_____
_____
_____

B. _____
_____
_____
_____

Piaget's Cognitive-Developmental Theory

1. True or False: Piaget's *cognitive-developmental theory* is consistent with the principles of behaviorism; that is, Piaget believed that knowledge is imparted in children through the use of reinforcement. Briefly explain your response. (p. 20)

_____
_____
_____

2. Describe Piaget's notion of *adaptation*. (p. 20)

_____
_____
_____

3. Match each of Piaget's stages with the appropriate description: (p. 21)

_____ During this stage, thought becomes more complex, and children develop the capacity for abstract reasoning

_____ This stage is characterized by the use of eyes, ears, and hands to explore the environment

_____ During this stage, children develop the capacity for abstract thought

_____ This stage is marked by the development of logical, organized reasoning skills

1. Sensorimotor
2. Preoperational
3. Concrete Operational
4. Formal Operational

4. What did Piaget use as his chief method for studying child and adolescent thought? (p. 21)

_____

5. Cite three contributions of Piaget's theory. (p. 21)

A. _____

_____

B. _____

_____

C. _____

_____

6. Describe two recent challenges to Piaget's theory. (pp. 21–22)

A. _____

_____

B. _____

_____

Recent Theoretical Perspectives

Information Processing

1. Briefly describe the *information-processing view* of child development. (p. 22)

_____

_____

_____

2. Information processing theorists often use _____ to map the precise steps individuals use to solve problems and complete tasks. (p. 23)

3. In what basic way are information processing and Piaget's theory alike? In what basic way are they different? (p. 24)

Alike: _____

Different: _____

4. Cite one strength and two limitations of the information-processing approach. (p. 24)

Strength: _____

Limitation: _____

Limitation: _____

Ethology

1. Ethology is the study of

_____. (p. 24)

2. Contrast the notion of a critical period with that of a sensitive period. (p. 24)

Critical period: _____

_____

_____

Sensitive period: _____

_____

_____

3. Explain how John Bowlby used the principles of ethology to understand the infant-caregiver relationship. (p. 25)

_____

_____

_____

_____

4. Briefly explain what is studied in the field of *evolutionary developmental psychology*. (p. 25)

_____

_____

_____

Vygotsky's Sociocultural Theory

1. Cite one benefit of cross-cultural and multicultural research. (p. 26)

_____

_____

2. Explain the importance of social interaction according to Vygotsky's sociocultural theory. (p. 26)

_____

_____

_____

3. Compare and contrast the theories of Piaget and Vygotsky. (p. 26)

_____

_____

_____

_____

_____

_____

4. True or False: Because cultures select tasks for children's learning, children in every culture develop unique strengths not present in others. (p. 26)

5. Vygotsky's emphasis on culture and social experience led him to neglect _____ contributions to development. (p. 26)

Cultural Influences: !Kung Infancy—Acquiring Culture

1. Describe how caregivers in the !Kung society respond to infants' play with objects, and explain how such responses transmit cultural values. (p. 27)

_____

_____

_____

_____

Ecological Systems Theory

1. Briefly explain Bronfenbrenner's *ecological systems theory*. (p. 27)

    _____

    _____

    _____

2. Match each level of ecological systems theory with the appropriate description or example: (pp. 28–29)

    _____ Relationship between the child's home and school   1. Exosystem
    _____ The influence of cultural values   2. Microsystem
    _____ The parent's workplace   3. Mesosystem
    _____ The child's interaction with parents   4. Macrosystem

3. Describe Bronfenbrenner's concept of *bidirectional relationships* within the microsystem. (p. 28)

    _____

    _____

    _____

    _____

4. Bronfenbrenner's _____-*system* refers to temporal changes that affect development, such as the timing of the birth of a sibling. (p. 29)

5. True or False: In ecological systems theory, development is controlled neither by environmental circumstances nor by inner dispositions, but rather by the interaction of the two. (p. 29)

New Theoretical Directions: Development as a Dynamic System

1. Describe the *dynamic systems perspective*. (p. 29)

    _____

    _____

    _____

2. Based on dynamic systems theory, explain how individuals develop both universal traits and individual abilities. (p. 30)

Universal traits: _____

_____

Individual abilities: _____

_____

Comparing Child Development Theories

1. Identify the stand that each of the following modern theories take on the three basic issues of childhood and child development: (p. 32)

Theory	One Course of Development versus Many Courses of Development	Continuous versus Discontinuous Development	Nature versus Nurture
Psychoanalytic theory	_____	_____	_____
Behaviorism and social learning	_____	_____	_____
Piaget's cognitive-developmental theory	_____	_____	_____
Information processing	_____	_____	_____
Ethology	_____	_____	_____
Vygotsky's sociocultural perspective	_____	_____	_____
Dynamic systems theory	_____	_____	_____

1. What are *childhood social indicators*? (p. 31)

   _____

   _____

2. Cite at least five examples of childhood social indicators. (pp. 31–33)

   A. _____

   B. _____

   C. _____

   D. _____

   E. _____

3. What two types of families are at greatest risk for poverty? (pp. 31–33)

   A. _____

   B. _____

4. True or False: The United States is one of only two industrialized nations that fails to guarantee every citizen basic health care services. (p. 33)

5. True or False: The United States has a much lower rate of infant death than all other industrialized nations. (p. 33)

6. The rates of adolescent pregnancy and parenthood in the United States are among the (lowest / highest) in the industrialized world. (p. 33)

7. True or False: One out of every 65 American children experiences parental divorce each year, a rate exceeding that of all other countries. (p. 33)

8. True or False: The United States was among the first nations to develop a national system of high-quality child care. (p. 33)

1. Differentiate between social policy and public policy. (p. 34)

   A. Social policy: _____

   _____

   B. Public policy: _____

   _____

2. True or False: Among developed nations, the United States has served as a forerunner in the development of public policies to safeguard children. (p. 34)

3. Explain how public policy in the United States has been influenced by our cultural values. (pp. 34–35)

   _____

   _____

   _____

   _____

4. In _____ societies, people think of themselves as part of a group and stress group goals over individual goals. In _____ societies, on the other hand, people think of themselves as separate entities and are largely concerned with their own personal needs. (p. 35)

Progress in Meeting the Needs of American Children

1. Cite two grounds on which public policies aimed at fostering children's development can be justified. (p. 36)

   A. _____

   B. _____

2. The _____ is the international treaty which commits each cooperating country to work toward guaranteeing environments that foster children's development, protect them from harm, and enhance their community participation and self-determination. The United States (is / is not) one of the few countries in the world that has not yet ratified this treaty. (p. 36)

1. What is the primary aim of the Access Program? (p. 37)

   _____

2. Explain how the program uses collaboration between schools, students, and parents to meet its objectives. (p. 37)

   _____

   _____

   _____

   _____

   _____

3. True or False: Research findings show that the program was effective in helping participating adolescents gain access to a college education. (p. 37)

4. Explain how the Access Program illustrates the ability of researchers to assist communities in making programs more effective. (p. 37)

   _____

ASK YOURSELF . . .

Review: Why are there many theories of child development? Cite three basic issues on which almost all theories take a stand. (p. 9)

_____

_____

_____

_____

_____

Apply: A school counselor advises a parent, "Don't worry about your teenager's argumentative behavior. It shows that she understands the world differently than she did as a young child." What stance is the counselor taking on the issue of continuous or discontinuous development? Explain. (p. 9)

_____

_____

_____

_____

_____

Connect: Cite an aspect of your development that differs from a parent's or grandparent's when he or she was your age. How might contexts explain this difference? (p. 9)

_____

_____

_____

_____

_____

Review: Suppose we could arrange a debate between John Locke and Jean-Jacques Rousseau on the nature–nurture controversy. Summarize the argument each historical figure is likely to present. (p. 14)

_____

_____

_____

_____

_____

Review: Explain how Darwin, Hall and Gesell, and Binet each contributed to the scientific study of children. (p. 14)

_____

_____

_____

_____

_____

Review: Cite similarities and differences between Freud's and Erikson's view of development. (p. 22)

_____

_____

_____

_____

_____

Review: What aspect of behaviorism made it attractive to critics of psychoanalytic theory? How does Piaget's theory respond to a major limitation of behaviorism? (p. 22)

_____

_____

_____

_____

_____

Review: Why is the field of child development divided over its loyalty to Piaget's ideas? (p. 22)

_____

_____

_____

_____

_____

Apply: A 4-year-old becomes frightened of the dark and refuses to go to sleep at night. How would a psychoanalyst and a behaviorist differ in their views of how this problem developed? (p. 22)

_____

_____

_____

_____

_____

Connect: Although social learning theory focuses on social development and Piaget's theory on cognitive development, they have enhanced our understanding of other domains as well. Mention an additional domain addressed by each theory. (p. 22)

_____

_____

_____

_____

_____

Review: What features of Vygotsky's sociocultural theory distinguish it from Piaget's cognitive-developmental theory? (p. 31)

_____

_____

_____

_____

_____

Review: Explain how each recent theoretical perspective regards children as active, purposeful beings who contribute to their own development. (p. 31)

_____

_____

_____

_____

_____

Apply: Return to the Biology and Environment box on page 10. How does the story of John and Gary illustrate bi-directional influences within the microsystem, as described by ecological systems theory? (p. 31)

_____

_____

_____

_____

_____

Connect: How does ecological systems theory differ from psychoanalytic theory in its explanation of parents' influence on children's development? (p. 31)

_____

_____

_____

_____

_____

Review: What do childhood social indicators reveal about the health and well-being of children in the United States? (p. 38)

_____

_____

_____

_____

_____

Connect: How do cultural values, special interests, economic decisions, and child development research affect children's development? What levels of Bronfenbrenner's ecological systems theory contain these influences? (p. 38)

_____

_____

_____

_____

_____

Connect: How have American cultural values impeded government support for children and families and ratification of the U.N. Convention on the Rights of the Child? (p. 38)

_____

_____

_____

_____

_____

SUGGESTED STUDENT READINGS

Goldhaber, D. E. (2000). *Theories of human development: integrative perspectives.* Mountain View, CA: Mayfield. Presents an extensive summary and critique of historical and current developmental theories, including Bandura's social-cognitive theory, Piaget's cognitive-developmental theory, Freud's and Erikson's psychoanalytic theories, social learning theory, information processing, ethology, Vygotsky's sociocultural theory, and the lifespan perspective.

Lieberman, D. A. (2001). *Learning: Behavior and cognition (3rd ed.).* Belmont, CA: Wadsworth/Thomas Learning. For those interested in ethology and evolutionary developmental psychology, this book illustrates how the learning principles used in animal research can be applied to human behavior and development.

Richardson, K. (1999). *The origins of human potential: Evolution, development, and psychology.* New York: Routledge. Presents a refreshing perspective on the development of cognitive competence. The author uses dynamic systems theory to illustrate the complexity of genetic and environmental factors and how these interactions contribute to cognitive development.

Violato, C., Oddone-Paolucci, E., & Genuis, M. (Eds.). (2000). *The changing family and child development.* Aldershot, England: Ashgate Publishing. An interdisciplinary approach to the development of resiliency in childhood, this book highlights the importance of early childhood experiences, family dynamics, the role of society, and the impact of nonmaternal care on child development.

PUZZLE 1.1

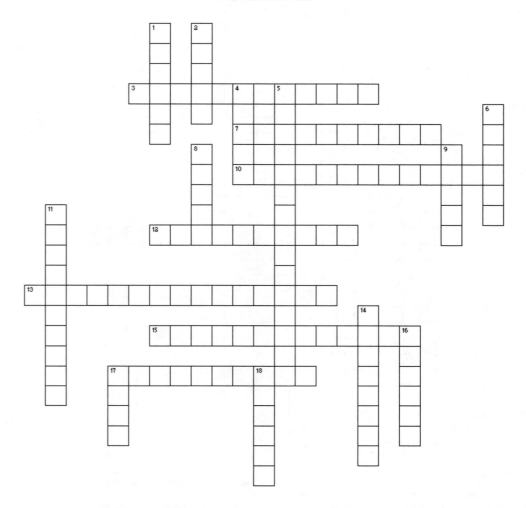

Across

3. In _____ societies, people define themselves as part of a group and stress group over individual goals.
7. Childhood social _____ are measures of children's health, living conditions, and psychological well-being that lend insight into their overall status in community, state, or nation
10. Branch of psychology devoted to understanding changes experienced throughout the lifespan
12. View of development as gradually adding on more of the same types of skills that were there to begin with
13. Medieval view of the child as a miniature adult
15. View of development in which new ways of understanding and responding to the world emerge at specific time
17. The ability to adapt effectively in the face of threats to development

Down

1. An orderly, integrated set of statements that describes, explains, and predicts behavior
2. _____ savage: Rousseau's view of the child as naturally endowed with a sense of right and wrong and with an innate plan for orderly, healthy growth

4. _____ development: field devoted to understanding human constancy and change from conception to adolescence
5. In _____ societies, people think of themselves as separate entities and are largely concerned with their own personal needs.
6. _____ policy: laws and government programs aimed at improving current conditions
8. _____ development: interdisciplinary field devoted to understanding changes experienced throughout the lifespan
9. A qualitative change in thinking, feeling, and behaving that characterizes a specific period of development
11. Genetically determined, naturally unfolding course of growth
14. Unique combinations of genetic and environmental circumstances that can result in markedly different paths of development
16. _____ policy: any planned set of actions directed at solving a social problem or attaining a social goal
17. Tabula _____: Locke's view of the child as a blank slate whose character is shaped by experience
18. _____-nurture controversy: disagreement about whether genetic or environmental circumstances are more important determinants of development

PUZZLE 1.2

Across

4. _____ systems theory: views the child as developing within a complex system of relationships affected by multiple levels of the environment
5. _____ period: time that is optimal for certain capacities to emerge and in which the individual is especially responsive to environmental influences
6. Approach concerned with the adaptive value of behavior and its evolutionary history
8. Freud's _____ theory emphasizes management of early sexual and aggressive drives
9. Behavior _____: procedures combining modeling and conditioning to eliminate undesirable behaviors and increase desirable responses
11. In ecological systems theory, social settings that do not contain children but that affect their experiences in immediate settings
12. Vygotsky's _____ theory focuses on how social interaction contributes to development.
13. _____ processing: approach that views the human mind as a symbol-manipulating system through which information flows
15. _____ developmental psychology: seeks to understand the adaptive value of species-wide cognitive, emotional, and social competencies as they change over time
17. In ecological systems theory, connections between children's immediate settings

19. Social _____ theory: emphasizes the role of modeling in the development of behavior
20. In ecological systems theory, temporal changes in children's environments

Down

1. Erikson's _____ theory of development focuses on resolution of psychological conflicts over the lifespan
2. In ecological systems theory, the activities and interaction patterns in the child's immediate surroundings
3. In ecological systems theory, cultural values, laws, customs, and resources that influence experiences and interactions at inner levels of the environment
7. _____ perspective: approach to personality development introduced by Freud; assumes children move through a series of stages in which they confront conflicts between biological drives and social expectations
10. Approach that emphasizes the study of directly observable events
14. _____ approach: age-related averages are computed to represent typical development
16. Piaget's _____-developmental theory suggests that children actively construct knowledge as they manipulate and explore their world.
18. _____ systems perspective: the child's mind, body, and physical and social worlds form an integrated system

PRACTICE TEST

1. Our knowledge of child development is interdisciplinary. What does this mean? (p. 4)
   a. Our knowledge of child development is based exclusively on research conducted by people in the field of child development.
   b. Child development is not recognized as a distinct field of study.
   c. Individuals from diverse fields have contributed to our knowledge of child development.
   d. Child development is part of a larger discipline known as developmental psychology.

2. An orderly, integrated set of statements that describes, explains, and predicts behavior is a: (p. 6)
   a. strategy.
   b. theory.
   c. hypothesis.
   d. design.

3. How do theories differ from opinion? (p. 6)
   a. Theories are based on scientific research.
   b. Theories must be scientifically confirmed.
   c. Theories offer a more complete picture of behavior.
   d. Theories and opinions do not differ.

4. Stage theories conform to which of the following perspectives of development? (p. 8)
   a. nature
   b. nurture
   c. continuous
   d. discontinuous

5. In medieval times: (p. 11)
   a. childhood was not recognized as a separate phase of the lifecycle.
   b. children were regarded as evil and stubborn.
   c. childhood experiences were regarded as crucial for healthy development.
   d. toys and games were designed to amuse children.

6. The idea that children are neither innately good nor evil, but rather are shaped by their experiences, is known as: (p. 11)
   a. preformationism.
   b. original sin.
   c. tabula rasa.
   d. noble savage.

7. Which of the following theorists emphasized the concepts of natural selection and survival of the fittest? (p. 12)
   a. Locke
   b. Rousseau
   c. Gessell
   d. Darwin

8. In the normative approach to child study: (p. 13)
   a. researchers jot down day-to-day descriptions and impressions of a youngster's behavior beginning in early infancy.
   b. researchers take measures of behavior on large numbers of children and then compute age-related averages to represent typical development.
   c. researchers investigate children's cognitive development through the use of clinical interviews, in which children describe their thinking.
   d. researchers use flowcharts to map the precise steps that individuals take to solve problems and complete tasks.

9. The first successful intelligence test, created by Alfred Binet, represented an improvement over previous tests primarily because: (p. 14)
   a. it was able to reduce intelligence to its simplest elements.
   b. it measured abilities indirectly.
   c. it was culturally unbiased.
   d. it was based on a well-developed theory.

10. According to Freud's theory, which of the following is the conscious, rational part of personality which redirects biological impulses so that they are expressed in socially acceptable ways? (p. 16)
    a. id
    b. ego
    c. superego
    d. conscience

11. Which of the following theories is noted for its focus on the unique developmental history of each child? (p. 16)
    a. behaviorism
    b. social learning theory
    c. psychoanalytic theory
    d. information processing

12. Behaviorism focuses on the study of: (p. 18)
    a. unconscious motives for behavior.
    b. imitation as a mechanism for learning new behaviors.
    c. cognitive reasoning underlying behavior.
    d. directly observable events.

13. An approach that emphasizes the role of modeling, or observational learning, in the development of behavior is known as: (p. 19)
    a. psychosocial theory.
    b. social learning theory.
    c. cognitive-developmental theory.
    d. behaviorism.

14. According to Piaget's theory, each of the four stages of development is characterized by: (p. 21)
    a. advances in motor development.
    b. increased capacity to process information.
    c. a distinct psychosocial crisis.
    d. qualitatively distinct ways of thinking.

15. New evidence challenging Piaget's theory suggests that he: (p. 21)
    a. overestimated the competencies of young children.
    b. underestimated the competencies of young children.
    c. overlooked several important areas of cognitive development.
    d. used overly simplified measures in his studies of cognitive development.

16. Which of the following techniques is used by information-processing theorists to map the precise steps that individuals use to solve problems and complete tasks? (p. 23)
    a. cognitive maps
    b. schematic representation
    c. flowcharts
    d. mental operations charts

17. Which of the following theories is concerned with the adaptive value of behavior and its evolutionary significance? (p. 24)
    a. ethology
    b. ecological systems theory
    c. sociocultural theory
    d. bioecological theory

18. A _____ period is a time that is optimal for certain capacities to emerge because the individual is especially responsive to environmental influences. (p. 25)
    a. sensitive
    b. critical
    c. resiliency
    d. maturation

19. Evolutionary developmental psychology is the study of: (p. 25)
    a. childhood social indicators.
    b. the adaptive value of species-wide cognitive, emotional, and social competencies as those competencies change over time.
    c. temporal changes in a child's environment and the impact of such changes on the individual child's development.
    d. children's ability to adapt in the face of threats to development.

20. According to _____, cognitive development is a socially mediated process. (p. 26)
    a. Piaget
    b. Vygotsky
    c. Bronfenbrenner
    d. Hull

21. Since Bronfenbrenner's ecological systems theory emphasizes the joining of biological dispositions and environmental forces in molding children's development, he characterized his perspective as a _____ model. (p. 27)
    a. sociocultural
    b. psychosocial
    c. bioecological
    d. ethological

22. Jennifer's mother volunteers as a room mother. This connection between home and school illustrates Bronfenbrenner's: (p. 28)
    a. mesosystem.
    b. exosystem.
    c. microsystem.
    d. macrosystem.

23. Dynamic systems theory focuses on: (p. 29)
    a. the impact of changes occurring in the child's mind, body, and physical and social worlds.
    b. describing universal features of development.
    c. children's ability to learn through modeling.
    d. consistencies across various systems, or domains, of development.

24. Laws and government programs designed to improve current conditions, such as those of children and families are called: (p. 34)
    a. legal policies.
    b. domestic policies.
    c. public policies.
    d. democratic policies.

25. American public policies to safeguard children and youths: (p. 36)
    a. are superior to those found in most other industrialized nations.
    b. lag behind those of other developed countries.
    c. are often ineffective due to inadequate knowledge and resources.
    d. are rapidly improving as the United States moves towards a more collectivist ideology.

CHAPTER 2
RESEARCH STRATEGIES

BRIEF CHAPTER SUMMARY

Researchers face many challenges as they plan and implement studies of children. An understanding of research strategies enables students to separate dependable information from misleading results and to conduct their own investigations. Research usually begins with a hypothesis—a prediction about behavior drawn directly from a theory—or with a research question. The researcher then selects one or more research methods to use in the investigation, such as systematic observations, self-reports, psychophysiological methods, clinical methods, or ethnography. Once the researcher chooses the research methods, it is important to make sure that the procedures are reliable and valid—two keys to scientifically sound research. Next, the researcher chooses a research design, an overall plan for the study that permits the best possible test of the research idea. Two main types of designs, the correlational design and the experimental design, are used in research on human behavior. Longitudinal, cross-sectional, and longitudinal-sequential designs are uniquely suited for studying development. In the microgenetic design, researchers have the opportunity to watch change as it occurs.

Research involving children raises special ethical concerns because they are more vulnerable than adults to physical and psychological harm. Ethical guidelines for research, along with special committees and agencies, determine if the benefits of research outweigh the risks and help ensure that children's rights are protected.

LEARNING OBJECTIVES

After reading this chapter, you should be able to:

2.1   Explain the difference between a hypothesis and a research question, and discuss why it is important to be knowledgeable about research strategies. (p. 42)

2.2   Describe the common research methods used to study children, and explain the strengths and limitations of each. (pp. 43–52)

2.3   Explain why reliability and validity are keys to scientifically sound research, and indicate how these concepts apply to research methods and to the overall findings and conclusions of research studies. (pp. 52–53)

2.4 Describe correlational and experimental research designs, and explain the strengths and limitations of each. (pp. 53–57)

2.5 Describe four research methods used to study development, noting the strengths and limitations of each, and explain why experimental and developmental designs are sometimes combined. (pp. 57–62)

2.6 Describe children's research rights, and explain why research involving children raises special ethical concerns. (pp. 63–65)

STUDY QUESTIONS

From Theory to Hypothesis

1. Research usually begins with a _____, or a prediction about behavior drawn directly from a theory. (p. 42)

2. When little or no theory exists on a topic of interest, investigators may start with a _____. (p. 42)

3. Cite two reasons why it is important to learn about research strategies. (p. 42)

   A. _____

   _____

   B. _____

   _____

Common Methods Used to Study Children

Systematic Observation

1. Compare and contrast naturalistic and structured observation techniques, noting one strength and one limitation of each approach. (p. 44)

   _____

   _____

   _____

_____

_____

2. Name and describe three procedures used to collect systematic observations. (p. 44)

    A. _____

    B. _____

    C. _____

3. Discuss three limitations of systematic observation. (p. 45)

    A. _____

    B. _____

    C. _____

    _____

4. List two ways that researchers can minimize observer influence when collecting systematic observations. (p. 45)

    A. _____

    B. _____

5. Define *observer bias*, and explain how researchers guard against this problem. (p. 45)

    _____

Self-Reports: Interviews and Questionnaires

1. Explain how clinical interviews differ from structured interviews, and note the benefits of each technique. (p. 45)

    Clinical: _____

    _____

    Structured: _____

    _____

2. Summarize the limitations of the clinical interview technique. (p. 46)

_____

_____

_____

3. True or False: Researchers can eliminate problems with inaccurate reporting (on the part of interviewees) by conducting structured interviews rather than clinical interviews. (p. 46)

Psychophysiological Methods

1. Psychophysiological methods measure the relationship between _____ processes and _____. Investigators who rely on these methods want to find out which _____ structures contribute to development and individual differences. (p. 47)

2. List several commonly used physiological measures that are sensitive to an individual's psychological state. (p. 47)

_____

_____

3. _____, which yield three-dimensional pictures of brain activity, provide the most precise information on which brain regions are specialized for certain functions. (p. 47)

4. Describe two limitations of psychophysiological methods. (p. 47)

A. _____

B. _____

The Clinical or Case Study Method

1. Cite the primary aim of the clinical method. (p. 48)

_____

2. The clinical method has been used to find out what contributes to the accomplishments of _____-extremely gifted children who attain the competence of an adult in a particular field before age 10. (p. 48)

3. Discuss the drawbacks of using the clinical method. (p. 48)

_____

_____

_____

Methods for Studying Culture

1. When comparing several cultural groups, researchers can use _____ and _____ procedures. (p. 50)

2. _____ is a research method aimed at understanding a culture or distinct social group. This goal is achieved through _____, a technique in which the researcher lives with the cultural community and participates in all aspects of daily life. (p. 51)

3. Cite two limitations of the ethnographic method. (p. 52)

A. _____

B. _____

Biology and Environment: Case Studies of Prodigies

1. Case studies suggest that a unique _____ disposition to excel in a particular field combines with intense _____ and highly _____ early child rearing to permit full expression of the child's special capacity. (p. 49)

2. When parents are overly _____ and care only about their child's gifts rather than about the child him- or herself, prodigious children can end up disengaged, depressed, and resentful. (p. 49)

Social Issues: Education
Immigrant Youths: Amazing Adaptation

1. True or False: Students who are first-generation (foreign-born) and second-generation (American-born with immigrant parents) achieve in school as well or better than do students of native-born parents. (p. 50)

2. Compared with their agemates, adolescents from immigrant families are (more / less) likely to commit delinquent and violent acts, to use drugs and alcohol, and to have early sex. (p. 50)

3. Discuss two ways in which family and community exert an influence on the academic achievement of adolescents from immigrant families. (p. 50)

A. _____

B. _____

Reliability and Validity: Keys to Scientifically Sound Research

Reliability

1. Define *reliability*. (p. 52)

_____

2. Explain how reliability is determined for the following research methods: (p. 52)

Observational research: _____

_____

Self-report and psychophysiological methods: _____

_____

Clinical and ethnographic studies: _____

_____

Validity

1. For research methods to have high validity, they must
_____. (p. 53)

2. True or False: Reliability is essential for valid research. Briefly explain your response. (p. 53)

_____

_____

_____

3. Cite two ways that researchers can ensure that the methods they use are valid. (p. 53)

A. _____

_____

B. _____

_____

General Research Designs

Correlational Design

1. Describe the basic features of the correlational design. (p. 53)

_____

_____

_____

2. True or False: The correlational design is preferred by researchers because it allows them to infer cause and effect. Explain your answer. (p. 54)

_____

_____

_____

3. Investigators examine relationships among variables using a(n) _____, a number that describes how two measures, or variables, are associated with one another. (p. 54)

4. A correlation coefficient can range from _____ to _____. The magnitude of the number shows the _____ of the relationship between the two variables, whereas the sign indicates the _____ of the relationship. (p. 54)

5. For a correlation coefficient, a positive sign means that as one variable increases, the other _____; a negative sign indicates that as one variable increases, the other _____. (p. 54)

6. A researcher determines that the correlation between warm, consistent parenting and child delinquency is –.80. Explain what this indicates about the relationship between these two variables. (p. 54)

_____

_____

7. If the same researcher had found a correlation of +.45, what would this have indicated about the relationship between warm, consistent parenting and child delinquency? (p. 54)

_____

_____

8. Explain the difference between a correlation of –1.00 and a correlation of +1.00. (p. 54)

_____

_____

Experimental Design

1. What is the primary distinction between a correlational design and an experimental design? (p. 54)

_____

_____

2. The (independent / dependent) variable is anticipated by the researcher to cause changes in the (independent / dependent) variable. (p. 54)

3. What is the feature of an experimental design that enables researchers to infer a cause-and-effect relationship between the variables? (p. 54)

_____

_____

4. By using _____ assignment of participants to treatment conditions, investigators are able to control for characteristics that could reduce the accuracy of their findings. This technique is sometimes combined with _____, in which participants are measured ahead of time on the factor in question and groups are deliberately made equivalent on characteristics likely to distort the results. (p. 55)

Modified Experimental Designs

1. In _____ experiments, researchers randomly assign people to treatment conditions in natural settings. (p. 55)

2. True or False: Natural experiments differ from correlational research because groups of participants are carefully chosen to ensure that their characteristics are as much alike as possible. (p. 55)

Designs for Studying Development

The Longitudinal Design

1. Explain the procedure used in a longitudinal design. (p. 57)

    _____

    _____

2. List two advantages of the longitudinal design. (p. 57)

    A. _____

    _____

    B. _____

    _____

3. Provide an example of one research question that could be studied using a longitudinal design. (p. 57)

    _____

    _____

4. In longitudinal research, _____ is a common problem because people move away or drop out, and the ones who remain are likely to differ in important ways from those who continue. (p. 58)

5. What are *practice effects*? (p. 58)

    _____

    _____

6. _____ effects refer to the influence of cultural-historical change on the accuracy of longitudinal research findings. (p. 58)

The Cross-Sectional Design

1. In the cross-sectional design, groups of people differing in _____ are studied at the same point in time. (p. 58)

2. In cross-sectional designs, researchers (do / do not) need to worry about selective attrition, practice effects, and changes in the field of child development. (p. 60)

3. Describe two problems associated with conducting cross-sectional research. (p. 60)

   A. _____

   _____

   B. _____

   _____

Improving Developmental Designs

1. In the _____ design, researchers merge longitudinal and cross-sectional research strategies. List three advantages of this design. (p. 60)

   A. _____

   _____

   B. _____

   _____

   C. _____

   _____

2. A recent modification of the longitudinal approach, called the _____ design, allows researchers to track change while it is occurring. (p. 61)

3. Microgenetic research is especially useful for studying (cognitive / physical) development. (p. 61)

4. List three reasons why microgenetic studies are difficult to carry out. (p. 61)

   A. _____

   _____

   B. _____

   _____

   C. _____

   _____

5. Longitudinal and cross-sectional research provide only (correlational / causal) inferences about development, but when a longitudinal or cross-sectional design is combined with an experimental strategy, researchers have evidence for (correlational / causal) associations. (p. 62)

Cultural Influences—The Impact of Historical Times on Development: The Great Depression and World War II

1. During the Great Depression, adolescent (boys / girls / boys and girls) became increasingly focused on college and career aspirations. (p. 59)

2. Cite evidence suggesting that cultural-historic events have a differential impact, depending on the age at which they take place. (p. 59)

   _____

   _____

   _____

Ethics in Research on Children

1. Discuss the special ethical concerns of conducting research on children. (p. 63)

   _____

   _____

2. Describe children's research rights. (p. 63)

   A. Protection from harm: _____

   _____

B. Informed consent: _____

_____

C. Privacy: _____

_____

D. Knowledge of results: _____

_____

E. Beneficial treatments: _____

_____

3. For children under _____ years and older, their own informed consent should be obtained in addition to _____ consent prior to participation in research. (p. 64)

4. In _____, the investigator provides a full account and justification of research activities to participants in a study in which deception was used. (p. 64)

From Research to Practice—Children's Research Risks: Developmental and Individual Differences

1. Whereas younger children have special difficulties understanding the research process, older children are more susceptible to procedures that threaten _____. (p. 65)

2. Cite one example of how a child's background and prior experiences may introduce special vulnerabilities with regard to the research process. (p. 65)

_____

_____

_____

ASK YOURSELF . . .

Review: Why might a researcher prefer to observe children in the laboratory rather than the natural environment? How about the natural environment rather than the lab? Cite factors that can distort the naturalness of systematic observation, regardless of where the information is gathered. (p. 52)

_____

_____

_____

_____

_____

Review: What strengths and limitations do the clinical method and ethnography have in common? (p. 52)

_____

_____

_____

_____

Apply: A researcher wants to study the thoughts and feelings of children who have experienced their parents' divorce. Which method is best suited for investigating this question? Why? (p. 52)

_____

_____

_____

_____

Connect: Why is it better for a researcher to use multiple research methods rather than just one method in a testing a hypothesis or answering a research question? (p. 52)

_____

_____

_____

_____

_____

Review: Explain why a research method *must be* reliable to be valid, yet reliability *does not guarantee* validity. (p. 53)

_____

_____

_____

_____

_____

Connect: Review the limitations of systematic observation on page 45. How do observer influence and observer bias relate to reliability and validity in research? (p. 53)

_____

_____

_____

_____

_____

Review: Why can we infer cause-and-effect in experimental research but not in correlational research? (p. 57)

_____

_____

_____

_____

_____

Review: Why are natural experiments less precise than laboratory and field experiments? (p. 57)

_____

_____

_____

_____

_____

Apply: A researcher compares children who went to summer leadership camps with children who attended athletic camps. She finds that those who attended leadership camps are friendlier. Should the investigator tell parents that sending children to leadership camps will cause them to be more sociable? Why or why not? (p. 57)

_____

_____

_____

_____

_____

Connect: Reread the description of the study investigating antisocial boys and their friendships on page 44. What type of research design did the researchers use, and why? (p. 57)

_____

_____

_____

_____

_____

Review: Explain how cohort effects can distort the findings of both longitudinal and cross-sectional studies. How does the longitudinal-sequential design reveal cohort effects? (p. 62)

_____

_____

_____

_____

Review: What design is best suited to studying processes of change, and why? When researchers use this design, what factors can threaten the validity of their findings? (p. 62)

_____

_____

_____

_____

_____

Apply: A researcher wants to find out if children enrolled in child-care centers in the first few years of life do as well in school as those who are not in child care. What developmental design is appropriate for answering this question? Explain.

_____

_____

_____

_____

_____

Apply: Suppose a researcher asks you to enroll your baby in a 10-year longitudinal study. What factors would lead you to agree and stay involved? Do your answers shed light on why longitudinal studies often have biased samples?

_____

_____

_____

_____

_____

Review: Why is the use of deception in research more risky with children than with adults? (p. 64)

_____

_____

_____

_____

_____

Review: Explain why researchers must consider children's age-related capacities to ensure that they are protected from harm and have freely consented to research. (p. 64)

_____

_____

_____

_____

_____

Apply: When a researcher engages in naturalistic observation of preschoolers' play, a child says, "Stop watching me!" Using the research rights in Table 2.4, how should the researcher respond, and why? (p. 64)

_____

_____

_____

_____

_____

SUGGESTED STUDENT READINGS

Greig, P., & Taylor, J. (1999). *Doing research with children.* London: Sage Publications Ltd. Reviews the various techniques and approaches, including the unique ethical and legal concerns, that are associated with child development research. This book provides a framework for studying children which can be utilized by students, practitioners, educators, and others working in the field of child development.

Hoagwood, K., Jensen, P. S., & Fisher, C. (1996). *Ethical issues in mental health research with children and adolescents.* Mahwah, NJ: Erlbaum. Presents evidence that individuals with mental, emotional, or behavioral difficulties may require special ethical treatment in research studies. Includes 65 real-life cases and useful suggestions for addressing different ethical issues.

McBurney, D. H. (2001). *Research methods (5th ed).* Belmont, CA: Wadsworth/Thomas Learning. For those interested in exploring the various research methods used in psychology, this book presents a review of relevant literature, along with a discussion of how the Internet has become a valuable resource in psychological research. In addition, the author provides real-world examples and activities to enhance the reader's understanding of the research process.

Whitehouse, H. (Ed.). (2001). *The debated mind: Evolutionary psychology verses ethnography.* New York: Berg. A collection of articles examining the relationship between nature, nurture, and culture. The goal of this particular work is to integrate the nature-nurture debate with ethnographic perspectives and create an interdisciplinary framework for studying development.

PUZZLE 2.1

Across

1. Natural _____: researcher studies already existing treatments in natural settings.
4. A number describing how two variables are related is called a correlation _____.
6. A prediction about behavior drawn from a theory
7. Risks-versus-_____ ratio: comparison of the costs of a research study against its potential value
8. Participant observation of a culture
9. _____ observation: researcher goes in to the natural environment to observe the behavior of interest
12. ___-_____ design: groups of people differing in age are studied at the same point in time
13. In a _____ design, the researcher presents children with a novel task and follows their mastery over a series of sessions.
16. Design in which the researcher gathers information without altering the participants' experience
17. Observer _____: observer sees and records what is expected rather than actual behavior
18. Full account and justification of research activities
19. Extent to which research methods accurately measure what the researcher intended to measure

Down

2. Methods that measure the relationship between physiological processes and behavior
3. Longitudinal-_____ design: participants born in different years are followed over time
5. Experiment in which participants are randomly assigned to treatment conditions in natural settings
10. Observer _____: tendency of participants to react to the presence of an observer and behave in unnatural ways
11. _____ from harm: right of research participants to be safeguarded from physical or psychological harm
14. Consistency, or repeatability, of measures of behavior
15. Observation method in which the researcher evokes the behavior of interest in a laboratory setting

PUZZLE 2.2

Across

3. _____ effects: changes in participants' natural responses as a result of repeated testing
4. In _____ sampling, the observer records all instances of a particular behavior during a specified period of time.
5. Interview method in which the researcher asks all participants the same questions in the same way
7. Variable manipulated by the researcher
8. Sampling procedure in which the researcher records whether or not a behavior occurred during a sample of short time intervals
10. Clinical _____ method: uses a flexible, conversational style
11. Effects of cultural-historical change on the accuracy of findings
12. Variable expected to be influenced by the experimental manipulations
13. Experiment permitting the maximum possible control over treatment conditions
17. Design in which one group of participants is studied repeatedly at different ages
18. _____ record: researcher records a description of a participant's entire stream of behavior

Down

1. Informed _____: right of research participants to have explained to them all aspects of a study that might affect willingness to participate
2. Longitudinal samples become biased due to _____ attrition.
6. Design in which the researcher randomly assigns participants to two or more treatment conditions; permits inferences about cause and effect
9. Ensures equivalency of research groups with regard to factors that are likely to distort findings
14. _____ assignment: even-handed procedure for assigning participants to treatment groups
15. _____, or case study, method
16. Failure to select research participants who are representative of the population of interest is known as _____ sampling.

PRACTICE TEST

1. A _____ is a prediction about behavior drawn directly from a theory. (p. 42)
   a. hypothesis
   b. research question
   c. dependent variable
   d. research design

2. A researcher interested in the development of aggression in young children goes into a preschool to observe classroom behavior. She keeps a record of all aggressive acts occurring during her observation. This is an example of a(n) (p. 44):
   a. structured observation.
   b. naturalistic observation.
   c. ethnographic observation.
   d. field experiment.

3. _____ observation permits greater control over the research situation than does naturalistic observation. (p. 44)
   a. Clinical
   b. Correlational
   c. Longitudinal
   d. Structured

4. A description of everything said and done over a certain time period is called: (p. 44)
   a. time sampling.
   b. a specimen record.
   c. a clinical interview.
   d. a longitudinal study.

5. An observer watches a student in the classroom setting and records each instance in which she raises her hand. This would be: (p. 45)
   a. time sampling.
   b. event sampling.
   c. a specimen record.
   d. a longitudinal study.

6. A researcher observes a child doing seatwork at his desk for a period of 10 seconds and then records his behavior on a checklist during the next 5 seconds. This is called: (p. 45)
   a. time sampling.
   b. biased sampling.

c. a specimen record.

d. event sampling.

7. Researchers can minimize observer influence by: (p. 45)

a. using observers who are unaware of the investigator's hyptheses.

b. using observers who are unfamiliar to the child.

c. asking individuals who are part of the child's natural environment to do the observing.

d. conducting structured, rather than naturalistic, observations.

8. In a clinical interview, the researcher: (p. 46)

a. asks each participant the same set of questions in the same way.

b. uses a flexible, conversational style.

c. focuses on past experiences and global judgments rather than current information and specific characteristics.

d. targets observable behaviors rather than subjective reports of thoughts, feelings, and experiences.

9. Psychophysiological research is useful because: (p. 47)

a. interpretation of physiological responses does not require inferential reasoning.

b. few environmental factors exert an influence on physiological responses.

c. investigators have established clear causal links between physiological and psychological reactions.

d. it helps to identify the perceptions, thoughts, and emotions of infants and young children.

10. The clinical method: (p. 48)

a. stresses the importance of understanding the individual.

b. relies almost exclusively on experimental research designs.

c. is the most systematic and objective approach available for studying children.

d. emphasizes universal norms for behavior.

11. Ethnography aims to understand a culture or distinct social group through: (p. 51)

a. structured observation.

b. case study reports.

c. participant observation.

d. clinical interviews with members of the group.

12. One limitation of ethnographic research is that: (p. 52)

a. members of the culture or group under study are typically aware of the purpose of the research and may adjust their behavior in an effort to please the investigator.

b. findings cannot be assumed to generalize beyond the people and settings in which the research was originally conducted.

c. group members may provide inaccurate reports of their thoughts, feelings, and experiences.

d. information is often collected unsystematically and subjectively.

13. _____ is absolutely essential for valid research. (p. 52)

a. Subjectivity

b. Reliability

c. Use of an experimental design

d. Use of a correlational design

14. A test is intended to measure first graders' mathematical ability and includes numerous word problems. The fact that the test may measure verbal ability as well as mathematical ability means that test results may be: (p. 53)

a. cross-sectional.

b. unreliable.

c. invalid.

d. correlational.

15. In a correlational design: (p. 53)

a. researchers gather information on already existing groups of individuals, generally in natural life circumstances.

b. researchers randomly assign participants to various treatment groups to examine group differences.

c. researchers examine the behavior of interest in a laboratory setting.

d. researchers establish causal associations between variables.

16. In a study on the association between time spent studying and exam scores, an investigator finds a correlation of +.91. What does this correlation coefficient indicate about the relationship between these two variables? (p. 54)

a. As study time increases, exam scores also increase.

b. As study time increases, exam scores decrease.

c. There is a moderate relationship between time spent studying and exam scores.

d. There is almost no relationship between time spent studying and exam scores.

17. An experimental design permits inferences about cause and effect because: (p. 54)

a. experimental studies are conducted in natural settings rather than laboratory settings.

b. the researcher controls changes in the independent variable.

c. the researcher controls changes in the dependent variable.

d. the researcher systematically assigns participants to specific treatment conditions based on their known characteristics.

18. A researcher is interested in studying peer relationships. He recruits a sample of kindergarten children and examines changes in their relationships with peers over the next ten years. This is an example of a: (p. 57)
    a. cross-sectional design.
    b. longitudinal-sequential design.
    c. microgenetic design.
    d. longitudinal design.

19. Imagine that a researcher concludes that 5-year-olds in the 1950's learned more slowly than do 5-year-olds of today. Which of the following poses a threat to the accuracy of such a finding? (p. 58)
    a. biased sampling
    b. investigator bias
    c. cohort effects
    d. selective attrition

20. In a _____ design, groups of people differing in age are studied at the same point in time. (p. 58)
    a. longitudinal
    b. cross-sectional
    c. longitudinal-sequential
    d. microgenetic

21. An advantage of the longitudinal-sequential design is that: (p. 60)
    a. it allows researchers to infer cause-and-effect relationships.
    b. it eliminates problems caused by practice effects.
    c. it allows researchers to determine the presence of cohort effects.
    d. it is not affected by selective attrition.

22. The microgenetic design: (p. 61)
    a. allows researchers to track development as it takes place.
    b. emphasizes structured observations of children's behavior in natural settings.
    c. eliminates threats to research reliability caused by observer bias.
    d. enables researchers to measure the relationship between physiological processes and behavior.

23. Researchers sometimes combine longitudinal or cross-sectional designs with _____ designs in order to explore causal relationships between variables. (p. 62)
    a. microgenetic
    b. clinical
    c. experimental
    d. self-report

24. Which of the following is true of children's research rights with regard to informed consent? (p. 64)
    a. For children under age 18, only parental consent should be obtained.
    b. In most cases, researchers need only obtain the child's informed consent; parental consent is rarely required.
    c. For children 7 years and older, their own informed consent should be obtained in addition to parental consent.
    d. Unless the research presents a risk of potential harm to the child, researchers are not required to obtain informed consent from the child or the parent.

25. Debriefing refers to: (p. 64)
    a. providing research participants with a full account and justification of research activities.
    b. the right of research participants to be protected from physical and psychological harm.
    c. the right of research participants to have explained to them all aspects of the study that may affect their willingness to participate.
    d. children's right to be informed of research results in language that is appropriate to their level of understanding.

CHAPTER 3
BIOLOGICAL FOUNDATIONS, PRENATAL DEVELOPMENT, AND BIRTH

BRIEF CHAPTER SUMMARY

Because nature has prepared us for survival, all humans have features in common. Yet each human being is also unique. Human biological foundations include the genetic code and basic genetic principles that contribute to individual differences in appearance and behavior and to various abnormalities and disorders. During the most rapid phase of human growth, the prenatal period, complex transactions between heredity and environment begin to shape the course of development. Genetic counseling and prenatal diagnosis help people make informed decisions about conceiving or carrying a pregnancy to term. The vast changes that take place during pregnancy are divided into three periods: the period of the zygote, the period of the embryo, and the period of the fetus. Environmental supports such as maternal health and nutrition are necessary for normal prenatal growth, but damaging influences such as teratogens, inadequate maternal diet, and severe maternal emotional stress can threaten the child's health and survival. Prenatal vitamin supplements can benefit women during pregnancy and also can prevent certain birth complications and defects.

Childbirth takes place in three stages: dilation and effacement of the cervix, delivery of the baby, and birth of the placenta. Childbirth practices, like other aspects of family life, are molded by the society of which baby and mother are a part. Natural, or prepared, childbirth tries to overcome the idea that birth is a painful ordeal that requires extensive medical intervention. Interest in home birth, which has always been popular in certain industrialized nations, has increased in the United States. In complicated deliveries, labor and delivery medication is essential; but used routinely, it can cause problems. Oxygen deprivation, prematurity, and low birth weight are serious birth complications. Infants born underweight or prematurely face developmental risks, but interventions to ensure a supportive home environment can help restore these children's growth.

The field of behavioral genetics is devoted to discovering the hereditary and environmental origins of the great diversity of complex human characteristics. These two basic determinants of development are bidirectional and continue to influence the individual's emerging characteristics from infancy through adolescence.

LEARNING OBJECTIVES

After reading this chapter, you should be able to:

3.1   Distinguish between genotypes and phenotypes. (p. 70)

3.19 Describe several interventions for preterm infants, including infant stimulation and parent training. (pp. 109–111)

3.20 Summarize findings from the Kauai study relating to the long-term consequences of birth complications. (p. 111)

3.21 Cite the goals of behavioral genetics. (pp. 112–114)

3.22 Describe methods used by behavioral geneticists to infer the role of heredity in human characteristics, and note the limitations of these techniques. (pp. 114–116)

3.23 Describe concepts that explain how heredity and environment work together to influence complex human characteristics. (pp. 116–119)

STUDY QUESTIONS

1. _____ are directly observable characteristics, which depend in part on the individual's _____, the complex blend of genetic information that influences all of our unique characteristics. (p. 70)

Genetic Foundations

1. Rodlike structures in the nucleus of a cell that store and transmit genetic information are called _____. (p. 70)

2. Humans have (23 / 46) pairs of chromosomes in each cell. (p. 70)

The Genetic Code

1. Chromosomes are made up of a chemical substance called _____. It looks like a twisted ladder and is composed of segments called _____. (p. 70)

2. The process through which DNA duplicates itself so that each new body cell contains the same number of chromosomes is called _____. (p. 71)

The Sex Cells

1. Sex cells, or _____, are formed through the process of (mitosis / meiosis). (p. 71)

2. True or False: Sex cells contain only half the number of chromosomes normally present in body cells. (p. 71)

3. Describe the process of cell duplication known as *mitosis*. (p. 71)

_____

_____

_____

_____

_____

4. True or False: The crossing over of chromosomes during meiosis creates new hereditary combinations unique to the individual. (p. 71)

5. When the sperm and ova unite at fertilization, the cell that results is called a
   _____. (p. 73)

Multiple Offspring

1. Match the following terms with the appropriate description. (p. 73)

_____ The most common type of multiple birth	1. Identical, or monozygotic, twins
_____ Older maternal age and use of fertility drugs are major causes of this type of twinning	2. Fraternal, or dizygotic, twins
_____ These twins share the same genetic makeup	
_____ This type of twinning may result from environmental influences such as temperature changes, variation in oxygen levels, and late fertilization of the ovum	
_____ These twins are genetically no more alike than ordinary siblings	

Boy or Girl?

1. The 22 pairs of matching chromosomes are called _____. The 23rd pair consists of _____ chromosomes, which determine the sex of the child. (p. 74)

2. Explain how the sex of the new organism is determined. (p. 74)

_____

_____

_____

_____

Patterns of Genetic Inheritance

1. Each of two or more forms of a gene located at the same place on the chromosome is called a(n) _____. (p. 74)

2. If the alleles from both parents are alike, the child is _____ and will display the inherited trait. If the alleles inherited from the mother and father are different, then the child is _____, and the relationship between the alleles will determine the trait that will appear. (p. 74)

3. Explain the nature of *dominant-recessive inheritance*, and provide one example of this type of inheritance. (p. 74)

_____

_____

_____

_____

4. A heterozygous individual who can pass a recessive trait to his or her offspring is called a _____. (p. 74)

5. One of the most common recessive disorders is _____, which affects the way the body breaks down proteins contained in many foods. (p. 74)

6. _____ genes enhance or dilute the effects of other genes. (p. 75)

7. True or False: Serious disorders typically result from dominant alleles. (p. 75)

8. What is *codominance*? (p. 75)

_____

_____

_____

9. True or False: Males are more likely to be affected by X-linked inheritance than are females. (p. 75)

10. Name two X-linked conditions or disorders. (pp. 76–77)

    A. _____

    B. _____

11. _____ occurs when alleles are chemically marked in such a way that one pair member is activated, regardless of its makeup. (p. 77)

12. Explain how harmful genes are created. (p. 78)

    _____

    _____

    _____

13. Describe *polygenic inheritance*, and give an example of a trait that is determined by this pattern of inheritance. (p. 78)

    _____

    _____

    _____

    _____

Chromosomal Abnormalities

1. Most chromosomal defects are the result of mistakes during _____, when the ovum and sperm are formed. (p. 78)

2. _____, the most common chromosomal abnormality, often results from a defect in the 21st chromosome. For this reason, the disorder is sometimes called _____. (p. 79)

3. List the physical and behavioral characteristics of Down syndrome. (p. 79)

    A. Physical: _____

    _____

    _____

B. Behavioral: _____

_____

_____

4. True or False: The risk of Down syndrome rises with maternal age. (p. 79)

5. Disorders of the sex chromosomes result in (more / less) serious consequences than do disorders of the autosomes. (p. 79)

6. Most children with sex chromosome disorders (do / do not) suffer from mental retardation. (p. 79)

Reproductive Choices

Genetic Counseling

1. What is the purpose of genetic counseling, and who is most likely to seek this service? (p. 80)

_____

_____

_____

_____

Prenatal Diagnosis and Fetal Medicine

1. _____ are procedures that permit detection of developmental problems before birth. (p. 81)

2. Cite four types of prenatal diagnostic methods. (p. 81)

A. _____

B. _____

C. _____

D. _____

3. True or False: The techniques used in fetal medicine rarely result in birth complications such as premature labor and miscarriage. (p. 83)

4. The _____ Project is an international research program aimed at deciphering the chemical makeup of human genetic material. (p. 84)

Social Issues: The Pros and Cons of Reproductive Technologies

1. Explain the following reproductive technologies: (pp. 82–83)

   Donor insemination: _____

   _____

   _____

   In vitro fertilization: _____

   _____

   _____

2. True or False: Children conceived through in vitro fertilization typically exhibit a variety of behavioral and adjustment problems and have insecure attachments to their parents. (pp. 82–83)

3. Discuss some of the concerns surrounding the use of donor insemination and in vitro fertilization. (pp. 82–83)

   _____

   _____

   _____

   _____

4. Describe some of the risks involved with surrogate motherhood. (pp. 82–83)

   _____

   _____

   _____

   _____

Conception

1. Approximately once every 28 days, an ovum is released from one of a woman's two
   _____, and it travels through one of the two
   _____, which are long, thin structures that lead to the uterus.
   (p. 85)

The Period of the Zygote

1. The period of the zygote lasts about _____ weeks. (p. 87)

2. Match each term with the appropriate description. (p. 87)

   _____ will provide protective covering and nourishment
   to the new organism

   _____ a hollow, fluid-filled ball that is formed by a tiny
   mass of cells four days after fertilization

   _____ will become the new organism

   1. blastocyst
   2. embyronic disk
   3. trophoblast

3. List two functions of the amniotic fluid. (p. 87)

   A. _____

   B. _____

4. True or False: As many as 30% of zygotes do not make it through the first two weeks. (p. 87)

5. The _____ permits food and oxygen to reach the developing organism and
   waste products to be carried away. (pp. 87–88)

6. The placenta is connected to the developing organism by the _____
   _____. (p. 88)

The Period of the Embryo

1. The period of the embryo lasts from implantation through the _____ week of pregnancy. (p. 88)

2. True or False: The most rapid prenatal changes take place during the period of the embryo.
   (p. 88)

3. Why is the embryo especially vulnerable to interference with healthy development? (p. 88)

_____

_____

_____

4. List the organs and structures which will be formed from each of the following layers of the embryonic disk. (p. 88)

Ectoderm: _____

_____

Mesoderm: _____

_____

Endoderm: _____

_____

5. Summarize prenatal growth during the second month of pregnancy. (p. 89)

_____

_____

_____

The Period of the Fetus

1. The period of the fetus is sometimes referred to as the
   _____ phase. (p. 89)

2. Prenatal development is divided into _____, or three equal period of time. (p. 89)

3. The white, cheese-like substance that completely covers the fetus to protect the skin from chapping in the amniotic fluid is called _____. (p. 89)

4. _____ is a white, downy hair that covers the entire body of the fetus. (p. 89)

5. What major milestone in brain development is reached at the end of the second trimester? (p. 89)

_____

6. The age at which the baby can first survive if born early is called the *age of* _____. When does this typically occur? _____ (p. 90)

7. Describe the research findings on the relationship between fetal activity patterns and infant temperament at 3 and 6 months of age. (p. 90)

_____

_____

_____

_____

8. True or False: Research shows that the fetus develops a preference for the tone and rhythm of the mother's voice during the last weeks of pregnancy. (p. 91)

Prenatal Environmental Influences

Teratogens

1. Define the term *teratogen*, and describe four factors that affect the impact of teratogens on prenatal development. (p. 91)

Definition: _____

_____

A. _____

_____

B. _____

_____

C. _____

_____

D. _____

_____

2. A _____ *period* is a limited time span in which a part of the body or a behavior is biologically prepared to develop rapidly and is especially vulnerable to its surroundings. (p. 92)

3. True or False: The fetal period is the time when teratogens are most likely to cause serious defects. (p. 92)

4. When taken by mothers 4 to 6 weeks after conception, _____, a sedative widely available in some countries during the early 1960's, produced deformities of the embryo's developing arms and legs, and less frequently, caused damage to the ears, heart, kidneys, and genitals. (p. 93)

5. True or False: Heavy caffeine intake during pregnancy is associated with prematurity, miscarriage, and newborn withdrawal symptoms. (p. 93)

6. Describe the difficulties faced by babies who are prenatally exposed to heroine, cocaine, or methadone. (p. 94)

_____

_____

_____

_____

7. Explain why it is difficult to isolate the precise damage caused by prenatal exposure to cocaine. (p. 94)

_____

_____

_____

8. Summarize physical and behavioral effects of maternal smoking during the prenatal period. (pp. 94–95)

_____

_____

_____

_____

9. True or False: If the mother stops smoking at any time during the pregnancy, even during the last trimester, she reduces the chances that her baby will be negatively impacted. (p. 94)

10. Explain the mechanisms through which smoking harms the fetus. (p. 95)

_____

_____

_____

_____

11. True or False: Passive smoking has not been linked with any adverse effects on the infant. (p. 95)

12. Infants who have a cluster of physical and behavioral abnormalities and whose mothers drank heavily throughout most or all of pregnancy are said to have _____ _____; infants who show some, but not all, of these deficits and whose mothers drank in smaller quantities during pregnancy are said to suffer from _____ _____. (p. 95)

13. List some of the common impairments evidenced by children with FAS. (p. 95)

_____

_____

_____

14. True or False: The physical and mental impairments seen in babies with FAS typically lessen by the time the individual reaches adolescence or early adulthood. (p. 95)

15. Describe two ways in which alcohol produces its devastating effects. (p. 96)

A. _____

_____

B. _____

_____

16. True or False: There is no precise dividing line between safe and dangerous drinking levels during pregnancy. (p. 96)

17. Match each of the following environmental pollutants with its effect on development. (p. 96)

_____ This teratogen, commonly found in paint chippings from old buildings and other industrial materials, is related to prematurity, low birth weight, brain damage, and physical defects

_____ In the 1950's, children prenatally exposed to this teratogen in a Japanese community displayed mental retardation, abnormal speech, and uncoordinated movements

_____ Women who ate fish contaminated with this substance gave birth to babies with slightly reduced birth weights, smaller heads, and later memory and intellectual deficits

1. Mercury
2. Lead
3. PCBs

18. _____ (3 day German measles) is a teratogen that inflicts the greatest damage when it strikes during the (embryonic / fetal) period. (p. 97)

19. When women carrying the AIDS virus become pregnant, they pass the deadly virus to the developing organism approximately _____ to _____ percent of the time. (p. 97)

20. True or False: Most infants prenatally exposed to the AIDS virus survive 8 to 10 years after the appearance of symptoms. (p. 97)

Other Maternal Factors

1. Regular moderate exercise during pregnancy is associated with (increased / decreased) birth weight. (p. 98)

2. Summarize the behavioral and health problems of prenatally malnourished infants. (p. 98)

_____

_____

_____

_____

3. List the vitamin and mineral supplements which have been found to reduce prenatal complications and birth defects. (p. 99)

A. _____   B. _____

C. _____   D. _____

E. _____

4. Describe the mechanisms through which maternal stress affects the developing organism, and note outcomes associated with severe emotional stress during pregnancy. (pp. 99–100)

Mechanisms: _____

_____

_____

Outcomes: _____

_____

_____

5. True or False: Research shows that healthy women in their forties experience far more prenatal difficulties than do women in their twenties. (p. 100)

6. The physical immaturity of teenage mothers (does / does not) lead to pregnancy complications. (p. 100)

Childbirth

1. Name and describe the three stages of labor. (pp. 101–102)

A. _____

_____

_____

B. _____

_____

_____

C. _____

_____

_____

The Baby's Adaptation to Labor and Delivery

1. True or False: The production of stress hormones is adaptive for infants during childbirth. (p. 103)

The Newborn Baby's Appearance

1. The average newborn is _____ inches long and _____ pounds in weight. (p. 103)

2. At birth, the head is very (small / large) in relation to the trunk and legs. (p. 103)

Assessing the Newborn's Physical Condition: The Apgar Scale

1. List the five characteristics assessed by the Apgar Scale, and note which is the least reliable of these measures. (p. 104)

   A. _____

   B. _____

   C. _____

   D. _____

   E. _____

   Least reliable: _____

2. On the Apgar Scale, a score of _____ or better indicates that the infant is in good physical condition; a score between _____ and _____ indicates that the baby requires special assistance; a score of _____ or below indicates a dire emergency. (p. 104)

Biology and Environment: What Controls the Timing of Birth?

1. Name the placental hormone believed to initiate the complex hormonal system that controls the timing of birth. (pp. 102–103)

   _____

2. Explain how the "CRH-cortisol circuit" helps ensure that labor will occur only when the fetus is ready to survive outside of the womb. (pp. 102–103)

_____

_____

_____

Approaches to Childbirth

Natural, or Prepared, Childbirth

1. What is the theory behind the natural childbirth approach? (p. 105)

_____

_____

_____

2. List and describe three components of a typical natural childbirth program. (p. 105)

A. _____

_____

B. _____

_____

C. _____

_____

3. Research suggests that social support (is / is not) an important part of the success of natural childbirth techniques. (p. 105)

Home Delivery

1. Home births are typically handled by certified _____, who have degrees in nursing and additional training in childbirth management. (p. 106)

2. True or False: For healthy women assisted by a trained professional, it is just as safe to give birth at home as in a hospital. (p. 106)

Labor and Delivery Medication

1. True or False: Some form of medication is used in 85 to 90% of births in the United States. (p. 106)

2. Discuss three problems with the routine use of labor and delivery medications. (pp. 106–107)

   A. _____

   _____

   B. _____

   _____

   C. _____

   _____

Birth Complications

Oxygen Deprivation

1. _____ refers to oxygen deprivation during the birth process. (p. 107)

2. Infants in the _____ position are turned in such a way that the buttocks or feet would be delivered first. (p. 107)

3. Under what conditions can the Rh factor cause problems for the developing fetus? (p. 107)

   _____

   _____

   _____

4. True or False: First-born children are more likely than later-born children to be affected by Rh incompatibility. (p. 107)

5. True or False: Although anoxic infants are often behind their agemates in intellectual and motor progress in early childhood, most catch up by elementary school. (p. 108)

Preterm and Low-Birth-Weight Infants

1. Babies are considered premature if they are born _____ weeks before the end of a full 38-week pregnancy or if they weigh less than _____ pounds. (p. 108)

2. True or False: Birth weight is the best available predictor of infant survival and healthy development. (p. 108)

3. List the problems associated with low birth weight. (p. 108)

_____

_____

_____

_____

4. Distinguish between preterm and small-for-date babies. (p. 109)

Preterm: _____

_____

Small-for-date: _____

_____

5. Of the two types of babies, (preterm / small-for-date) infants usually have more serious problems. (p. 109)

6. Describe the characteristics of preterm infants and explain how those characteristics may influence the behavior of parents. (p. 109)

_____

_____

_____

_____

_____

7. Discuss several methods of stimulation used to foster the successful development of preterm infants. (p. 110)

_____

_____

_____

_____

_____

8. True or False: Research suggests that all preterm infants, regardless of family characteristics, require continuous, high-quality interventions well into the school years in order to maintain developmental gains. (p. 110)

Understanding Birth Complications

1. Summarize important findings from the Kauai study regarding the development of infants who experienced birth complications. (p. 111)

_____

_____

_____

_____

_____

Cultural Influences: A Cross-National Perspective on Health Care and Other Policies for Parents and Newborn Babies

1. _____ refers to the number of deaths in the first year of life per 1,000 live births. (pp. 112–113)

2. True or False: Black infants are more than twice as likely as white infants to die in the first year of life. (pp. 112–113)

3. _____ _mortality_, the rate of death in the first month of life, accounts for 67% of the infant death rate in the United States. (pp. 112–113)

4. List the two leading causes of neonatal mortality. (pp. 112–113)

   A. _____

   B. _____

5. Discuss the factors largely responsible for the relatively high rates of infant mortality in the United States. (pp. 112–113)

_____

_____

_____

_____

6. Discuss factors linked to lower infant mortality rates. (pp. 112–113)

_____

_____

_____

_____

Heredity, Environment, and Behavior: A Look Ahead

1. _____ is a field devoted to uncovering the contributions of nature and nurture as they relate to individual differences in human traits and abilities. (p. 113)

2. True or False: All behavioral geneticists agree that both heredity and environment are involved in every aspect of development. (p. 113)

The Question, "How Much?"

1. What are two methods used by behavioral geneticists to infer the role of heredity in human characteristics? (p. 114)

   A. _____

   B. _____

2. What are *heritability estimates*? (p. 114)

   _____

   _____

   _____

3. Heritability estimates are obtained from _____, which compare characteristics of family members. (p. 114)

4. True or False: Heritability estimates for intelligence and personality are approximately .50, indicating that genetic makeup can explain half of the variance in these traits. (p. 114)

5. What is a *concordance rate*? (p. 114)

   _____

   _____

   _____

6. What do concordance rates of 0 and 100 mean? (p. 114)

0: _____

_____

100: _____

_____

7. When a concordance rate is much higher for (identical / fraternal) twins, then heritability is believed to play a major role. (p. 114)

8. Discuss the limitations of heritability estimates and concordance rates. (p. 115)

_____

_____

_____

_____

_____

_____

The Question, "How?"

1. The concept of _____ emphasizes that each person responds to the environment in a unique way because of his or her genetic makeup. (p. 116)

2. Define the term *canalization*. (p. 116)

_____

_____

3. Infant perceptual and motor development seem to be (more strongly / less strongly) canalized, while intelligence and personality are (more strongly / less strongly) canalized. (p. 116)

4. According to the concept of _____, our genes influence the environments to which we are exposed. (p. 116)

5. Describe passive, evocative, and active genetic-environmental correlations. (pp. 116–117)

Passive: _____

_____

_____

Evocative: _____

_____

_____

Active: _____

_____

_____

6. The tendency to choose environments that complement our own heredity is called
   _____. (p. 117)

7. Define the term *epigenesis*. (p. 117)

_____

_____

**Biology and Environment: Uncoupling Genetic-Environmental Correlations
for Mental Illness and Antisocial Behavior**

1. True or False: Adopted children whose biological mothers have psychological disorders are more likely to develop mental illness when reared in maladaptive homes than when reared in healthy homes. (p. 118)

ASK YOURSELF . . .

Review: Explain the genetic origins of PKU and Down syndrome. Cite evidence indicating that both heredity and environment contribute to the development of children with these disorders. (p. 80)

_____

_____

_____

_____

_____

Review: Using your knowledge of X-linked inheritance, explain why males are more vulnerable to miscarriage, infant death, and genetic disorders. (p. 80)

_____

_____

_____

_____

_____

Apply: Gilbert's genetic makeup is homozygous for dark hair. Jan's is homozygous for blond hair. What proportion of their children are likely to be dark-haired? Explain. (p. 80)

_____

_____

_____

_____

_____

Connect: Referring to ecological systems theory (Chapter 1, pages 27–29), explain why parents of children with genetic disorders often experience increased stress. What factors, within and beyond the family, can help these parents support their children's development? (p. 80)

_____

_____

_____

_____

_____

Review: Why is genetic counseling called a *communication process?* Who should seek it? (p. 84)

_____

_____

_____

_____

_____

Apply: A woman over age 35, who has just learned she is pregnant, wants to find out as soon as possible whether her embryo has a genetic defect. She also wants to minimize injury to the developing organism. Which prenatal diagnostic method is she likely to choose? (p. 84)

_____

_____

_____

_____

_____

Review: Why is the period of the embryo regarded as the most dramatic prenatal phase? Why is the period of the fetus called the "growth and finishing" phase? (p. 91)

_____

_____

_____

_____

_____

Apply: Amy, 2 months pregnant, wonders how the developing organism is being fed. "I don't look pregnant yet, so does that mean not much development has occurred?" she asks. How would you respond to Amy? (p. 91)

_____

_____

_____

_____

_____

Connect: How does brain development relate to fetal behavior? (p. 91)

_____

_____

_____

_____

_____

Review: What is a sensitive period? How is it relevant to understanding the impact of teratogens? (p. 100)

_____

_____

_____

_____

_____

Review: Why is it difficult to determine the effects of many environmental agents, such as drugs and pollution, on the embryo and fetus? (p. 100)

_____

_____

_____

_____

_____

Apply: Nora, pregnant for the first time, has heard about the teratogenic impact of alcohol and tobacco. Nevertheless, she believes that a few cigarettes and a glass of wine a day won't be harmful. Provide Nora with research-based reasons for not smoking or drinking. (p. 100)

_____

_____

_____

_____

_____

Connect: List teratogens and other maternal factors that affect brain growth during the prenatal period. Why is the central nervous system often affected when the prenatal environment is compromised? (p. 100)

_____

_____

_____

_____

_____

Review: Name and briefly describe the three stages of labor. (p. 107)

_____

_____

_____

_____

_____

Review: Describe the ingredients and benefits of natural childbirth. What aspect contributes greatly to favorable outcomes, and why? (p. 107)

_____

_____

_____

_____

_____

Apply: Jenny is thinking about having her baby at home. What should she consider in making her decision? (p. 107)

_____

_____

_____

_____

_____

Connect: How do findings on the timing of birth illustrate bidirectional influences between mother and fetus? How do they illustrate the roles of both nature and nurture? (p. 107)

_____

_____

_____

_____

_____

Review: Cite five possible causes of anoxia during childbirth. How do anoxic newborns fare in development? (p. 111)

_____

_____

_____

_____

_____

Review: Sensitive care can help preterm infants recover, but they are less likely to receive such care than are full-term newborns. Explain why. (p. 111)

_____

_____

_____

_____

_____

Apply: Cecilia and Adena each gave birth to a 3-pound baby 7 weeks preterm. Cecilia is single and on welfare. Adena and her husband are happily married and earn a good income. Plan an intervention for helping each baby develop. (p. 111)

_____

_____

_____

_____

_____

Connect: List factors in this chapter that increase the chances that an infant will be born underweight. How many of these factors could be prevented through better health care for expectant mothers? (p. 111)

_____

_____

_____

_____

_____

Review: Why did one group of experts conclude that heritability estimates cannot yield firm conclusions about the relative strength of heredity and environmental influences? (p. 119)

_____

_____

_____

_____

Review: What is epigenesis, and how does it differ from range of reaction and genetic-environmental correlation? (p. 119)

_____

_____

_____

_____

_____

Apply: Bianca's parents are accomplished musicians. At age 4, Bianca began taking piano lessons. By age 10, she was accompanying the school choir. At age 14, she asked if she could attend a special music high school. Explain how genetic–environmental correlation promoted Bianca's talent. (p. 119)

_____

_____

_____

_____

Connect: How do the findings shown in Figure 3.19 in the Biology and Environment box on page 118 illustrate the idea that unique blends of heredity and environment lead to both similarities and differences in behavior? (p. 119)

_____

_____

_____

_____

SUGGESTED STUDENT READINGS

Baker, D. L., Schuette, J. L., & Uhlmann, W. R. (Eds.). (1998). *A guide to genetic counseling.* New York: Wiley-Liss. A detailed presentation of the components, theoretical framework, goals, and unique approaches used in genetic counseling.

Kleinfeld, J., Morse, B., Wescott, S. (Eds.). (2000). *Fantastic Antone grows up: adolescents and adults with fetal alcohol syndrome.* Fairbanks, AK: University of Alaska Press. Primarily written as a guide for parents and caregivers, presents real-life accounts of the unique experiences of adolescents and young adults living with fetal alcohol syndrome.

Moore, K. L., & Persaud, T. V. N. (1998). *Before we are born (5th ed.).* Philadelphia: Saunders. A detailed presentation of prenatal development, emphasizing basic facts and concepts of normal and abnormal growth from a biological perspective.

Tracey, N. (Ed.). (2000). *Parents of premature infants: Their emotional world.* London: Whurr Publishers, Ltd. A series of in-depth interviews which focus on the emotions, thoughts, and fantasies of parents of premature infants.

PUZZLE 3.1

Across

4. Each of two or more forms of a gene located at the same place on the chromosomes
5. Human sperm and ova
7. Directly observable characteristics
9. Genetic _____: alleles are chemically marked in such a way that one pair member is activated, regardless of its makeup
10. Long, double-stranded molecules that make up chromosomes (abbr.)
12. Having two identical alleles at the same place on a pair of chromosomes
13. The genetic makeup of an individual
15. Exchange of genes between chromosomes next to each other during meiosis (2 words)
17. Rodlike structures in the cell nucleus that store and transmit genetic information

Down

1. A heterozygous individual who can pass a recessive trait to his or her offspring
2. _____ counseling: helps couples assess the likelihood of giving birth to a baby with a hereditary disorder and choose the best course of action in view of the risks and family goals
3. A segment of DNA along the length of a chromosome
6. The process of cell duplication
8. Having two different alleles at the same place on a pair of chromosomes
11. The 22 matching chromosome pairs in each cell
14. _____ genes enhance or dilute the effects of other genes.
16. _____ diagnostic methods are medical procedures that permit detection of developmental problems before birth.
18. A sudden but permanent change in a segment of DNA
19. The process of cell division
20. _____ chromosomes: the 23rd pair of chromosomes; XX in females, XY in males

PUZZLE 3.2

Across

2. Fetal Alcohol _____: condition of children who display some, but not all, of the defects of FAS
4. Age of _____: age at which the fetus can survive if born early
6. Outer membrane that forms a protective covering around the prenatal organism
7. Organ that separates the mother's bloodstream from that of the fetus or embryo but permits exchange of nutrients and waste products
9. Cell resulting from the union of the sperm and ova at conception
11. When present in the fetus's blood but not in the mothers, the _____ factor can cause the mother to build up antibodies that destroy the fetus's red blood cells.
14. Inner membrane that forms a protective covering around the prenatal organism and encloses it in amniotic fluid
15. Scale used to assess the newborn's physical condition immediately after birth
18. Pattern of inheritance in which, under heterozygous conditions, the influence of only one allele is apparent
20. Childbirth approach designed to reduce pain and medical intervention
21. White, cheeselike substance covering the fetus and preventing the skin from chapping in the amniotic fluid
24. Infants born several weeks or more before their due date
25. White, downy hair that covers the entire body of the fetus

Down

1. Position of the baby in the uterus such that the buttocks or feet would be delivered first
3. Infants whose birth weight is below normal when the length of the pregnancy is taken into account (3 words)
5. Pattern of inheritance in which both alleles influence the person's characteristics
8. Twins that result from the release and fertilization of two ova; genetically no more alike than ordinary siblings; also known as dizygotic twins
10. Any environmental agent that causes damage during the prenatal period
12. Pattern of inheritance in which many genes determine the characteristic in question
13. Long cord connecting the prenatal organism to the placenta that delivers nutrients and removes waste products (2 words)
16. Twins that result when a zygote that has started to duplicate separates into two clusters of cells that develop into two individuals with the same genetic makeup
17. Prenatal organism from 2 to 8 weeks after conception, during which time the foundation for all body structures and internal organs are laid down
19. Fetal Alcohol _____: set of defects that results when women consume large amounts of alcohol during pregnancy
22. Pattern of inheritance in which a recessive gene is carried on the X chromosome
23. Prenatal organism from the beginning of the third month to the end of pregnancy, during which time completion of body structures and dramatic growth in size take place

PUZZLE 3.3

Across

2. The tendency to actively choose environments that complement our heredity (hyph.)
3. The percentage of instances in which both twins show a trait when it is present in one twin is referred to as a _____ rate.
4. _____ estimate: statistic that measures the extent to which individual differences in complex traits in a specific population are due to genetic factors
7. Each person's unique, genetically determined response to a range of environmental conditions (3 words)
8. _____ genetics is a field of study devoted to uncovering the hereditary and environmental origins of individual differences in human traits and abilities.

9. _____ studies compare the characteristics of family members to determine the importance of heredity in complex human characteristics.
10. The tendency of heredity to restrict the development of some characteristics to just one or a few outcomes

Down

1. The number of deaths in the first year of life per 1,000 live births (2 words)
5. Development resulting from ongoing bidirectional exchanges between heredity and all levels of the environment
6. _____-environmental correlation: idea that heredity influences the environments to which individuals are exposed

PRACTICE TEST

1. Directly observable physical and behavioral characteristics are called: (p. 70)
   a. genotypes.
   b. phenotypes.
   c. alleles.
   d. chromosomes.

2. Rodlike structures in the nucleus of a cell that store and transmit genetic information are called: (p. 70)
   a. gametes.
   b. genes.
   c. autosomes.
   d. chromosomes.

3. The process of cell duplication in which the DNA ladder splits down the middle and each base pairs with a new mate, creating two identical DNA ladders, is called: (p. 71)
   a. mitosis.
   b. meiosis.
   c. crossing over.
   d. genetic imprinting.

4. Monozygotic twins are: (p. 73)
   a. genetically identical.
   b. genetically no more alike than ordinary siblings.
   c. conceived when two separate ova are fertilized.
   d. the most common type of multiple birth.

5. The pattern of genetic inheritance, seen in heterozygous pairings, in which only one allele affects the child's characteristics is called: (p. 74)
   a. polygenic inheritance.
   b. X-linked inheritance.
   c. dominant-recessive inheritance.
   d. codominance.

6. Serious diseases are only rarely due to dominant alleles because: (p. 75)
   a. dominance requires that the same allele be inherited from both parents.
   b. other genes usually alter the effects of dominant alleles.
   c. children inheriting the harmful dominant allele would always develop the disorder and would seldom live long enough to pass on the trait.
   d. recessive genes usually overtake the harmful dominant allele.

7. Continuous traits, such as height and intelligence, are due to _____, in which many genes determine the characteristic. (p. 78)
   a. polygenic inheritance
   b. monogenic inheritance
   c. heterozygous inheritance
   d. homozygous inheritance

8. The most common chromosomal abnormality is: (p. 79)
   a. Klinefelter Syndrome.
   b. PKU.
   c. cystic fibrosis.
   d. Down syndrome.

9. The organ that separates the mother's bloodstream from the embryonic or fetal bloodstream, but permits exchange of nutrients and waste, is called the: (p. 87)
   a. amnion.
   b. chorion.
   c. placenta.
   d. umbilical cord.

10. The most rapid prenatal changes take place during the period of the _____. (p. 88)
    a. zygote
    b. fetus
    c. neonate
    d. embryo

11. _____ covers the baby's skin and prevents it from chapping in the amniotic fluid. (p. 89)
    a. Lanugo
    b. The amnion
    c. Vernix
    d. The placenta

12. Exposure to teratogens during the _____ period is associated with the most serious defects. (p. 92)
    a. embryonic
    b. zygotic
    c. fetal
    d. neonatal

13. Infants who are prenatally exposed to cocaine: (p. 94)
    a. rarely show addictions to the drug at birth.
    b. show few ill effects beyond the dangerous withdrawal period.
    c. typically have lasting difficulties.
    d. exhibit an easy temperament and are very receptive to cuddling.

14. The most well-known effect of smoking during pregnancy is: (p. 94)
    a. low birth weight.
    b. infant death.
    c. childhood behavioral problems.
    d. long-term respiratory difficulties.

15. What amount of alcohol is required to produce Fetal Alcohol Effects (FAE)? (p. 95)
    a. extreme maternal alcoholism
    b. more than two drinks per day
    c. as little as one ounce per day
    d. no precise amount has been determined

16. The AIDS virus: (p. 97)
    a. is transmitted from infected mothers to their unborn babies approximately 80% of the time.
    b. is now the leading cause of infant death in most Western nations.
    c. progresses especially rapidly in infants.
    d. progresses more slowly in infants than in older children and adults.

17. Prenatal malnutrition is known to cause: (p. 98)
    a. damage to the central nervous system (CNS).
    b. severe mental retardation.
    c. delayed motor development.
    d. serious cognitive impairments, including deficits in attention, memory, planning, and spatial abilities.

18. Which of the following takes place during Stage 1 of the childbirth process? (p. 101)
    a. delivery of the baby
    b. prelabor
    c. dilation and effacement of the cervix
    d. birth of the placenta

19. Natural, or prepared, childbirth: (p. 105)
    a. tries to overcome the idea that birth is a painful ordeal that requires extensive medical intervention.
    b. is typically handled by a certified midwife.
    c. is not conducive to father presence in the delivery room.
    d. is associated with increased risk of birth complications.

20. In cases where the mother is negative and the baby is positive, _____ can cause oxygen deprivation and may result in mental retardation, heart damage, and death at birth. (p. 107)
    a. eclampsia
    b. the Rh factor
    c. antibody incompatibility
    d. the androgen factor

21. An infant born two months early but weighing an appropriate amount for the time spent in the uterus is called: (p. 109)
    a. small-for-date.
    b. preterm.
    c. postterm.
    d. breech.

22. Which of the following is true regarding the use of stimulation with preterm infants? (p. 110)
    a. Doctors recommend that all preterm infants are placed in a highly stimulating environment in order to foster development.
    b. Research suggests that stimulation is harmful for fragile preterm infants.
    c. Preterm infants differ in their responses to stimulation, and therefore, the amount and kind of stimulation should be adjusted to fit the needs of the individual child.
    d. Studies suggest that stimulation is unrelated to developmental outcomes in preterm infants.

23. A statistic that measures the extent to which continuous traits, such as intelligence, can be traced to genetic factors is called a: (p. 114)
    a. heritability estimate.
    b. kinship estimate.
    c. concordance rate.
    d. canalization estimate.

24. Since all normal human infants eventually roll over, sit up, crawl, and walk, one can conclude that infant motor behavior is a strongly _____ trait. (p. 116)
    a. canalized
    b. imprinted
    c. instinctive
    d. encouraged

25. Identical twins reared apart, who nevertheless have many psychological traits and lifestyle characteristics in common, illustrate a form of genetic-environmental correlation called: (p. 117)
    a. range of reaction.
    b. canalization.
    c. niche-picking.
    d. evocation.

.

CHAPTER 4
INFANCY: EARLY LEARNING, MOTOR SKILLS, AND PERCEPTUAL CAPACITIES

BRIEF CHAPTER SUMMARY

Infant development proceeds at an astounding pace. The newborn baby enters the world with surprisingly sophisticated perceptual and motor abilities, a set of skills for interacting with people, and a capacity to learn that is put to use immediately after birth. Reflexes are the newborn's most obvious organized patterns of behavior. Some have survival value, others help parents and infants establish gratifying interaction, and others form the basis for motor skills that will develop later. Infants move in and out of six states of arousal that become more organized and predictable with age. Like children and adults, infants alternate between REM and NREM sleep, although they spend far more time in the REM state than they ever will again. Young infants are believed to have a special need for REM sleep; their brain-wave activity safeguards the central nervous system, and the rapid eye movements protect the health of the eye. Crying is the first way that babies communicate, letting parents know they need food, comfort, and stimulation. An infant's cry stimulates strong feelings of arousal and discomfort in almost anyone, and controversy exists on how quickly and how often parents should respond. Abnormal crying may indicate central nervous system distress.

The most widely used instrument for assessing the organized functioning of newborn infants is Brazelton's Neonatal Behavioral Assessment (NBAS). It has helped researchers understand individual and cultural differences in newborn behavior.

Babies come into the world with built-in learning capacities that permit them to profit from experience immediately. Infants are capable of two basic forms of learning: classical and operant conditioning. Habituation and recovery research provides a window into infant attention, perception, and cognition, and reveals that infants are naturally attracted to novel stimulation and that their recognition memory improves steadily with age. Newborn infants also have a primitive ability to imitate the facial expressions and gestures of adults.

According to dynamic systems theory of motor development, mastery of motor skills involves acquiring increasingly complex systems of action. Each new skill is jointly influenced by central nervous system maturation, movement possibilities of the body, goals the child has in mind, and environmental supports. Voluntary reaching plays a vital role in infant cognitive development and is integrated into increasingly elaborate motor skills.

Sensitivity to touch, taste, smell, and sound are well developed in the newborn. Newborns have a built-in sense of balance that is refined with experience and motor control, as their postural adjustments to self-movement take place unconsciously. Vision is the least mature of the baby's senses. Research on infants with severe visual impairments dramatically illustrates the interdependence of vision, social interaction, motor exploration, and understanding of the world. Depth perception develops as infants detect kinetic, binocular, and pictorial cues, and gradually babies move from focusing on the parts of a pattern to perceiving it as an organized whole. Experience in crawling facilitates coordination of action with depth information. The Gibsons' differentiation theory provides an overall account of perceptual development.

Research findings on the question of whether infancy is a sensitive period of development indicate that early experience combines with current conditions to affect the child's development.

LEARNING OBJECTIVES

After reading this chapter, you should be able to:

4.1   Name and describe major newborn reflexes, noting the functions served by each, and discuss the importance of assessing newborn reflexes. (p. 124–126)

4.2   Describe the six infant states of arousal, with particular attention to sleep and crying. (p. 126–133)

4.3   Describe Brazelton's Neonatal Behavioral Assessment Scale (NBAS), and explain its usefulness. (p. 133)

4.4   Explain how infants learn through classical conditioning, operant conditioning, habituation, and imitation. (p. 134–138)

4.5   Describe the sequence of motor development during the first 2 years of life. (p. 139–140)

4.6   Explain the dynamic systems theory of motor development, and discuss the support for this approach stemming from microgenetic and cross-cultural research. (p. 140–142)

4.7   Describe the development of reaching and grasping, and explain how early experiences affect these skills. (p. 142–144)

4.8   Describe infants' sensitivity to touch, taste, smell, and balance and self-movement, noting how each perceptual capacity influences other aspects of development. (p. 145–148)

4.9   Summarize the development of hearing in infancy, giving special attention to speech perception. (p. 148–150)

4.10 Summarize the development of vision in infancy, including acuity, color perception, depth perception, face perception, and object perception. (p. 150–159)

4.11 Explain the concept of intermodal perception. (p. 159–161)

4.12 Explain the differentiation theory of perceptual development. (p. 161–162)

4.13 Discuss research on early deprivation and enrichment, and explain how it sheds light on the question of whether infancy is a sensitive period of development. (p. 163–164)

STUDY QUESTIONS

The Organized Newborn

Newborn Reflexes

1. What is a *reflex*? (p. 124)

   _____

   _____

2. Match each reflex with the appropriate response or function descriptor. (p. 125)

_____ Spontaneous grasp of adult's finger	1. Eye blink
_____ When the sole of foot is stroked, the toes fan out and curl	2. Tonic neck
	3. Palmar grasp
_____ Helps infant find the nipple	4. Babinski
_____ Prepares infant for voluntary walking	5. Rooting
_____ Permits feeding	6. Sucking
_____ Infant lies in a "fencing position"	7. Swimming
_____ Protects infant from strong stimulation	8. Stepping
_____ In our evolutionary past, may have helped infant cling to mother	9. Moro
_____ Helps infants survive if dropped in water	

3. Briefly explain the adaptive value of newborn reflexes. (p. 125)

   _____

   _____

   _____

4. Discuss research findings concerning how early reflexive stimulation contributes to motor control. (p. 125)

_____

_____

_____

_____

5. When do most newborn reflexes disappear? (p. 125)

_____

6. Explain the importance of assessing newborn reflexes. (p. 126)

_____

_____

_____

Newborn States

1. Name and describe the six infant states of arousal. (p. 128)

A. _____

_____

B. _____

_____

C. _____

_____

D. _____

_____

E. _____

_____

F. _____

_____

2. Describe the characteristics of REM and NREM sleep. (p. 128)

REM: _____

_____

NREM: _____

_____

3. Why do infants spend more time in REM sleep than do children, adolescents, and adults? (p. 128)

_____

_____

4. What is the most effective way to soothe a crying baby when feeding and diaper changing do not work? (p. 131)

_____

5. True or False: Trends in infant crying behavior are likely due to normal difficulties in readjusting to the sleep-wake cycle as the central nervous system develops rather than resulting from parental response patterns. (p. 132)

6. How do the cries of brain-damaged babies and those who have experienced prenatal and birth complications differ from those of healthy infants, and how does this difference affect parental responding? (p. 132)

_____

_____

_____

Cultural Influences: Cultural Variations in Infant Sleeping Arrangements

1. True or False: Although rare in the United States, parent–infant cosleeping is common in many other countries around the world. (p. 127)

2. Explain the role of collectivist versus individualistic cultural values in determining infant sleeping arrangements. (p. 127)

_____

_____

_____

_____

1. What is *Sudden Infant Death Syndrome (SIDS)*? (p. 130)

    _____

    _____

2. True or False: In industrialized countries, SIDS is the leading cause of infant mortality between one week and twelve months of age. (p. 130)

3. True or False: Researchers have recently determined the precise cause of SIDS. (p. 130)

4. Describe some early physical problems that are common among SIDS victims. (p. 130)

    _____

    _____

    _____

5. Describe four environmental factors associated with SIDS. (p. 130)

    A. _____

    _____

    B. _____

    _____

    C. _____

    _____

    D. _____

    _____

Neonatal Behavioral Assessment

1. Which areas of behavior does the NBAS evaluate? (p. 133)

    _____

    _____

2. Since the NBAS is given to infants all around the world, researchers have been able to learn a great deal about individual and cultural differences in newborn behavior and the ways in which various child-rearing practices affect infant behavior. Briefly discuss these findings. (p. 133)

    _____

    _____

    _____

    _____

3. Why is a single NBAS score not a good predictor of later development, and what should be used in place of a single score? (p. 133)

    _____

    _____

4. How are NBAS interventions beneficial for the early parent–infant relationship? (p. 133)

    _____

    _____

Learning Capacities

1. Define *learning*. (p. 134)

    _____

2. _____ *conditioning* is a form of learning in which a neutral stimulus is paired with a stimulus that leads to a reflexive response. (p. 134)

3. Why is classical conditioning of great value to infants? (p. 134)

    _____

    _____

4. Match the following terms to the appropriate definitions. (p. 135)

    _____ A neutral stimulus that leads to a reflexive response, if learning occurs
    _____ A learned response exhibited toward a previously neutral stimulus
    _____ A reflexive response
    _____ A stimulus that automatically leads to a reflexive response

    1. Unconditioned Stimulus (UCS)
    2. Conditioned Stimulus (CS)
    3. Unconditioned Response (UCR)
    4. Conditioned Response (CR)

5. Using the above definitions as a guide (see question 4), outline the three steps involved in classical conditioning. (p. 134–135)

A. _____

_____

B. _____

_____

C. _____

_____

6. In classical conditioning, if the CS is presented alone enough times, without being paired with the UCS, the CR will no longer occur. This is referred to as
_____. (p. 135)

7. Young infants can be classically conditioned most easily when the association between the two stimuli has _____ value. (p. 135)

8. Explain the process of *operant conditioning.* (p. 135)

_____

_____

_____

9. Define the terms *reinforcer* and *punishment* as they relate to operant conditioning. (p. 135)

Reinforcer: _____

_____

Punishment: _____

_____

10. _____ refers to a gradual reduction in the strength of a response due to repetitive stimulation. The recovery seen when a new stimulus is introduced and responsiveness returns to a high level is referred to as _____. (p. 136)

11. Cite two limitations of habituation research. (p. 137)

A. _____

_____

B. _____

_____

12. True or False: Habituation and recovery to visual stimuli during infancy are among the best available predictors of intelligence in childhood and adolescence. (p. 137)

13. True or False: The imitation observed in newborns appears to represent active attempts to match what they "see" with what they "feel," much as it does in adults. (p. 138)

14. Describe what infants are able to learn through the process of imitation. (p. 138)

_____

_____

_____

Motor Development in Infancy

The Sequence of Motor Development

1. Distinguish between gross and fine motor development, and provide examples of each. (p. 139)

Gross: _____

_____

Examples: _____

Fine: _____

_____

Examples: _____

2. True or False: Although the *sequence* of motor development is fairly uniform, large individual differences exist in the *rate* of development. (p. 139)

3. Discuss the organization and direction of motor development in relation to the cephalocaudal and proximodistal trends. (p. 139)

Cephalocaudal: _____

_____

_____

Proximodistal: _____

_____

_____

Motor Skills as Dynamic Systems

1. According to the dynamic systems theory of motor development, mastery of motor skills involves acquisition of increasingly complex *systems of action*. Explain what this means. (p. 140)

_____

_____

_____

_____

2. List four factors that contribute to the development of each new motor skill. (p. 140)

A. _____

B. _____

C. _____

D. _____

3. True or False: Dynamic systems theory regards motor development as a genetically determined process. Briefly explain your response. (p. 141)

_____

_____

_____

4. What did Esther Thelen's microgenetic studies reveal about infant motor development? (p. 141)

_____

_____

_____

5. Give at least one example of how cultural variations in infant-rearing practices affect motor development. (p. 141–142)

_____

_____

_____

Fine Motor Development: Voluntary Reaching, Grasping, and Manipulation of Objects

1. The grasp reflex of the newborn period is replaced by the _____ grasp, a clumsy motion in which the fingers close against the palm. By the end of the first year, infants use the thumb and index finger opposably in a well-coordinated _____ grasp. (p. 143)

Perceptual Development in Infancy

Touch

1. True or False: Infants are born with a poorly developed sense of touch, and consequently, they are not sensitive to pain. (p. 145)

Taste and Smell

1. True or False: Infants not only have taste preferences, but they are also capable of communicating these preferences to adults through facial expressions. (p. 146)

2. True or False: Certain odor preferences are innate. (p. 146)

3. True or False: Newborn infants are attracted to the scent of a lactating woman, but they are unable to discriminate the smell of their own mother's breast from that of an unfamiliar lactating woman. (p. 146–147)

Balance and Self-Movement

1. Explain the concept of *optical flow*. (p. 147)

_____

_____

_____

2. Balance is a(n) (innate / learned) capacity. (p. 147)

Hearing

1. True or False: Infants can discriminate almost all of the speech sounds of any human language. (p. 148)

2. Cite the characteristics of human speech preferred by infants. (p. 148)

_____

_____

**From Research to Practice: Impact of Early Hearing Loss on Development—
The Case of Otitis Media**

1. What is *otitis media,* and how does it lead to hearing loss? (p. 149)

_____

_____

_____

2. Discuss the impact of otitis media on language development and academic functioning. (p. 149)

_____

_____

_____

_____

_____

3. List four ways to prevent the negative developmental outcomes of early otitis media. (p. 149)

A. _____

B. _____

C. _____

D. _____

Vision

1. Vision is the (most / least) mature of the newborn baby's senses. (p. 150)

2. Describe the newborn baby's visual acuity. (p. 150–151)

   _____

   _____

3. True or False: Infants have well-developed color vision at birth, and they are immediately capable of discriminating colors. (p. 151)

4. What is *depth perception,* and why is it important in infant development? (p. 152)

   Definition: _____

   _____

   Importance: _____

   _____

5. Describe Gibson and Walk's studies using the visual cliff, and cite the limitations of this approach for the study of infant depth perception. (p. 152)

   Studies: _____

   _____

   _____

   _____

   Limitations: _____

   _____

   _____

6. Name and describe the three cues for depth, and indicate the approximate age at which infants become sensitive to each. (p. 152)

   A. _____

   _____

   Age: _____

   B. _____

   _____

   Age: _____

   C. _____

   _____

   Age: _____

7. Summarize Karen Adolph's research findings regarding the relationship between crawling and depth perception. (p. 153)

   _____

   _____

   _____

   _____

8. The principle of _____, which accounts for early pattern preferences, states that if infants can detect a difference in contrast between two or more patterns, they will prefer the one with more contrast. (p. 155)

9. True or False: By 1 to 2 months of age, infants recognize aspects of their mother's facial features, and they look longer at her face than at an unfamiliar woman's face. (p. 157–158)

10. True or False: Size and shape constancy emerge gradually over time as infants acquire more advanced knowledge of objects in the environment. (p. 158)

11 Newborn babies (are / are not) sensitive to indicators of an object's boundaries. (p. 159)

Biology and Environment: Development of Infants with Severe Visual Impairments

1. True or False: Children with severe visual impairments show delays in motor, cognitive, language, and social development. (p. 154–155)

2. Discuss how severe visual impairments impact motor exploration and spatial understanding. (p. 154–155)

   _____

   _____

   _____

   _____

3. How do severe visual impairments affect the caregiver–infant relationship? (p. 154–155)

   _____

   _____

   _____

4. List three techniques that can help infants with severe visual impairments become aware of their physical and social surroundings. (p. 154–155)

   A. _____

   _____

   B. _____

   _____

   C. _____

   _____

Intermodal Perception

1. What is *intermodal perception*? (p. 159)

   _____

   _____

2. True or False: From birth, infants are capable of combining information from multiple sensory systems. Cite research evidence supporting your response. (p. 159)

_____

_____

_____

_____

Understanding Perceptual Development

1. Explain the *differentiation theory* of perceptual development. (p. 161)

_____

_____

_____

_____

2. According to differentiation theory, perception is guided by discovery of _____ the action possibilities a situation offers an organism with certain motor capabilities. (p. 161)

**Early Deprivation and Enrichment:
Is Infancy a Sensitive Period of Development?**

1. Discuss the findings of Michael Rutter's research with young children adopted from Romanian orphanages. (p. 163)

_____

_____

_____

_____

2. True or False: Children who spend their first two years in deprived institutionalized care usually remain delayed in all domains of development. (p. 163)

3. True or False: Toddlers enrolled in early learning centers, where they are given a full curriculum of reading, math, and science, show dramatic gains in cognitive development and perform better than agemates on tests of intelligence. (p. 164)

ASK YOURSELF . . .

Review: What functions does REM sleep serve in young infants? When newborns awaken, about how much time do they spend crying? Can sleep and crying tell us about the health of a baby's central nervous system? Explain. (p. 138)

_____

_____

_____

_____

_____

Review: Provide an example of classical conditioning, operant conditioning, and habituation / recovery in young infants. Why is each type of learning useful? Cite differences between habituation and operant conditioning research on infant memory, and explain them. (p. 138)

_____

_____

_____

_____

_____

Apply: After a difficult birth, 2-day-old Kelly scored poorly on the NBAS. How would you address her mother's concerns that Kelly might not develop normally? (p. 138)

_____

_____

_____

_____

Connect: Provide several examples of how the diverse capabilities of newborns contribute to their first social relationships. (p. 138)

_____

_____

_____

_____

_____

Review: Cite evidence indicating that motor development is not hardwired into the brain but rather is a joint product of biological, psychological, and environmental factors. (p. 144)

_____

_____

_____

_____

_____

Review: Using an example, explain how infants acquire new motor skills by modifying and reorganizing what the body can already do to fit a new task. (p. 144)

_____

_____

_____

_____

_____

Apply: Roseanne hung mobiles and pictures above her newborn baby's crib and surrounded it with a brightly colored, patterned bumper hoping this would stimulate her infant's motor development. Is Roseanne doing the right thing? Why or why not? (p. 144)

_____

_____

_____

_____

_____

Connect: Provide several examples of how motor development influences infants' social experiences. How do social experiences, in turn, influence motor development? (p. 144)

_____

_____

_____

_____

_____

Review: According to differentiation theory, perceptual development reflects infants' active search for invariant features. Provide examples from research on hearing, pattern perception, and intermodal perception. (p. 162)

_____

_____

_____

_____

_____

Review: Using research on crawling, show how motor and perceptual development support one another. (p. 162)

_____

_____

_____

_____

_____

Review: Do changes in pattern perception illustrate how infant development proceeds from a perceptual to a cognitive emphasis? Explain. (p. 162)

_____

_____

_____

_____

_____

Apply: After several weeks of crawling, Benji learned to avoid going headfirst down a steep incline. Now he has started to walk. Can his mother trust him not to try walking down the steep surface? Explain, using the concept of affordances. (p. 162)

_____

_____

_____

_____

_____

Connect: Illustrate how operant conditioning and habituation/recovery permit researchers to find out about infants' sensitivity to touch, taste, smell, sound, and visual stimulation. Cite examples for each sense. (p. 162)

_____

_____

_____

_____

_____

Review: Explain why either too much stimulation or too little stimulation for an extended time has adverse effects on infant development. (p. 166)

_____

_____

_____

_____

_____

Connect: What do research findings on the development of Eastern European orphanage children tell us about the issue of stability versus change in children's development? (see Chapter 1, page 9) (p. 166)

_____

_____

_____

_____

_____

SUGGESTED STUDENT READINGS

Barr, R. G., Hopkins, B., & Green, J. A. (Eds.). (2000). *Crying as a sign, symptom, and a signal: Clinical, emotional, and developmental aspects of infant and toddler crying.* New York: Cambridge University Press. Takes a multidisciplinary look at this important infant behavior, describes normative developmental patterns of crying, and discusses how they are manifested in various settings—emergency department, painful procedures, colic, temper tantrums, and nonverbal and mentally challenged infants.

Bruer, J. T. (1999). *The myth of the first three years.* New York: Free Press. Challenges the widely accepted belief that the first 3 years of life determine whether or not a child will develop into a successful, thinking person. Drawing on research on brain development, this book shows that learning and cognitive development occur not just in infancy and toddlerhood, but also throughout childhood and adulthood. Stresses the dangers of a view that overemphasizes early learning to the detriment of long-term parental and educational responsibilities.

Nelson, C. A. (Ed.). (2000). *The Minnesota symposia on child psychology, Vol. 31: The effects of early adversity on neurobehavioral development.* Mahwah, NJ: Lawrence Erlbaum Associates. A collection of chapters that examines the effects of early biological and/or psychological adversity on child development. Also illustrates the importance of a dynamic systems approach to the study of early development.

Spock, B., & Parker, S. J. (1998). *Dr. Spock's baby and child care.* New York: Pocket Books. The most recent edition of this classic book of advice to parents. Includes sections on infant feeding and nutrition, growth and development, sleep, toilet training, illness, and more.

PUZZLE 4.1

Across

1. An inborn, automatic response to stimulation
5. The unexpected death of an infant under 1 year of age that remains unexplained after thorough investigation (abbr.)
6. In classical conditioning, a reflexive response that is produced by an UCS (abbr.)
8. In classical conditioning, a new response produced by a CS that resembles the UCR (abbr.)
11. A gradual reduction in the strength of a response due to repetitive stimulation
12. A test developed to assess the behavioral status of the infant during the newborn period (abbr.)
14. In classical conditioning, a neutral stimulus that through pairing with an UCS leads to a new response (abbr.)
15. A "regular sleep" state in which the body is quiet and heart rate, breathing, and brain wave activity are slow and regular (abbr.)
16. States of _____: different degrees of sleep and wakefulness
17. Following habituation, an increase in responsiveness to a new stimulus

18. _____ conditioning: form of learning in which a spontaneous behavior is followed by a stimulus that changes the probability that the behavior will occur again

Down

2. In classical conditioning, decline of the CR as a result of presenting the CS enough times without the UCS
3. Learning by copying the behavior of another person; a.k.a. modeling or observational learning
4. In classical conditioning, a stimulus that leads to a reflexive response (abbr.)
7. _____ conditioning: a form of learning that involves associating a neutral stimulus with a stimulus that leads to a reflexive response
9. In operant conditioning, a stimulus that increases the occurrence of a response
10. In operant conditioning, removing a desirable stimulus or presenting an unpleasant one to decrease the occurrence of a response
13. An "irregular" sleep state in which brain wave activity is similar to that of the waking state (abbr.)

PUZZLE 4.2

Across

1. _____ theory: view that perceptual development involves detection of increasingly fine-grained, invariant features in the environment

5. The visual _____ is an apparatus used to study depth perception in infants.

6. The _____ systems theory of motor development views new motor skills as reorganizations of previously mastered skills that lead to more effective ways of exploring and controlling the environment

7. Poorly coordinated, primitive reaching movements of newborn babies

8. _____ flow: movements in the visual field signaling that the body is in motion, leading to postural adjustments so the body remains upright

10. _____ trend: pattern of growth that proceeds from head to tail

11. Size _____: perception of an object's size as stable, despite changes in the size of its retinal image caused by changes in distance

12. Visual _____ : fineness of visual discrimination

14. _____ constancy: perception of an object's shape as stable, despite changes in its retinal image because of being seen from different vantage points

15. _____ trend: pattern of growth that proceeds from the center of the body outward

16. Well-coordinated grasp involving thumb and forefinger opposition

17. Depth cues that rely on each eye receiving a slightly different view of the visual field

18. Depth cues created by movements of the body or of objects in the environment

Down

2. In the differentiation theory of perceptual development, _____ features are those that remain stable in a constantly changing perceptual world.

3. _____ are the action possibilities a situation offers an organism with certain motor capabilities; play a major role in perceptual differentiation

4. _____ perception combines information from more than one sensory system.

9. Depth cues such as those that artists use to make a painting look three-dimensional, including receding lines, texture changes, and overlapping objects

13. Clumsy grasp of the young infant in which fingers close against the palm

14. Contrast _____: ability to detect contrast, or differences in light levels between adjacent regions in a pattern

117

PRACTICE TEST

1. The _____ reflex helps a breast-fed baby to find the mother's nipple. (p. 125)
   a. rooting
   b. sucking
   c. tonic neck
   d. Moro

2. A careful assessment of a newborn's reflexes provides the pediatrician with important information about the infant's: (p. 126)
   a. muscle tone.
   b. sensory capacities.
   c. responsiveness to physical stimulation.
   d. nervous system.

3. REM sleep: (p. 128)
   a. accounts for a lesser percentage of sleep time in infants than in children and adults.
   b. seems to fulfill young infants' need for stimulation since they spend such little time in an alert state.
   c. is a "regular" sleep state in which the body is almost motionless, and the heart rate, breathing, and brain wave activity are slow and regular.
   d. is less frequent in the fetus and in preterm infants than in full- term infants.

4. The most effective way to sooth a crying baby is to: (p. 131)
   a. lift the baby to the shoulder.
   b. swaddle the baby.
   c. offer a pacifier.
   d. play rhythmic sounds.

5. The cries of brain-damaged infants and those who have experienced prenatal and birth complications are often: (p. 132)
   a. more difficult for adults to interpret.
   b. weak and sporadic.
   c. shrill and piercing.
   d. easier to sooth than the cries of other infants.

6. Which of the following is true? (p. 133)
   a. A single Neonatal Behavioral Assessment Scale (NBAS) score is a good predictor of later development.
   b. NBAS "recovery curves", which estimate the baby's ability to recover from the stress of birth, successfully predict intelligence into the preschool years.
   c. Although widely used in the United States, the biased nature of the NBAS has not allowed successful exploration of cultural differences in newborn behavior.
   d. NBAS-based interventions have proven unsuccessful at facilitating a positive parent-infant relationship.

7. In classical conditioning, the _____ must consistently produce a reflexive reaction before learning can take place. (p. 134)
   a. unconditioned stimulus (UCS)
   b. conditioned stimulus (CS)
   c. unconditioned response (UCR)
   d. conditioned response (CR)

8. In classical conditioning, if the conditioned stimulus (CS) is presented alone enough times, without being paired with the unconditioned stimulus (UCS), the conditioned response (CR) will no longer occur. This is known as: (p. 135)
   a. dishabituation.
   b. termination.
   c. extinction.
   d. disassociation.

9. Which of the following is true with regard to classical conditioning? (p. 134)
   a. Infants are easily conditioned by pairing any two stimuli.
   b. Infants are conditioned most easily to fear responses.
   c. Classical conditioning is most effective when the neutral stimulus is presented several minutes after the unconditioned stimulus (UCS).
   d. Classical conditioning is valuable to infants because it makes the environment more orderly and predictable.

10. Which of the following best reflects the views of infant behavior suggested by classical conditioning and operant conditioning perspectives? (p. 136)
    a. In classical conditioning, infants are viewed as passive learners, whereas in operant conditioning, infants are viewed as active learners.
    b. In operant conditioning, infants are viewed as passive learners, whereas in classical conditioning, infants are viewed as active learners.
    c. Both classical and operant conditioning perspectives view infants as active learners.
    d. Both classical and operant conditioning perspectives view infants as passive learners.

11. In operant conditioning, a stimulus that increases the likelihood of a response is a: (p. 135)
    a. punishment.
    b. reward.
    c. reinforcer.
    d. conditioned stimulus.

12. After repeatedly listening to a particular tone for a period of time, an infant shows a gradual reduction in responding to this tone. When a new tone is introduced, the infant returns to a high level of responding. This increase in responsiveness to the new stimulus is known as: (p. 136)
    a. habituation.
    b. recovery.
    c. differentiation.
    d. extinction.

13. Research on infants' habituation and recovery allows researchers to explore early: (p. 136)
    a. motor development.
    b. imitation skills.
    c. attention and memory.
    d. extinction responses.

14. Crawling, standing, and walking are examples of: (p. 139)
    a. fine motor development.
    b. gross motor development.
    c. coordinated motor development.
    d. dynamic motor development.

15. The _____ trend refers to a pattern of physical growth which proceeds from the center of the body outward. (p. 139)
    a. intermodal
    b. cephalocaudal
    c. proximodistal
    d. inverse

16. According to the dynamic systems theory of motor development: (p. 140)
    a. new skills are acquired by revising and combining earlier accomplishments.
    b. new skills are acquired independently of previously learned skills.
    c. motor development is a genetically determined process.
    d. the pathways to motor skill acquisition are universal.

17. In which sequence do infants develop voluntary reaching and grasping behaviors? (p. 143)
    a. pincer grasp, ulnar grasp, prereaching
    b. ulnar grasp, pincer grasp, prereaching
    c. prereaching, ulnar grasp, pincer grasp
    d. prereaching, pincer grasp, ulnar grasp

18. Research on the sense of smell indicates that: (p. 146)
    a. infants do not have a well-developed sense of smell until several months after birth.
    b. newborn infants recognize the smell of their own mother's breast and amniotic fluid.
    c. odor preferences are gradually developed through environmental exposure to a variety of scents.
    d. infants can distinguish pleasant and unpleasant odors but cannot identify the location of an odor, and therefore, cannot defend themselves from unpleasant odors by turning their heads in the other direction.

19. Newborn infants: (p. 148)
    a. prefer pure tones to complex sounds.
    b. are most attentive to low-pitched, monotonous patterns of sound.
    c. can discriminate all but a few sounds of any human language.
    d. can only discriminate the speech sounds of their native language.

20. Because the visual system is not yet well-developed, _____, or fineness of discrimination, is limited in newborn infants. (p. 150)
    a. depth perception
    b. tunnel vision
    c. binocular vision
    d. visual acuity

21. _____ depth cues, the first to which infants are sensitive, are created by movements of the body or of objects in the environment. (p. 152)
    a. Kinetic
    b. Binocular
    c. Pictorial
    d. Invariant

22. According to the principle of contrast sensitivity, infants 2 months of age and older would prefer to look at: (p. 155)
    a. a large, bold checkerboard.
    b. a small, complex checkerboard.
    c. a simple pattern with a lot of color.
    d. an image representing a familiar object.

23. From the start, infants expect sight, sound, and touch to go together, a capacity called: (p. 159)
    a. intermodal perception.
    b. sensory perception.
    c. systematic perception.
    d. integrative perception.

24. According to the differentiation theory of perceptual development: (p. 161)
    a. infants seek out variant, or ever-changing, features of the environment.
    b. infants seek out invariant, or stable, features of the environment.
    c. infants have an innate capacity to give order to their environment.
    d. infants impose meaning on their perceptions, thereby constructing categories of objects and events in the environment.

25. Which of the following best reflects the development of infants reared in deprived institutionalized care? (p. 163)
    a. Even when adopted prior to 6 months of age, these infants fail to show physical and cognitive catch-up relative to agemates.
    b. When adopted prior to age 2, these infants show dramatic cognitive catch-up but fail to catch up to peers physically.
    c. When infants spend the first two years or more in deprived institutionalized care, all domains of development remain greatly delayed.
    d. As long as these children are adopted before they reach school-age, they catch up to agemates in all areas of development.

CHAPTER 5
PHYSICAL GROWTH

BRIEF CHAPTER SUMMARY

During the first two decades of life, the human body changes continuously and dramatically, until it reaches the mature adult state. Numerous biological and environmental factors regulate and control the course of human growth. Compared to other animals, primates (including humans) experience a prolonged period of physical growth.

Physical development during infancy and childhood follows the cephalocaudal and proximodistal trends. Exceptions to these basic growth trends occur during puberty, when growth proceeds in the reverse direction, and sex-related differences in body proportions appear. The best way of estimating a child's overall physical maturity is to use skeletal age, a measure of development of the bones of the body. Body growth is controlled by a complex set of hormonal secretions released by the pituitary gland and regulated by the hypothalamus. Individual and cultural differences in body size and rate of maturation are influenced by both heredity and environment. Secular trends in physical growth have taken place in industrialized nations, due to improved health and nutrition. Physical growth is an asynchronous process because different body systems have their own unique, carefully timed patterns of maturation.

During the first few years, the human brain grows faster than any other organ. Studies indicate that brain growth spurts coincide with major cognitive changes and that there may be sensitive periods in which appropriate stimulation is necessary.

Both heredity and nutrition are factors affecting physical growth. Breast-feeding is especially suited to infants' growth needs, and the importance of nutrition is evident in the dietary diseases of marasmus and kwashiorkor. In industrialized countries, obesity is a growing problem with health, psychological, and social consequences. The most effective treatments are family based and focus on changing behaviors. Infectious disease can combine with poor nutrition to undermine healthy physical development. Nonorganic failure to thrive and psychosocial dwarfism illustrate the role of affection and stimulation to children's healthy physical growth.

Puberty is a time of dramatic physical change leading to an adult-sized body and sexual maturity. The psychological impact of pubertal events is a product of both biological and social forces. Adolescents' physical changes and their new powers of reasoning may lead to a rise in family tensions, but the conflict that takes place is generally mild. The timing of puberty has a major impact on psychological adjustment. For some adolescent girls, cultural ideals combine with family and individual psychological problems to produce the serious eating disturbances of anorexia nervosa and bulimia. American adolescents receive mixed messages from adults and the larger culture about sexual activity, which contributes to high rates of sexually transmitted disease and teenage pregnancy, abortion, and parenthood.

LEARNING OBJECTIVES

After reading this chapter, you should be able to:

5.1 Describe the course of physical growth from birth through adolescence, including changes in body size, proportions, and composition, and note sex differences in patterns of physical growth. (pp. 170–173)

5.2 Describe changes in gross motor skills across childhood and adolescence. (p. 173)

5.3 Describe skeletal growth, including the usefulness of skeletal age for estimating physical maturity. (pp. 173–175)

5.4 Discuss hormonal influences on physical growth. (pp. 175–178)

5.5 Discuss factors that contribute to worldwide variations, secular trends, and asynchronies in physical growth. (pp. 178–181)

5.6 Describe the development and functions of neurons and glial cells. (pp. 181–182)

5.7 Describe the development of the cerebral cortex, and explain the concepts of brain lateralization and brain plasticity, noting the link between brain lateralization and handedness. (pp. 182–185)

5.8 Describe the development and functions of the cerebellum, the reticular formation, and the corpus callosum. (p. 185)

5.9 Discuss evidence supporting brain growth spurts as sensitive periods of development. (pp. 185–186)

5.10 Describe evidence indicating that heredity is an important factor in physical growth. (pp. 186–187)

5.11 Discuss age-related nutritional needs, including the importance of breast-feeding and the influence of the social environment on children's food preferences. (pp. 187–189)

5.12 Discuss the causes, symptoms, consequences, and treatment of marasmus and kwashiorkor. (pp. 189–190)

5.13 Discuss the incidence, causes, consequences, and treatment of obesity. (pp. 190–191)

5.14 Explain how disease interacts with malnutrition to affect physical growth, and describe the importance of oral rehydration therapy (ORT) and immunization in protecting children from infectious disease. (pp. 191–192)

5.15 Describe the growth disorders known as nonorganic failure to thrive and psychosocial dwarfism, noting common symptoms and family circumstances associated with these disorders. (pp. 192–193)

5.16 Describe sexual maturation in girls and boys, noting genetic and environmental influences on pubertal timing. (pp. 193–196)

5.17 Cite evidence indicating that puberty is not an inevitable period of storm and stress. (p. 196)

5.18 Discuss adolescents' reactions to the physical changes of puberty, noting factors that influence feelings and behavior. (pp. 196–200)

5.19 Discuss the impact of maturational timing on adolescent adjustment, noting sex differences, as well as immediate and long-term consequences. (pp. 201–202)

5.20 Describe the symptoms of anorexia nervosa and bulimia nervosa, and cite factors within the individual, the family, and the larger culture that contribute to these disorders. (pp. 202–204)

5.21 Discuss personal, familial, and cultural influences on adolescent sexual attitudes and behavior. (pp. 204–206)

5.22 Discuss biological and environmental contributions to homosexuality. (pp. 206–208)

5.23 Discuss the risk of sexually transmitted disease (STD), particularly AIDS, during adolescence. (p. 208)

5.24 Discuss factors related to adolescent pregnancy and parenthood, including correlates, consequences, prevention strategies, and interventions for teenage parents. (pp. 208–212)

STUDY QUESTIONS

The Course of Physical Growth

Changes in Body Size

1. Physical growth during infancy is (slower / faster) than physical growth during childhood and adolescence. (p. 170)

2. List and describe two types of growth curves used to track height and weight changes. (pp. 170–171)

   A. _____

   _____

   _____

   B. _____

   _____

   _____

3. Based on established norms, discuss sex differences in patterns of physical growth. (p. 171)

   _____

   _____

   _____

   _____

4. True or False: The velocity curve shows that from infancy through adolescence children tend to grow at a constant rate rather than in spurts. (p. 171)

Changes in Body Proportions

1. True or False: Physical growth during infancy and childhood follows the cephalocaudal and proximodistal trends. Briefly explain your answer. (p. 171)

   _____

   _____

   _____

2. True or False: An exception to the basic growth trend occurs during puberty, when growth proceeds in the reverse direction. (p. 171)

Changes in Muscle-Fat Makeup

1. Describe sex differences in muscle-fat makeup from infancy to adolescence. (pp. 172–173)

_____

_____

_____

_____

Changes in Gross Motor Skills

1. As children's bodies become less top-heavy, their center of gravity shifts downward, toward the trunk resulting in improved _____, which will pave the way for new motor skills. (p. 173)

2. Describe the principle of *dynamic systems of action* as it relates to children's motor development. (p. 173)

_____

_____

_____

From Research to Practice: Sex Differences in Gross Motor Development

1. Distinguish the types of motor abilities in which boys and girls show a differential advantage during early and middle childhood. (pp. 176–177)

Boys: _____

_____

Girls: _____

_____

2. True or False: Sex differences in physical growth during childhood are solely responsible for boys' superiority in many gross motor capacities. (pp. 176–177)

3. True or False: Although high school girls' sports participation has increased dramatically over the past several decades, it still falls short of boys' participation. (pp. 176–177)

4. Discuss ways to increase girls' participation in sports and confidence that they can do well at athletics. (pp. 176–177)

_____

_____

_____

_____

Skeletal Growth

1. The best way of estimating a child's physical maturity is to use _____ , a measure of development of the bones of the body. (p. 173)

2. Explain how epiphyses can be used to estimate skeletal age. (p. 173)

_____

_____

_____

3. When skeletal ages are examined, (African-American / Caucasian) children and (boys / girls) tend to be slightly ahead. (p. 175)

4. At birth, the bones of the skull are separated by six gaps, or "soft spots," called _____. Explain their function. (p. 175)

_____

_____

_____

Hormonal Influences on Physical Growth

1. The most important hormones for human growth are released by the _____ *gland*, located near the base of the brain near the hypothalamus. (p. 176)

2. Describe the impact of growth hormone (GH) and thyroxine on physical growth and indicate what happens when children have deficiencies of these hormones. (p. 177)

GH: _____

_____

Thyroxine: _____

_____

Impact of hormonal deficiencies: _____

_____

_____

3. During sexual maturation, boys' testes release large quantities of the androgen _____, which leads to muscle growth, body and facial hair, and other male sex characteristics, as well as contributing to gains in body size. (p. 178)

4. In girls, the release of _____ causes the breasts, uterus, and vagina to mature and the body to take on feminine proportions. (p. 178)

5. True or False: Estrogens are found only in females, and androgens are found only in males. (p. 178)

Worldwide Variations in Body Size

1. Explain two factors that account for the vast differences in body size and rate of growth among children around the world. (p. 179)

A. _____

_____

B. _____

_____

Secular Trends

1. Explain what is meant by the term *secular trends in physical growth.* (p. 180)

    _____

    _____

    _____

2. Cite the two factors largely responsible for recent secular gains in physical development. (p. 180)

    A. _____

    B. _____

Asynchronies in Physical Growth

1. Describe the *general growth curve*, which represents changes in body size from infancy to adolescence. (p. 180)

    _____

    _____

    _____

    _____

2. List two exceptions to the trend depicted by the general growth curve. (p. 180)

    A. _____

    B. _____

Development of the Brain

Development of Neurons

1. What are *neurons* and what is their function? (p. 181)

    _____

    _____

    _____

2. Between neurons, there are tiny gaps, or _____, across which messages pass. (p. 181)

3. The peak period of development in any brain area is marked by the greatest rate of _____, or death of surrounding neurons to make room for growth of neural fibers that form synaptic connections. (p. 181)

4. Explain the process of *synaptic pruning*. (p. 181)

   _____

   _____

   _____

5. About half of the brain's volume is made up of _____ *cells*, whose most important function is _____, the coating of neural fibers with an insulating fatty sheath that improves the efficiency of message transfer. (p. 182)

Development of the Cerebral Cortex

1. True or False: The cerebral cortex is the largest, most complex brain structure, containing the greatest number of neurons and synapses. (p. 182)

2. Describe the different functions controlled by the left and right hemispheres of the brain. (p. 182)

   Left: _____

   Right: _____

3. Explain the concepts of *lateralization* and *brain plasticity*, noting how the two are related. (pp. 182–183)

   Lateralization: _____

   _____

   _____

   Brain plasticity: _____

   _____

   _____

Relationship: _____

_____

_____

4. The brain is (more / less) plastic during the early years than during later years in life. (p. 183)

5. The brains of left-handers tend to be (more / less) strongly lateralized than those of right-handers. (p. 183)

6. Describe two theories regarding the origins of handedness. (p. 184)

A. _____

_____

_____

B. _____

_____

_____

Other Advances in Brain Development

1. Note how developmental changes in the following brain structures impact children's physical and/or cognitive skills. (p. 185)

Cerebellum: _____

_____

_____

Reticular formation: _____

_____

_____

Corpus callosum: _____

_____

_____

Brain Growth Spurts and Sensitive Periods of Development

1. Cite evidence of sensitive periods in human brain development. (pp. 185–186)

_____

_____

_____

_____

_____

Factors Affecting Physical Growth

Heredity

1. True or False: When diet and health are adequate, height and rate of physical growth are largely determined by heredity. (p. 186)

2. Describe the phenomenon of *catch-up growth*. (p. 186)

_____

_____

_____

Nutrition

1. Describe several nutritional and health benefits of breast-feeding. (pp. 187–188)

_____

_____

_____

_____

_____

2. Discuss the benefits of breast-feeding as they relate to mothers and infants in poverty-stricken regions of the world. (p. 188)

_____

_____

_____

_____

3. True or False: It is normal for children's appetite to decline in early childhood. (p. 188)

4. The most common nutritional problem of adolescence is _____ deficiency. (p. 189)

5. Describe the causes of *marasmus* and *kwashiorkor*, two dietary diseases associated with severe malnutrition, and summarize the developmental outcomes associated with these extreme forms of malnutrition. (p. 189)

    Marasmus: _____

    _____

    Kwashiorkor: _____

    _____

    Outcomes: _____

    _____

    _____

    _____

6. Nearly 25 percent of American children suffer from _____, a greater-than-20-percent increase over average body weight, based on the child's age, sex, and physical build. (p. 190)

7. (Low-SES / Middle-SES) children are most likely to be obese. Cite three factors that contribute to this trend. (pp. 190–191)

    A. _____

    _____

    B. _____

    _____

    C. _____

    _____

8. Describe parental feeding practices that contribute to childhood obesity, along with their consequences for children's eating habits. (pp. 190–191)

Parental feeding practices: _____

_____

_____

Consequences: _____

_____

_____

9. Summarize research findings on the relationship between TV viewing and childhood obesity. (p. 191)

_____

_____

_____

_____

10. Summarize the effects of obesity on emotional and social development. (p. 191)

_____

_____

_____

_____

11. The most effective interventions for childhood obesity are _____-based and focus on changing behavior. Furthermore, weight loss is greater when treatments focus on both dietary and lifestyle changes, including regular vigorous _____. (p. 191)

Infectious Diseases

1. Explain how malnutrition and disease interact to undermine physical growth. (p. 192)

_____

_____

_____

_____

2. In developing countries, most growth retardation and deaths due to diarrhea can be prevented with nearly cost-free _____ *therapy*, in which sick children are given a glucose, salt, and water solution to replace lost body fluids. (p. 192)

3. True or False: Among industrialized nations, the United States has the highest rates of immunization. Briefly explain your response, providing reasons for this pattern. (p. 192)

_____

_____

_____

Emotional Well-Being

1. What is *nonorganic failure to thrive,* and what are some common symptoms? (p. 192)

_____

_____

_____

_____

2. Describe family circumstances associated with nonorganic failure to thrive. (p. 193)

_____

_____

_____

_____

3. Explain the features that help distinguish psychosocial dwarfism from normal shortness. (p. 193)

_____

_____

_____

_____

Puberty: The Physical Transition to Adulthood

1. Distinguish between primary and secondary sexual characteristics. (p. 193)

Primary: _____

_____

Secondary: _____

_____

Sexual Maturation in Girls

1. _____ is the scientific name for the first menstruation. It occurs (early / late) in the sequence of pubertal events. (p. 194)

2. Menarche typically happens at around age _____ for North American girls. (p. 194)

3. Explain the adaptive value of the timing of menarche in relation to other pubertal milestones. (pp. 194–195)

   _____

   _____

Sexual Maturation in Boys

1. The first sign of puberty in boys is _____. (p. 195)

2. The growth spurt occurs much (earlier / later) in the sequence of pubertal events for boys than for girls. (p. 195)

3. Around age 13, _____, or first ejaculation, occurs. (p. 195)

Individual and Group Differences in Pubertal Growth

1. True or False: Heredity contributes significantly to the timing of puberty. (p. 195)

2. What factor is largely responsible for the secular trend toward earlier menarche? (p. 195)

   _____

3. Describe factors responsible for variations in the timing of menarche. (p. 195)

   _____

   _____

   _____

   _____

Is Puberty an Inevitable Period of Storm and Stress?

1. True or False: The overall rate of psychological disturbance rises dramatically from childhood to adolescence, suggesting that emotional disturbance is a routine feature of this phase of development. (p. 196)

2. Margaret Mead suggested that (biological / social) factors are entirely responsible for teenagers' adjustment to puberty. (p. 196)

3. Explain why adolescence is typically a more difficult period in industrialized societies than in nonindustrialized societies. (p. 196)

_____

_____

_____

Reactions to Pubertal Changes

1. Discuss two factors that affect girls' reactions to menarche. (p. 197)

   A. _____

   _____

   _____

   B. _____

   _____

   _____

2. Overall, boys seem to get (more / less) social support for the physical changes of puberty than do girls. (p. 197)

3. Many tribal and village societies celebrate puberty with a _____
   _____— a community-wide event that marks an important change
   in privilege and responsibility. Contrast this experience with that of adolescents in Western
   societies. (p. 197)

   _____

   _____

_____

_____

Cultural Influences: Adolescent Initiation Ceremonies

1. What is the purpose of an *adolescent initiation ceremony*? (pp. 198–199)

   _____

   _____

2. Describe three features typically included in an adolescent initiation ceremony. (pp. 198–199)

   A. _____

   _____

   _____

   B. _____

   _____

   _____

   C. _____

   _____

   _____

3. Adolescent initiation ceremonies are more common in (simple / complex) societies. (pp. 198–199)

Pubertal Change, Emotion, and Social Behavior

1. Research shows that adolescents report (more / less) favorable moods than do school-age children and adults. (p. 197)

2. Discuss three factors that contribute to adolescent moodiness. (pp. 197–200)

   A. _____

   _____

   B. _____

   _____

C. _____

_____

3. True or False: Both situational factors and hormonal influences affect teenagers' moodiness. (pp. 199–200)

4. Describe changes in the parent-child relationship that take place during adolescence. (p. 200)

_____

_____

_____

_____

5. The conflict that takes place between parents and adolescents is generally (mild / severe). Briefly explain your response. (p. 200)

_____

_____

_____

Early versus Late Maturation

1. Discuss research findings on the effects of maturational timing for the following groups of adolescents: (p. 201)

Early maturing boys: _____

_____

Late maturing boys: _____

_____

Early maturing girls: _____

_____

Late maturing girls: _____

_____

2. Cite two factors that appear to account for trends in the effects of maturational timing. (p. 201)

   A. _____

   B. _____

3. Discuss the impact of maturational timing on adolescents' body images. (p. 201)

   _____

   _____

   _____

   _____

4. (Early / Late) maturers of both sexes are psychologically stressed and show declines in academic performance. (pp. 201–202)

5. True or False: When long-term outcomes are examined, many of the effects of maturational timing on adjustment seen in adolescence appear to reverse themselves in adulthood. (p. 202)

Puberty and Adolescent Health

Eating Disorders

1. What is *anorexia nervosa*? (p. 203)

   _____

   _____

   _____

2. True or False: Most anorexics have a realistic body image, and therefore, recognize when they become severely underweight. (p. 203)

3. Describe the physical symptoms of anorexia nervosa. (p. 203)

   _____

   _____

   _____

4. Cite the cultural, individual, and familial factors that give rise to anorexia nervosa. (p. 203)

Cultural: _____

_____

Individual: _____

_____

Familial: _____

_____

5. Cite three approaches to treating anorexia nervosa, and note which is the most successful. (pp. 203–204)

A. _____

B. _____

C. _____

Most Successful: _____

6. True or False: Over 90 percent of anorexics make a full recovery. (p. 204)

7. What is *bulimia nervosa*? (p. 204)

_____

_____

_____

8. Bulimia nervosa is (more / less) common than anorexia nervosa. (p. 204)

9. How do bulimics tend to differ from anorexics, and what impact does this have for the treatment of the disorder? (p. 204)

Differences: _____

_____

_____

Impact: _____

_____

_____

Sexuality

1. Contrast the messages that adolescents receive from parents and the media regarding sexual activity, and note the impact of such contradictory messages on adolescents' understanding of sex. (p. 204)

Parents: _____

_____

Media: _____

_____

Impact: _____

_____

2. Summarize trends in adolescent sexual attitudes and behavior over the past 40 years. (p. 205)

_____

_____

_____

3. True or False: Most sexually active adolescents engage in sexual relations with only one partner at a time and engage in relatively low levels of sexual activity. (p. 205)

4. Summarize personal, familial, peer, and educational variables linked to early and frequent teenage sexual activity. (pp. 204–205)

Personal: _____

_____

Familial: _____

_____

Peer: _____

_____

Educational: _____

_____

5. Discuss cognitive and social factors that contribute to adolescents' reluctance to use contraception. (p. 206)

Cognitive: _____

_____

_____

Social: _____

_____

_____

6. Cite characteristics of adolescents who are more likely to use contraception. (p. 206)

_____

_____

7. About _____ to _____ percent of adolescents discover that they are gay or lesbian. (p. 206)

8. True or False: Recent research findings indicate that heredity makes a significant contribution to homosexuality. Briefly explain your response. (p. 206)

_____

_____

_____

9. Describe family factors associated with homosexuality. (p. 208)

_____

_____

_____

1. Describe the three-phase sequence that homosexual adolescents and adults move through in coming out to themselves and others. (p. 207)

    A. _____

    _____

    _____

    B. _____

    _____

    _____

    C. _____

    _____

    _____

2. For most homosexual individuals, a first sense of their sexual orientation appears between the ages of _____ and _____. In what context does this commonly occur? (p. 207)

    _____

3. True or False: Most adolescents resolve their feelings of confusion and discomfort at being attracted to same-sex individuals by crystallizing a gay, lesbian, or bisexual identity quickly—with a flash of insight into their sense of being different. (p. 207)

4. Discuss the process of disclosure, or coming out, noting factors that are important for reaching this phase of acceptance. (p. 207)

    _____

    _____

    _____

    _____

5. True or False: Coming out has the potential to foster many aspects of adolescents' development, including self-esteem, psychological well-being, and relationships with family, friends, and co-workers. (p. 207)

Sexually Transmitted Disease

1. True or False: Adolescents have the highest rate of sexually transmitted disease (STD) of any age group. (p. 208)

2. True or False: It is much easier for a female to infect a male with an STD than it is for a male to infect a female. (p. 208)

Adolescent Pregnancy and Parenthood

1. The adolescent pregnancy rate in the United States is much (lower / higher) than that of most other industrialized countries. List three ways in which the United States differs from these nations that might account for this discrepancy. (p. 208)

   A. _____

   B. _____

   C. _____

2. Why is teenage parenthood a much bigger problem today than it was 30 years ago? (pp. 208–209)

   _____

3. Summarize the consequences of adolescent parenthood in relation to the following areas: (p. 209)

   Educational attainment: _____

   _____

   _____

   Marital patterns: _____

   _____

   _____

   Economic circumstances: _____

   _____

   _____

4. Cite three maternal factors that are associated with better outcomes for teenage mothers and their children. (pp. 209–211)

A. _____

B. _____

C. _____

5. List three components of effective sex education programs. (p. 211)

A. _____

B. _____

C. _____

6. True or False: In Western Europe, where contraceptives are readily available to adolescents, teenage sexual activity is no higher than in the United States, and pregnancy, childbirth, and abortion rates are much lower. (p. 211)

7. Cite at lease three characteristics of effective school intervention programs for adolescent mothers. (p. 211)

A. _____

B. _____

C. _____

Social Issues: Health: Like Mother, Like Child—Intergenerational Continuity in Adolescent Parenthood

1. Based on the research of Janet Hardy, discuss factors that predict the intergenerational continuity of teenage childbearing, noting differences in the predictors for second-generation daughters and sons. (p. 210)

Daughters: _____

_____

_____

Sons: _____

_____

_____

2. True or False: Hardy found that when children born to teenage mothers did not repeat the pattern of early childbearing, their development was no longer compromised. Explain your response. (p. 210)

_____

_____

_____

ASK YOURSELF . . .

Review: Explain why sex differences in physical growth play little role in boys' childhood advantage over girls in athletic skills. (p. 181)

_____

_____

_____

_____

_____

Review: Describe the role of the pituitary gland in body growth, brain development, and sexual maturation. (p. 181)

_____

_____

_____

_____

_____

Apply: At birth, Joey's anterior fontanel had started to close prematurely. At age 3 months, Joey had surgery to open it. Considering the function of the fontanels, why was early surgery necessary? (p. 181)

_____

_____

_____

_____

_____

Connect: What do secular trends in physical growth and cohort effects, discussed on page 58 of Chapter 2, have in common? Why should a researcher engaged in a longitudinal or cross-sectional study of physical growth be concerned about cohort effects? (p. 181)

_____

_____

_____

_____

_____

Review: How does stimulation affect early brain development? Cite evidence at the level of neurons and at the level of the cerebral cortex. (p. 181)

_____

_____

_____

_____

_____

Review: Explain why the overproduction of synapses and synaptic pruning are adaptive processes that foster brain development. (p. 186)

_____

_____

_____

_____

_____

Apply: Lucia had a mild brain hemorrhage shortly after birth. Using what you know about brain plasticity, explain why her doctors believe her mental development will be normal, or near normal. (p. 186)

_____

_____

_____

_____

_____

Connect: On the basis of the findings on sensitive periods in this chapter and in Chapter 4, which infant enrichment program would you choose—one that emphasizes gentle talking and touching, exposure to sights and sounds, and simple social games, or one that includes work and number drills and classical music lessons? Explain. (p. 186)

_____

_____

_____

_____

_____

Review: Explain why breast-feeding offers babies protection against disease and early death in poverty-stricken regions of the world. (p. 193)

_____

_____

_____

_____

_____

Review: How does disease prevention, through immunization and ORT, play a role in preventing malnutrition? (p. 193)

_____

_____

_____

_____

_____

Apply: Ten-month-old Shaun is below average in height and painfully thin. He has one of two serious growth disorders. Name them, and indicate what clues you would look for to tell which one Shaun has. (p. 193)

_____

_____

_____

_____

_____

Connect: Use ecological systems theory (Chapter 1, page 28) to show how bidirectional influences between caregiver and child combine with factors in the surrounding environment to put children at risk for obesity. (p. 193)

_____

_____

_____

_____

_____

Review: Many people believe that the rising sexual passions of puberty cause rebelliousness in adolescents. Where did this belief originate? Explain why it is incorrect. (p. 202)

_____

_____

_____

_____

_____

Review: List factors that contribute to pubertal timing. Then summarize the consequences of early versus late maturation for adolescent development. (p. 202)

_____

_____

_____

_____

_____

Apply: Regina wonders why her 14-year-old daughter Cloe spends hours alone in her room and no longer wants to join in weekend family activities. Explain why Cloe's behavior is adaptive. (p. 202)

_____

_____

_____

_____

Connect: How might adolescent moodiness contribute to psychological distancing between parents and adolescents? (Hint: Think about bidirectional influences in parent–child relationships.) (p. 202)

_____

_____

_____

_____

Review: Compare the risk factors for anorexia nervosa and bulimia nervosa. How do treatments and outcomes differ in the two disorders? (p. 212)

_____

_____

_____

_____

Review: Describe the unfavorable life experiences associated with early and frequent sexual activity. (p. 212)

_____

_____

_____

_____

Apply: Sixteen-year-old Jamal knows he is homosexual but wonders what has made him this way. What could you tell Jamal about the research findings on genetic and environmental links to homosexuality? (p. 212)

_____

_____

_____

_____

Connect: How do various correlates and consequences of adolescent parenthood promote intergenerational continuity in teenage births? (p. 212)

_____

_____

_____

_____

_____

SUGGESTED STUDENT READINGS

Alsaker, F. D., & Flammer, A. (Ed.). (1998). *The adolescent experience: European and American adolescents in the 1990s.* Mahwah, NJ: Erlbaum. Presents the results of a large longitudinal study of adolescents from 13 different countries. Includes hundreds of features of adolescence that are more or less characteristic of culture, age, and gender.

Hayman, L. L., Mahon, M. M., & Turner, J. R. (1999). *Health behavior in childhood and adolescence.* Mahwah, NJ: Erlbaum. Presents multidisciplinary research on the interrelationships among behavior, health, and illness in childhood and adolescence within a developmental-contextual framework. Discusses major diseases of childhood and adolescence, chronic childhood conditions, and childhood precursors of adult-onset disease.

Johnson, N. G., Roberts, M. C., & Worell, J. P. (Eds.). (1999). *Beyond appearance: A new look at adolescent girls.* Washington, DC: American Psychological Association. An edited volume that explores key topics to understanding girls' adolescent development, including gender-role behaviors, body image issues, relationships with family and friends, sexual decision making, and school- and community-based experiences.

Junn, E. N. & Boyatzis, C. J. (Eds.). (2000). *Annual editions: Child growth and development 2000/2001 (7th ed.).* Guilford, CT: Dushkin/McGraw-Hill. A compilation of selected articles taken from journals, magazines, and newspapers, this book presents current perspectives on child growth and development. Appropriate for students, researchers, and anyone interested in the field of child development.

PUZZLE 5.1

Across

1. _____ dwarfism: growth disorder caused by severe emotional deprivation; observed between 2 and 15 years of age
3. The _____ gland, located near the base of the brain, releases hormones affecting physical growth.
6. A disease usually appearing between 1 and 3 years of age that is caused by a diet low in protein
8. A structure located at the base of the brain that initiates and regulates pituitary secretions
10. Oral _____ therapy: treatment for diarrhea in which sick children are given a glucose, salt, & water solution
11. A greater-than-20-percent increase over average body weight, based on the child's age, sex, and physical build
12. An estimate of physical maturity based on the development of the bones of the body (2 words)
19. _____ curve: growth curve that plots average height and weight at each age
20. _____ hormone: pituitary hormone affecting the development of all body tissues except the central nervous system and the genitals

Down

2. Changes in body size and rate of growth from one generation to the next are known as _____ _____ in physical growth. (2 words)
4. A disease usually appearing in the first year of life; caused by a diet low in all essential nutrients
5. _____ curve: growth curve that plots the average amount of growth at each yearly interval
7. Hormone released by the thyroid gland; necessary for central nervous system development and body growth
9. _____ failure to thrive: growth disorder usually present by 18 months of age; caused by lack of affection and stimulation
13. Growth centers in the bones
14. Hormones produced chiefly by the ovaries; cause the breasts, uterus, & vagina to mature and the body to take on feminine proportions
15. Hormones produced chiefly by the testes; influence the pubertal growth spurt, the appearance of hair, and male sex characteristics
16. Physical growth that returns to its genetically determined path after being delayed by environmental factors is called _____ growth.
17. Soft spots that separate the bones of the skull at birth
18. The _____ growth curve represents changes in overall body size—rapid growth during infancy, slower gains in early and middle childhood, and rapid growth again in adolescence

PUZZLE 5.2

Across

2. _____ nervosa: eating disorder in which individuals starve themselves because of a compulsive fear of getting fat
4. First menstruation
5. The largest structure of the human brain is the _____ cortex.
9. The _____ cerebral hemisphere is the hemisphere of the brain responsible for skilled motor action.
15. Specialization of functions of the two hemispheres of the cortex
16. _____ nervosa: eating disorder in which individuals engage in binge eating followed by deliberate vomiting, purging with laxatives, and strict dieting
17. Conception of and attitude toward one's physical appearance (2 words)
18. _____ cells are responsible for myelinization of neural fibers.
19. _____ sex characteristics: features visible on the outside of the body that serve as signs of physical maturity but do not involve the reproductive organs
21. Biological changes during adolescence that lead to an adult-sized body and sexual maturity

Down

1. Nerve cells that store and transmit information to the brain
3. A ritual announcing to the community that a young person is ready to make the transition from childhood into adolescence or full adulthood is known as an adolescent _____ ceremony.
6. _____ formation: structure in the brain stem that maintains alertness and consciousness
7. Brain structure that aids in balance and control of body movements
8. First ejaculation of seminal fluid
10. Brain _____ refers to the ability of other parts of the brain to take over functions of damaged regions.
11. Process in which neural fibers are coated with an insulating fatty sheath that improves the efficiency of message transfer
12. _____ sexual characteristics: physical features that involve the reproductive organs
13. Synaptic _____ is the loss of connective fibers by seldom-stimulated neurons.
14. _____ cell death: death of many surrounding neurons during the peak period of development of any brain area to make room for growth of neural fibers that form synaptic connections
19. The gap between neurons, across which messages are sent
20. Corpus _____: large bundle of fibers that connects the two hemispheres of the brain

PRACTICE TEST

1. Which type of growth curve plots the average height and weight of a sample of children at each age? (p. 170)
   a. developmental curve
   b. maturity curve
   c. velocity curve
   d. distance curve

2. Which of the following provides the best estimate of a child's physical maturity? (p. 173)
   a. comparison of the child's physical growth to universal growth norms for his/her age
   b. measures of the child's muscle-fat makeup
   c. measures of the development of the bones of the body
   d. examination of the child's gross motor skills

3. A gland located near the base of the brain that releases hormones affecting physical growth is the: (p. 176)
   a. adrenal gland.
   b. growth gland.
   c. thyroid gland.
   d. pituitary gland.

4. The _____ depict(s) rapid growth during infancy, slower gains in early and middle childhood, and rapid growth again in adolescence. (p. 180)
   a. universal growth norms
   b. synchronous growth trend
   c. general growth curve
   d. holistic growth pattern

5. _____ are nerve cells in the brain that store and transmit information. (p. 181)
   a. Glial cells
   b. Neurons
   c. Synapses
   d. Epiphyses

6. The process in which neural fibers are coated with an insulating fatty sheath that improves the efficiency of message transfer is called: (p. 182)
   a. myelinization.
   b. synaptic pruning.
   c. neural sheathing.
   d. brain plasticity.

7. Brain plasticity refers to: (p. 183)
   a. the specialization of functions of the two hemispheres of the brain.
   b. the ability of other parts of the brain to take over the functions of damaged regions.
   c. the extent of neural development at a particular period of development.
   d. the loss of neural connections resulting from inadequate stimulation.

8. Which of the following is true of breast-feeding during infancy? (pp. 187–188)
   a. Breast-feeding is not recommended for women in developing countries because breast milk does not contain sufficient nutrients to protect against malnutrition and infection.
   b. Breast-feeding is rare among American mothers, and rates of breast-feeding have declined over the last two decades.
   c. Breast-feeding is essential for children's healthy psychological development.
   d. Breast milk provides infants with nutrients ideally suited for early rapid brain development.

9. Marasmus is caused by: (p. 189)
   a. overeating during the first year of life.
   b. a severe iron deficiency.
   c. a diet low in protein.
   d. a diet low in all essential nutrients.

10. Obese children: (p. 191)
    a. rarely maintain their overweight status into adulthood.
    b. most often come from middle- or high-SES families.
    c. are more responsive to internal hunger cues than are normal-weight children.
    d. report greater feelings of depression and display more behavior problems than their normal-weight agemates.

11. Research indicates that the best treatment for childhood obesity is: (p. 191)
    a. family-based interventions that focus on changing behavior.
    b. placing the child on a strict, low-calorie diet.
    c. daily exercise for the child.
    d. behavior modification plans which reinforce exercise and punish inactivity.

12. Nonorganic failure to thrive: (p. 192)
    a. is associated with a known biological cause.
    b. is caused by a lack of stimulation and affection.
    c. results from an inadequate diet in early infancy.
    d. is associated with long-term deficits, even when treated early.

13. Menarche is the scientific name for: (p. 194)
    a. first ejaculation in males.
    b. first menstruation in females.
    c. maturation of the reproductive organs.
    d. outward signs of sexual maturity, including breast development in females and the appearance of underarm and pubic hair in both sexes.

14. The first sign of puberty in males is: (p. 195)
    a. spermarche.
    b. the appearance of pubic hair.
    c. enlargement of the testes.
    d. deepening of the voice.

15. Boys' and girls' reactions to pubertal changes are: (p. 195)
    a. overwhelmingly positive.
    b. similar in all cultures around the world.
    c. dependent upon the age of pubertal onset.
    d. dependent upon prior knowledge of such changes.

16. Compared to school-age children and adults, adolescents: (p. 198)
    a. experience decreased moodiness.
    b. report less favorable moods.
    c. have more stable moods.
    d. are more likely to report negative mood during times of the day spent with friends.

17. Which of the following groups are more likely to have positive self-images during adolescence? (p. 201)
    a. late maturing boys and girls
    b. early maturing boys and girls
    c. late maturing boys and early maturing girls
    d. early maturing boys and late maturing girls

18. Research on the consequences of maturational timing shows that: (p. 202)
    a. early maturing adolescents tend to seek out younger companions in an effort to better fit in with peers.
    b. school context, such as the grade and sex composition of the school, has little or no impact on maturational timing effects.
    c. maturational timing effects seen in adolescence tend to reverse in the long-term (i.e., early maturing boys and late maturing girls show a decline in adjustment, whereas late maturing boys and early maturing girls show improved adjustment)
    d. maturational timing has no long-term consequences

19. Anorexia nervosa: (p. 203)
    a. is more common among girls from middle-SES families than girls from low-SES families.
    b. is characterized by a loss of 25 to 50 percent of one's body weight.
    c. is more prevalent among girls with serious adjustment problems, particularly school failure.
    d. is fairly easy to treat, resulting in a full recovery in most cases.

20. Which of the following is true? (pp. 203–204)
    a. Anorexia nervosa is more common than bulimia nervosa.
    b. Anorexia is caused by hereditary characteristics, while bulimia results from environmental variables.
    c. Anorexics are often responsible and well-behaved, whereas bulimics often lack self-control, engaging in problem behaviors such as shoplifting and alcohol abuse.
    d. Anorexics feel guilty and depressed about their eating habits and are usually desperate for help, while bulimics often deny that any problem exists, making the disorder more difficult to treat.

21. According to research, which of the following factors is linked with increased contraceptive use among sexually active adolescents? (p. 206)
    a. sexual contact with multiple partners
    b. imitation of the sexually-responsible role-models seen in many prime-time TV shows.
    c. having a good relationship with parents and being able to talk openly with them about sex and contraceptives
    d. participation in sex education courses

22. Homosexuality: (pp. 206–208)
    a. results entirely from hereditary causes, most notably the level and impact of prenatal sex hormones.
    b. is caused by growing up with a same-sex parent who is cold, rejecting, or distant.
    c. likely results from a variety of biological and environmental combinations.
    d. has a prevalence rate of approximately 15 to 20 percent in the adolescent population.

23. Which of the following is true of sexually transmitted disease (STD) during adolescence? (p. 208)
    a. Adolescents have the highest incidence of STD of any age group.
    b. Homosexual adolescents are at greater risk for STD than are heterosexual adolescents.
    c. The United States has the lowest rate of STD of all industrialized nations.
    d. Over 90% of high school students are not aware of the basic facts about AIDS.

24. Adolescent mothers: (pp. 209–210)
    a. are as likely as other adolescent girls to finish high school.
    b. usually have a good understanding of child development.
    c. tend to have children who achieve poorly in school and who engage in disruptive social behavior.
    d. rarely experience pregnancy and birth complications.

25. The most effective aspect of sex education programs for preventing adolescent pregnancy is: (p. 211)
    a. teaching sexual facts.
    b. providing information about and ready access to contraceptives.
    c. teaching skills for handling sexual situations through creative discussion and role plays.
    d. promoting the value of abstinence.

CHAPTER 6
COGNITIVE DEVELOPMENT: PIAGETIAN, CORE KNOWLEDGE, AND VYGOTSKIAN PERSPECTIVES

BRIEF CHAPTER SUMMARY

Influenced by his background in biology, Piaget viewed cognitive development as an adaptive process in which thinking gradually achieves a better fit with external reality. By acting on the environment, children move through four invariant and universal stages—sensorimotor, preoperational, concrete operational, and formal operational—during which the exploratory behaviors of infants are transformed into the abstract, logical intelligence of adolescence and adulthood. Piaget's stage sequence, which emphasizes that stages are invariant and universal, groups together similar qualitative changes in many schemes that occur during the same period of development.

According to Piaget, specific psychological structures, or schemes, change with age through the exercise of two important intellectual functions: adaptation and organization. Piaget described infants' special means of adapting their first schemes as the circular reaction—stumbling onto a new experience caused by the baby's own motor activity, and then trying to repeat the event. He considered revisions in the circular reaction so important that he named the six sensorimotor substages after them.

Many studies suggest that infants display a variety of understandings earlier than Piaget believed. Recent evidence indicates that cultural practices and schooling have a profound effect on Piagetian task performance. Concrete and formal operations may not emerge universally in middle childhood and adolescence, and they seem to be greatly affected by training, context, and cultural conditions.

Piaget's theory has had a major impact on education, with its emphasis on discovery learning, sensitivity to children's readiness to learn, and acceptance of individual differences. Piaget's contributions to the field of child development are gigantic—greater than those of any other theorist. Nevertheless, virtually all experts agree that children's cognition is not as broadly stagelike as Piaget believed. Information-processing theorists believe that thought processes are similar at all ages—just present to a greater or lesser extent—and that uneven performance across tasks can largely be accounted for by variations in children's knowledge and experience.

According to the core knowledge perspective, infants begin life with innate, core domains of thought that support early, rapid cognitive development. Each core domain has a long evolutionary history, is essential for survival, and develops independently, resulting in uneven, domain-specific changes. This view maintains that physical and psychological explanations emerge before biological explanations and, because biological processes are more difficult to understand, young children often use psychological concepts to theorize about biological events. Core knowledge researchers have enriched our understanding of children's thinking by testing intriguing ideas about why certain cognitive skills emerge early and develop rapidly. However, so far, the core knowledge perspective has not offered greater clarity than Piaget's theory on how cognition changes.

Vygotsky's sociocultural theory, a third major theory of cognitive development, also views children as active seekers of knowledge, but rich social and cultural contexts profoundly affect the way their cognitive world is structured. Whereas Piaget concluded that young children's language is egocentric and nonsocial, Vygotsky reasoned that children speak to themselves for self-guidance and self-direction. Because language helps children think about their own behavior and select courses of action, Vygotsky regarded it as the foundation for all higher cognitive processes. Vygotsky believed that through joint activities with more mature members of society, children come to master activities and think in ways that have meaning in their culture. He believed that children learn best when tasks are in their zone of proximal development, a range of tasks that the child cannot yet handle alone but can accomplish with the help of adults and more skilled peers. In accord with his emphasis on social experience and language as vital forces for cognitive development, Vygotsky regarded make-believe play as a unique, broadly influential zone of proximal development in which children advance themselves as they try out a wide variety of challenging skills.

Vygotsky's theory has also influenced education through concepts and techniques such as assisted discovery, peer collaboration, reciprocal teaching, and cooperative learning. A new Vygotsky-inspired educational approach transforms classrooms into communities of learners, where no distinction is made between adult and child contributions; all collaborate and develop. An evaluation of Vygotsky's theory indicates that its emphasis on the role of language may not accurately describe cognitive development in all cultures. Also, by focusing on the cultural line of development, his theory does not describe exactly how elementary cognitive processes contribute to higher cognitive processes derived from social experience.

LEARNING OBJECTIVES

After reading this chapter, you should be able to:

6.1 Describe Piaget's cognitive-developmental theory, noting key concepts of this approach. (pp. 218–220)

6.2 Describe the major cognitive achievements of Piaget's six sensorimotor substages. (pp. 220–222)

6.3 Discuss recent research on sensorimotor development, noting its implications for the accuracy of Piaget's sensorimotor stage. (pp. 222–229)

6.4 Describe advances in mental representation during the preschool years, including changes in make-believe play. (pp. 229–234)

6.5 Describe what Piaget believed to be the deficiencies of preoperational thought. (pp. 234–235)

6.6 Discuss recent research on preoperational thought, and note the implications of such findings for the accuracy of Piaget's preoperational stage. (pp. 235–240)

6.7   Describe the major characteristics of concrete operational thought, including limitations of cognition during this stage. (pp. 241–243)

6.8   Discuss recent research on concrete operational thought, noting the implications of recent findings for the accuracy of Piaget's concrete operational stage. (pp. 243–245)

6.9   Describe the major characteristics of Piaget's formal operational stage, and discuss the consequences of adolescent's newfound capacity for abstract thought. (pp. 245–247)

6.10 Discuss recent research on formal operational thought and its implications for the accuracy of Piaget's formal operational stage. (pp. 247–249)

6.11 Describe three educational principles derived from Piaget's theory. (p. 249)

6.12 Discuss two recent challenges to Piaget's theory. (pp. 250–251)

6.13 Summarize the core knowledge perspective of cognitive development, and discuss the limitations of this approach. (pp. 251–256)

6.14 Explain Vygotsky's sociocultural theory of cognitive development, noting the importance of social experience and language. (pp. 256–259)

6.15 Contrast Piaget's view of children's private speech with that of Vygotsky. (pp. 257–258)

6.16 Explain how Vygotsky's concept of the zone of proximal development expands our understanding of early cognitive development. (p. 258)

6.17 Describe features of social interaction that foster cognitive development. (p. 259)

6.18 Discuss Vygotsky's view of the role of make-believe play in development. (pp. 259–260)

6.19 Discuss how Vygotsky's ideas have been applied in educational settings. (pp. 260–263)

6.20 Summarize the strengths and limitations of Vygotsky's theory. (pp. 263–264)

STUDY QUESTIONS

1. True or False: Piaget believed that human infants start out as cognitive beings. Briefly explain your response. (p. 218)

   _____

   _____

2. Explain why Piaget's theory is regarded as a *constructivist* approach to cognitive development. (p. 218)

   _____

   _____

   _____

Basic Characteristics of Piaget's Stages

1. List the four stages of cognitive development outlined in Piaget's theory. (p. 219)

   A. _____

   B. _____

   C. _____

   D. _____

2. True or False: Piaget's stages are invariant, meaning that they always follow a fixed order, and no stage can be skipped. (p. 219)

3. Piaget's stages are (culturally-specific to children in the United States and Western Europe / universal to children everywhere). (p. 219)

Piaget's Ideas about Cognitive Change

1. According to Piaget, specific psychological structures, or organized ways of making sense of experience called _____, change with age. (p. 219)

2. What are *mental representations*, and how are they related to cognitive development? (p. 219)

   _____

   _____

   _____

3. List and define the two processes that account for changes in schemes. (p. 219)

A. _____

_____

B. _____

_____

4. During _____, we use our current schemes to interpret the external world. In _____, we create new schemes or adjust old ones to produce a better fit with the environment. (p. 219)

5. Based on Piaget's theory, explain how the balance between assimilation and accommodation changes over time. (p. 220)

_____

_____

_____

6. Piaget used the term _____ to sum up the back-and-forth movement between cognitive equilibrium and disequilibrium that leads to more effective schemes. (p. 220)

The Sensorimotor Stage (Birth to 2 Years)

1. Match each of the following sensorimotor substages with the appropriate description (p. 221)

_____ Infants' primary means of adapting to the environment is through reflexes	1. Substage 1
_____ Infants engage in goal-directed behavior and begin to attain object permanence	2. Substage 2
	3. Substage 3
_____ Toddlers repeat behaviors with variation, producing new effects	4. Substage 4
_____ Infants' adaptations are oriented toward their own bodies	5. Substage 5
_____ Infants' attention begins to turn outward toward the environment	6. Substage 6
_____ Toddlers gain the ability to create mental representations	

2. The _____ (2 words) occurs when infants stumble onto a new experience caused by their own motor activity and then try to repeat the event again and again, thereby strengthening the response into a new schema. (p. 220)

3. Explain the differences between primary, secondary, and tertiary circular reactions. (p. 221)

Primary: _____

_____

Secondary: _____

_____

Tertiary: _____

_____

4. Eight- to 12-month-old infants gain an understanding that objects exist even when they are out of sight, a principle known as _____. They typically make the _____ *search error*, however, searching only in the first hiding place when an object has been moved from one hiding place to another. (p. 222)

5. _____ *imitation* is the ability to remember and copy the behavior of models who are not immediately present. (p. 222)

6. Mental representation makes possible _____ *play*, in which children act out everyday and imaginary activities. (p. 222)

Follow-up Research on Infant Cognitive Development

1. True or False: More recent studies suggest that Piaget overestimated infant capabilities. (p. 222)

2. Explain the *violation-of-expectation method*, which is often used by researchers to examine infants' grasp of object permanence and other aspects of physical reasoning. (p. 222)

_____

_____

_____

_____

3. Explain why the violation-of-expectation method is controversial. (p. 223)

_____

_____

_____

4. True or False: Recent research findings by Baillergeon and colleagues indicate that infants as young as 2 to 3 months of age show an understanding of object permanence. (p. 223)

5. True or False: Infants demonstrate the A-not-B search error because of memory deficits; that is, they cannot remember an object's new location after it has been hidden in more than one place. Discuss research evidence supporting your response. (p. 224)

_____

_____

_____

_____

6. True or False: Although Piaget's theory suggests that infants are incapable of mental representation until about 18 months of age, new studies show that infants exhibit deferred imitation, a form of representation, as early as six weeks of age. (p. 225)

7. The earliest categories used by infants are _____, based on similar overall appearance or prominent object part. By the end of the first year, categories become _____, based on common functions and behavior. (p. 226)

8. By 10 to 12 months of age, infants engage in _____ *problem solving*, meaning that they take a strategy from one problem and apply it to other relevant problems. (p. 226)

Evaluation of the Sensorimotor Stage

1. True or False: New studies reveal that while Piaget underestimated the age at which cognitive capacities emerge, these cognitive attainments do, in fact, develop in the neat, stepwise fashion that Piaget predicted. (pp. 227–229)

The Preoperational Stage (2 to 7 Years)

1. What is the most obvious change as children move from the sensorimotor stage to the preoperational stage? (p. 229)

_____

Advances in Mental Representation

1. How does language increase the efficiency of cognition? (p. 230)

   _____

   _____

2. According to Piaget, (language / sensorimotor activity) gives rise to representational thought. (p. 230)

3. According to Piaget, how is make-believe play related to cognitive development? (p. 230)

   _____

   _____

   _____

4. List three advances in make-believe play during early childhood, and give an example of each. (pp. 230–231)

   A. _____

   _____

   Example: _____

   B. _____

   _____

   Example: _____

   C. _____

   _____

   Example: _____

5. What is *sociodramatic play*? (p. 231)

   _____

6. List several advantages of make-believe play. (p. 231)

   A. _____

   B. _____

   C. _____

7. True or False: Recent research indicates that the creation of imaginary companions is a sign of maladjustment. (p. 231)

8. List the three-stage sequence through which drawing skills typically progress and the approximate age at which each is reached. (p. 232)

   A. _____ Age: _____

   B. _____ Age: _____

   C. _____ Age: _____

9. Describe evidence indicating that culture has a significant impact on the development of drawing skills. (p. 233)

   _____

   _____

   _____

10. _____ refers to the ability to view a symbolic object as both an object in its own right and a symbol. Provide an example. (p. 233)

   _____

   _____

Limitations of Preoperational Thought

1. According to Piaget, young children are not yet capable of *operations*. Define this term. (p. 234)

   _____

   _____

2. Piaget believed that _____, the tendency to focus on one's own viewpoint while ignoring other perspectives, is the most serious deficiency of preoperational thought. (p. 234)

3. The preoperational belief that inanimate objects have lifelike qualities is called
_____. (p. 234)

4. _____ refers to the idea that certain physical characteristics of objects remain the same even when their outward appearance changes. (p. 235)

5. Discuss the three aspects of thought highlighted by preoperational children's inability to conserve. (p. 235)

A. _____

_____

B. _____

_____

C. _____

_____

6. The most important illogical feature of preoperational thought is _____; that is, children of this stage cannot mentally go through a series of steps and then reverse direction, returning to the starting point. (p. 235)

7. Lack of logical operations leads preschoolers to have difficulty with
_____; that is, they cannot yet organize objects into classes and subclasses on the basis of similarities and differences. (p. 235)

Follow-up Research on Preoperational Thought

1. True or False: Even when researchers use familiar objects in visual displays, young children consistently give egocentric responses. (p. 236)

2. Explain why Piaget overestimated preschoolers' animistic beliefs. (pp. 236–237)

_____

_____

3. True or False: When preschoolers are given tasks that are simplified and made relevant to their everyday lives, they do better than Piaget might have predicted. (pp. 236–237)

4. By the second half of the first year, children have formed a variety of _____ categories, such as furniture, animals, and vehicles. Over the early preschool years, children's general categories differentiate as they form many _____-_____ categories, such as chairs, tables, dressers, and beds. Soon after, they break down these intermediate level categories into _____, such as rocking chairs and desk chairs. (p. 238)

5. What two capacities support preschoolers' categorization skills? (p. 238)

   A. _____

   B. _____

6. What experience helps children learn to distinguish between appearance and reality? (pp. 238–239)

   _____

   _____

Evaluation of the Preoperational Stage

1. Summarize conclusions regarding the accuracy of Piaget's preoperational stage. (p. 239)

   _____

   _____

   _____

   _____

2. Findings indicate that children attain logical operations (gradually / suddenly). (p. 239)

The Concrete Operational Stage (7 to 11 Years)

1. Why did Piaget view the concrete operational stage as a major turning point in cognitive development? (p. 241)

   _____

   _____

Concrete Operational Thought

1. The ability to pass _____ tasks provides clear evidence of *operations*. Name and describe two characteristics of thought which illustrate this ability. (p. 241)

   A. _____

   _____

   B. _____

   _____

2. Between ages 7 and 10, children pass Piaget's _____ problem, indicating that they are more aware of classification hierarchies and can focus on relations between a general category and two specific categories at the same time. Explain how this ability is evidenced in children's play activities. (p. 241)

   _____

   _____

   _____

3. The ability to order items along a quantitative dimension, such as length or weight, is called _____. The ability to perform this task mentally is known as _____. (p. 241)

4. Between the ages of 7 and 8, children start to perform *mental* _____, in which they align the self's frame to match that of a person in a different orientation. (p. 242)

5. What are *cognitive maps*, and how do they change from early to middle childhood? (p. 242)

   _____

   _____

   _____

   _____

Limitations of Concrete Operational Thought

1. Describe the major limitation of concrete operational thought. (pp. 242–243)

   _____

   _____

2. Explain what is meant by the term *horizontal décalage*. (p. 243)

_____

_____

Follow-up Research on Concrete Operational Thought

1. Research suggests that schooling and specific cultural experiences (do / do not) affect children's mastery of Piagetian tasks. (pp. 243–244)

2. True or False: Informal, nonschool experiences can foster operational thought. (p. 244)

3. True or False: The forms of logic required by Piagetian tasks appear to emerge spontaneously during childhood and are not heavily influenced by training context or cultural conditions. (p. 244)

The Formal Operational Stage (11 Years and Older)

1. Summarize the basic difference between concrete and formal operational reasoning. (p. 245)

_____

_____

_____

Hypothetico-Deductive Reasoning

1. What is *hypothetico-deductive reasoning*? (p. 245)

_____

_____

_____

Propositional Thought

1. What is *propositional thought*? (p. 246)

_____

_____

2. Although Piaget did not view _____ as playing a central role in cognitive development, he acknowledged that it is more important during adolescence. Briefly explain why this is the case. (p. 246)

_____

_____

_____

Consequences of Abstract Thought

1. Name and describe two distorted images of the relation between self and others that appear at adolescence, and state which of these distortions is the strongest. (p. 247)

   A. _____

   _____

   _____

   B. _____

   _____

   _____

2. True or False: The imaginary audience and the personal fable are probably the result of adolescent egocentrism, just as Piaget suggested. (p. 247)

Follow-up Research on Formal Operational Thought

1. True or False: School-age children show glimmerings of hypothetico-deductive reasoning, but they are not as competent as adolescents and adults. (p. 247)

2. School-age children fail to grasp the _____ of propositional reasoning—that the accuracy of conclusions drawn from premises rests on the rules of logic, not on real-world confirmation. (p. 247)

3. Explain why many college students and adults are not yet fully formal operational. (p. 248)

_____

_____

_____

4. How does the apparent lack of formal operational reasoning in some village and tribal societies pose a challenge to Piaget's theory? (p. 248)

_____

_____

_____

Piaget and Education

1. List and describe three educational principles derived from Piaget's theory. (p. 249)

A. _____

_____

B. _____

_____

C. _____

_____

Overall Evaluation of Piaget's Theory

1. Discuss three ways in which Piaget's theory has contributed to the field of child development. (p. 250)

A. _____

_____

B. _____

_____

C. _____

_____

Is Piaget's Account of Cognitive Change Clear and Accurate

1. Children's efforts to assimilate, accommodate, and reorganize structures (can / cannot) adequately explain patterns of cognitive change. (p. 250)

2. Explain why Piaget's theory has limited practical utility for deriving teaching strategies that foster children's optimum learning. (p. 250)

_____

_____

_____

Does Cognitive Development Take Place in Stages?

1. True or False: Most experts agree with Piaget's broad, stagelike conceptualization of children's cognitive development. (p. 250)

2. Summarize three contemporary perspectives that address the question of whether cognitive development takes place in stages. (pp. 250–251)

A. _____

_____

_____

B. _____

_____

_____

C. _____

_____

_____

Piaget's Legacy

1. True or False: Even today, Piaget's description of development is still fully accepted. (p. 251)

2. True or False: Piaget's findings have served as the starting point for virtually every major contemporary theory of children's development. (p. 251)

The Core Knowledge Perspective

1. Summarize the major tenants of the core knowledge perspective. (pp. 251–252)

_____

_____

_____

2. True or False: The core knowledge perspective assumes that each core domain develops independently. (p. 252)

3. Core knowledge theorists do not regard development as a general process; rather, they see it as _____-specific and uneven. (p. 252)

Infancy: Physical and Numerical Knowledge

1. Researchers have used the _____ method to determine whether infants display impressive physical and numerical understandings so early that some knowledge must be innate. (p. 252)

2. Discuss research findings indicating that infants as young as 2½ months of age are aware of basic object properties, and they quickly build on this knowledge. (p. 252)

_____

_____

_____

3. True or False: Research shows that 5-month-old infants are able to discriminate quantities up to three, and they can use that knowledge to perform simple arithmetic, such as addition and subtraction. (p. 252)

4. The findings of core knowledge researchers related to infants' numerical understanding are (controversial / well-accepted). (pp. 252–253)

Children as Naïve Theorists

1. Explain the *theory theory*. (p. 253)

_____

_____

_____

2. Compare theory theory to Piaget's theory of development, citing one similarity and one difference of these two perspectives. (p. 254)

Similarity: _____

_____

Difference: _____

_____

3. List four domains in which children develop naïve theories. (p. 254)

A. _____

B. _____

C. _____

D. _____

Biology and Environment: Children's Understanding of Health and Illness

1. Trace changes in children's understanding of health and illness from the preschool years into adolescence. (p. 255)

Preschool and early school-age (4- to 8-year-olds): _____

_____

Older school-age (9- to 10-year-olds): _____

_____

Early Adolescence: _____

_____

2. Describe factors that affect children's understanding of health and illness. (p. 255)

_____

_____

_____

Evaluation of the Core Knowledge Perspective

1. Cite two contributions of the core knowledge perspective. (p. 254)

A. _____

_____

B. _____

_____

2. Discuss a primary criticism of the core knowledge perspective. (pp. 254–256)

_____

_____

3. True or False: In explaining children's thinking across infancy and childhood, the core knowledge perspective emphasizes native endowment to the exclusion of environmental experience. (p. 256)

4. True or False: The core knowledge perspective has been extremely useful for helping to clarify how biology and environment jointly produce cognitive change. (p. 256)

5. True or False: One major limitation of the core knowledge perspective is that it pays little attention to children's learning through interaction with others. (p. 256)

Vygotsky's Sociocultural Theory

1. Summarize the primary differences between the core knowledge and Piagetian theories of development and Vygotsky's sociocultural theory. (p. 256)

_____

_____

_____

Private Speech

1. Contrast Piaget's view of children's private speech with that of Vygotsky. (p. 257)

Piaget: _____

_____

Vygotsky: _____

_____

2. Most research findings have supported (Piaget's / Vygotsky's) view of children's private speech. (p. 257)

3. Under what circumstances are children likely to use private speech? (p. 257)

_____

_____

4. True or False: Compared to their normally achieving agemates, children with learning problems engage in significantly less private speech. (p. 257)

Social Origins of Cognitive Development

1. Explain Vygotsky's concept of the *zone of proximal development*, noting how it is related to cognitive development. (p. 258)

_____

_____

_____

2. Identify and describe two features of social interaction that facilitate children's cognitive development. (p. 258)

A. _____

_____

B. _____

_____

3. _____ *participation* calls attention to both adult and child contributions to a cooperative dialogue, without specifying the precise features of communication. (p. 259)

Vygotsky's View of Make-Believe Play

1. According to Vygotsky, in what two ways does make-believe play foster cognitive development? (p. 259)

A. _____

_____

B. _____

_____

2. Research (does / does not) support Vygotsky's conclusion that make-believe play serves as a zone of proximal development. (p. 259)

From Research to Practice: Social Origins of Make-Believe Play

1. True or False: When adults participate, toddlers' make-believe play is more elaborate and advanced. (pp. 260–261)

2. Cite four ways in which parents and teachers can enhance children's development of make-believe play. (pp. 260–261)

   A. _____

   _____

   B. _____

   _____

   C. _____

   _____

   D. _____

   _____

Vygotsky and Education

1. Vygotskian classrooms go beyond independent discovery to promote _____ *discovery*, in which teachers guide children's learning by tailoring their interventions to each child's zone of proximal development. (p. 260)

2. Distinguish the components of education emphasized by Vygotsky during the preschool years from those that he emphasized once formal schooling begins. (p. 261)

   Preschool: _____

   _____

   _____

   Formal schooling: _____

   _____

   _____

Reciprocal Teaching

1. Explain the process of *reciprocal teaching*, including the four cognitive strategies used in this approach. (pp. 261–262)

    _____

    _____

    _____

    _____

Cooperative Learning

1. What is *cooperative learning,* and how does it foster development? (p. 262)

    _____

    _____

    _____

2. Explain why children in individualistic cultures have more difficultly working in groups than do children in collectivist cultures. (p. 262)

    _____

    _____

    _____

Evaluation of Vygotsky's Theory

1. True or False: Like that of Piaget, Vygotsky's theory emphasizes universal cognitive change. (p. 263)

2. True or False: According to Vygotsky, optimum learning results from children's independent efforts. Elaborate on your response. (p. 263)

    _____

    _____

3. Discuss two limitations of Vygotsky's theory. (p. 263)

    A. _____

    _____

    B. _____

    _____

1. Describe the daily experiences of children living in the Mayan village of the Yucatan, Mexico, and discuss how such experiences affect Mayan preschoolers' skills and behavior (relative to their Western agemates). (p. 264)

_____

_____

_____

_____

_____

_____

ASK YOURSELF . . .

Review: Explain how cognition changes in Piaget's theory, giving examples of assimilation, accommodations, and organization. (p. 229)

_____

_____

_____

_____

_____

Review: Using the text discussion on pages 220–227, construct your own table providing an overview of infants and toddler cognitive development. Which entries in the table are consistent with Piaget's sensorimotor stage? Which ones develop earlier than Piaget anticipated? (p. 229)

_____

_____

_____

_____

Apply: Ten-month-old Mimi's father holds up her favorite biscuit, deposits it under a napkin, and shows Mimi his empty hand. Mimi looks puzzled and fails to search for the biscuit. Explain why Mimi finds this object-hiding task difficult. (p. 229)

_____

_____

_____

_____

_____

Connect: Review research in Chapter 4, indicating that if infants are not tested in the same situation in which they were trained, they remember poorly (see page 137). After 12 months of age, memory becomes more flexible. Do similar changes in the flexibility of object-search behaviors, deferred imitation, and problem-solving occur around this time? Explain. (p. 229)

_____

_____

_____

_____

_____

Review: Select two of the following features of Piaget's preoperational stage: egocentrism, a focus on superficial perceptual appearances, difficulty reasoning about transformations, and lack of hierarchical classification. Cite findings that led Piaget to conclude that preschoolers are deficient in those ways. Then present evidence indicating that preschoolers are more capable thinkers than Piaget assumed. (p. 240)

_____

_____

_____

_____

_____

Review: Summarize evidence indicating that young preschoolers have difficulty with dual representation. Why is the mastery of dual representation important? (p. 240)

_____

_____

_____

_____

_____

Apply: Brett's preschool teacher creates many opportunities for sociodramatic play in his classroom. Brett's mother wonders whether Brett is learning anything from so much pretending. Using research findings, respond to her concern. (p. 240)

_____

_____

_____

_____

_____

Apply: At home, 4-year-old Will understands that his tricycle isn't alive and can't move by itself. Yet when Will went fishing with his family and his father asked, "Why do you think the river is flowing along?" Will responded, "Because it's alive and it wants to." What explains this contradiction in Will's reasoning? (p. 240)

_____

_____

_____

_____

_____

Review: Mastery of conservation provides one illustration of Piaget's horizontal décalage. Review the preceding sections. Then list additional examples showing that operational reasoning develops gradually during middle childhood. (p. 245)

_____

_____

_____

_____

Review: Cite evidence indicating that specific experiences influence children's performance on Piagetian concrete-operational tasks. (p. 245)

_____

_____

_____

_____

_____

Connect: Explain how advances in perspective taking contribute to school-age children's improved capacity to give directions and construct cognitive maps. (p. 245)

_____

_____

_____

_____

_____

Review: Using the concepts of hypothetico-deductive reasoning and propositional thought, illustrate the difference between school-age children's and adolescents' cognition. (p. 249)

_____

_____

_____

_____

_____

Review: Why do many college students have difficulty with Piaget's formal operational tasks? (p. 249)

_____

_____

_____

_____

_____

Apply: Thirteen-year-old Rosie had a crush on a boy who failed to return her affections. As she lay on the sofa feeling depressed, her mother assured her that there would be other boys. "Mom," Rosie snapped, "you don't know what it's like to be in love!" Which cognitive-distortion—the imaginary audience or the personal fable—does Rosie's thinking illustrate? Explain. (p. 249)

_____

_____

_____

_____

_____

Connect: How are questions raised about Piaget's formal operation stage similar to those raised about the concrete operational stage? (p. 249)

_____

_____

_____

_____

_____

Review: Cite examples of findings that have led contemporary researchers to question Piaget's account of (1) cognitive change and (2) development as taking place in stages. (p. 251)

_____

_____

_____

_____

_____

Connect: How are educational principles derived from Piaget's theory consistent with his emphasis on an active child who takes responsibility for her own learning? (p. 251)

_____

_____

_____

_____

_____

Review: What are core domains of thought? Cite an example of infants' innate knowledge in the physical domain and the numerical domain. Why do some researchers question whether infants actually have such knowledge? (p. 256)

_____

_____

_____

_____

_____

Review: Why do core knowledge researchers characterize young children as naïve theorists? Cite findings that support the theory. (p. 256)

_____

_____

_____

_____

Connect: Describe similarities and differences between Piaget's theory and the core knowledge perspective. (p. 256)

_____

_____

_____

_____

Review: Describe characteristics of social interaction that support children's cognitive development. How does such interaction create a zone of proximal development? (p. 264)

_____

_____

_____

_____

Review: Explain how make-believe play strengthens children's capacity to think before they act and follow social rules. (p. 264)

_____

_____

_____

_____

Apply: Tanisha sees her 5-year-old son, Toby, talking to himself while he plays. She wonders whether she should discourage this behavior. Using Vygotsky's theory and related research, explain why Toby's private speech is probably beneficial. (p. 264)

_____

_____

_____

_____

Connect: Explain how Piaget's and Vygotsky's theories complement one another in the way each views cognitive development. How would classroom practices by each theory be similar in some ways and different in others?

_____

_____

_____

_____

_____

SUGGESTED STUDENT READINGS

Berk, L. E. (2001). *Awakening children's minds: How parents and teachers can make a difference.* New York: Oxford University Press. Written for parents and teachers of young children, this book provides an overview of current theories of child development, straightforward advice for child rearing, and suggestions for concrete practice. Moreover, the author stresses the importance of parents and teachers in the development of competent, caring, and well-adjusted children.

Rogoff, B. (2002). *The cultural nature of human development.* New York: Oxford University Press. Presents a fascinating account of cultural influences on development, integrating research from cross-cultural psychology, anthropology, and sociocultural theory. The book examines multiple aspects of development, including cognition.

Rosengren, K. S., Johnson, C. N., & Harris, P. L. (Eds.). (2000). *Imagining the impossible: Magical, scientific, and religious thinking in children.* New York: Cambridge University Press. Examines the development of children's thinking in regards to imaginary entities, magic, and supernatural events. The goal of this book is to explore children's domain-specific knowledge, scientific reasoning, and the cognitive processes that underlie children's metaphysical thinking.

Roskos, K. A., & Christie, J. F. (Eds.). (2000). *Play and literacy in early childhood: Research for multiple perspectives.* Mahwah, NJ: Lawrence Erlbaum Associates. Explores the relationship between play and literacy by drawing on research from cognitive, ecological, and cultural perspectives. Also accompanying each chapter is a critical review of research by leading scholars in the field of child development.

PUZZLE 6.1

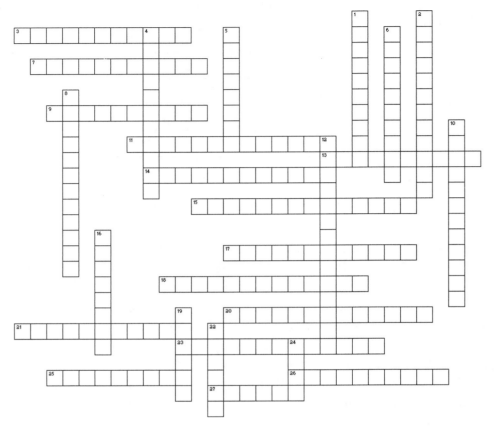

Across

3. The tendency to focus on one's own viewpoint and ignore other perspectives
7. Violation-of-_____ method: use of habituation procedures to examine infants' understanding of physical experience
9. The tendency to focus on one aspect of a situation to the neglect of other important features
11. _____ play: make-believe play with others
13. In Piaget's theory, mental operations of actions that obey logical rules
14. Use of current schemas to interpret the external world
15. Piaget's second stage in which rapid development of representation takes place
17. _____ classification: organization of objects into classes and subclasses based on similarities and differences
18. Back-and-forth movement between cognitive equilibrium and disequilibrium that leads to more effective schemas
20. Ability to mentally go through a series of steps and then reverse direction, returning to the staring point
21. Type of play in which children pretend, acting out everyday and imaginary events (two words; hyph.)
23. Use of old schemas and creation of new ones to produce a better fit with the environment
25. _____ thinking: belief that inanimate objects have lifelike qualities
26. Process of building schemas through direct interaction with the environment
27. _____ representation: internal depictions of information that the mind can manipulate

Down

1. Object _____ understanding that objects continue to exist when they are out of sight
2. The internal rearrangement and linking together of schemas so that they form a strongly interconnected cognitive system
4. _____ behavior: sequence of actions in which schemas are deliberately combined to solve a problem
5. _____ reaction: infants try to repeat a chance event caused by their own motor activity
6. _____ problem solving: taking a solution strategy from one problem and applying it to other relevant problems
8. Piaget's first stage, during which infants and toddlers "think" with their eyes, ears, and hands
10. The understanding that certain physical characteristics of objects remain the same, even when their outward appearance changes
12. _____ approach to cognitive development: children discover virtually all knowledge through their own activity
16. The ability to remember and copy the behavior of models who are not present is called _____ imitation.
19. A-not-B _____ error: if an object is moved from hiding place A to hiding place B, 8- to 12-month olds will search only in the first hiding place
22. A specific structure, or organized way of making sense of experience, that changes with age
24. _____ representation: viewing a symbolic object as both an object in its own right and a symbol

PUZZLE 6.2

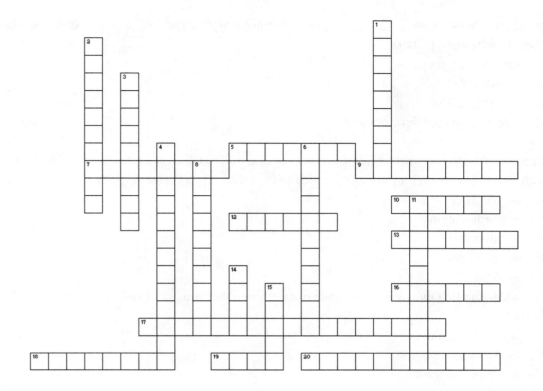

Across

5. _____ necessity: property of propositional thought which specifies that the accuracy of conclusions drawn from premises rests on rules of logic, not on real-world confirmation

7. _____ operational stage: Piaget's third stage, during which thought is logical, flexible, and organized in its application to concrete information

9. The ability to arrange items along a quantitative dimension, such as length or weight

10. _____ theory: assumes that children build on innate concepts to form nave theories in each core domain of thought

12. _____ participation: calls attention to both adult and child contributions to cooperative dialogue without specifying the precise features of communication

13. _____ speech: self-directed speech that children use to guide their own thinking and behavior

16. _____ operational stage: Piaget's highest stage, in which adolescents develop the capacity for abstract, scientific thinking

17. Process whereby two participants who begin a task with different understandings arrive at a shared understanding

18. Zone of _____ development: a range of tasks that the child cannot yet handle independently but can do with the help of more skilled partners

19. _____ knowledge perspective: assumes that infants begin life with innate special-purpose knowledge systems

20. Changing quality of support over a teaching session in which adults adjust the assistance they provide to fit the child's current level of performance

Down

1. Hypothetico-_____ reasoning begins with a theory of all possible factors that could affect an outcome and inferences about specific hypotheses, which are then tested in a systematic fashion.

2. In _____ teaching, a teacher and 2-4 pupils form a collaborative learning group

3. Adolescents' belief that they are the focus of everyone else's attention and concern is known as the _____ audience.

4. In _____ thought, adolescents evaluate the logic of verbal statements without referring to real-world circumstances.

6. _____ learning: groups of peers work toward common goals inference: the ability to seriate mentally

8. _____ inference: the ability to seriate mentally

11. _____ decalage: development within a Piagetian stage

14. Cognitive _____ are mental representations of large-scale spaces.

15. Personal _____: adolescents' belief that they are special and unique

191

PRACTICE TEST

1. In Piaget's theory, a(n) _____ is an organized way of making sense of experience that changes with age. (p. 219)
   a. scheme
   b. adaptation
   c. sensory register
   d. zone of proximal development

2. According to Piaget, when children create new schemas or adjust old ones to produce a better fit with the environment, they are using which of the following processes? (p. 219)
   a. assimilation
   b. accommodation
   c. equilibrium
   d. organization

3. The understanding that objects continue to exist when they are out of sight is referred to as: (p. 222)
   a. physical causality.
   b. mental representation.
   c. object permanence.
   d. stimulus constancy.

4. During Substage 6 of the sensorimotor stages, infants develop the ability to create _____, or internal images of absent objects and past events. (p. 222)
   a. schemas
   b. mental strategies
   c. symbolic images
   d. mental representations

5. To study infants' grasp of physical reasoning, researchers often use a violation-of-expectation method in which: (p. 222)
   a. infants are habituated to a physical event, and then researchers determine whether they dishabituate faster to a possible event or an impossible event.
   b. infants are asked to seek an object after it has been moved from one hiding place to another.
   c. infants are instructed to perform a response after seeing it modeled by an adult.
   d. infants are asked to retrieve an object that has been hidden from their view.

6. As children move from the sensorimotor to the preoperational stage, the most obvious change is: (p. 229)
   a. an increase in the child's use of senses and movements to explore the world.
   b. development of the capacity for abstract, scientific reasoning.
   c. an increase in mental representation.
   d. more logical, flexible, and organized thought.

7. Sociodramatic play refers to: (p. 231)
   a. make-believe play directed toward the self.
   b. make-believe play with others.
   c. play that is closely linked to the real-life conditions associated with it.
   d. make-believe play involving complex schema combinations.

8. Before age 3, children have difficulty with _____, or viewing a symbolic object as both an object in is own right and a symbol. (p. 233)
   a. dual representation
   b. sensorimotor relations
   c. hypothetical reasoning
   d. objectivity

9. According to Piaget, the most serious deficiency of preoperational thinking is: (p. 234)
   a. egocentrism.
   b. animistic thinking.
   c. centration.
   d. intersubjectivity.

10. Conservation refers to: (p. 235)
    a. children's tendency to focus on one aspect of a situation and neglect other important features.
    b. mental representation of actions that obey logical rules.
    c. the tendency to treat the initial and final states of a problem as completely unrelated.
    d. the notion that certain physical characteristics of objects remain the same, even when their outward appearance changes.

11. Follow-up research on preoperational thought shows that: (p. 236)
    a. when researchers give Piaget's tasks in just the way he designed them, preschoolers consistently perform at a much higher level than Piaget predicted.
    b. when preschoolers are given tasks that are simplified and made relevant to their everyday lives, they do better than Piaget predicted.
    c. Piaget overestimated preschoolers' cognitive abilities.
    d. children attain logical operations suddenly, shortly after they begin formal schooling.

12. The ability to pass conservation tasks provides clear evidence of _____ — mental actions that obey logical rules. (p. 241)
    a. transitive inference
    b. classification
    c. operations
    d. metacognitive awareness

13. Nadia can sort sticks of varying length into a sequence from shortest to longest. However, she cannot mentally infer that stick A is longer than stick C given that A is longer than B and that B is longer than C. Which of the following abilities does Nadia lack? (p. 241)
    a. decentration
    b. transitive inference
    c. class inclusion
    d. reversibility

14. Horizontal décalage refers to: (p. 243)
    a. consistent use of a mental strategy that leads to improvements in performance.
    b. patterns of development across the Piagetian stages.
    c. development within a Piagetian stage.
    d. the generation of a single correct answer to a problem.

15. When faced with a problem, adolescents begin with a general theory, deduce from it specific predictions about outcomes, and then test the predictions—a process that Piaget called: (p. 245)
    a. hypothetico-deductive reasoning.
    b. horizontal décalage.
    c. transitive inference.
    d. inductive reasoning.

16. An experimenter hides a poker chip in her hand and asks participants to indicate whether the following statement is true, false, or uncertain: "Either the chip in my hand is green or it is not green." A concrete operational child will indicate uncertainty, whereas a formal operational adolescent will respond "true." This response reflects the formal operational child's understanding of: (p. 246)
    a. causal reasoning.
    b. concrete thought.
    c. propositional thought.
    d. relativistic reasoning.

17. Adolescents' belief that they are the focus of everyone else's attention and concern is referred to as: (p. 247)
    a. the imaginary audience.
    b. the personal fable.
    c. narcissism.
    d. social phobia.

18. Research on Piaget's formal operational stage shows that: (p. 248)
    a. over 95% of college students easily pass Piaget's formal operational problems.
    b. most people are more likely to think abstractly in novel, rather than familiar, situations.
    c. development of formal operations is sudden, occurring in all contexts at once.
    d. in many tribal and village societies, formal operational tasks are not mastered at all.

19. A teacher in a Piagetian-based preschool wants to foster her students' cognitive development. Based on the educational principles derived from Piaget's theory, what would she do in order to accomplish this goal? (p. 249)
    a. present verbal lessons on a variety of subject areas
    b. promote children's self-paced discovery by providing a variety of materials and play areas
    c. frequently evaluate children's educational performance through comparison with same-age peers
    d. plan activities for the total class rather than for individuals or small groups in order to minimalize individual differences

20. According to the core knowledge perspective: (p. 251)
    a. individuals are born with innate knowledge systems, and therefore, environmental experience exerts little, if any, influence on cognitive development.
    b. infants begin life with innate knowledge systems which permit a ready grasp of new, related information, thereby supporting early, rapid development of certain aspects of thought.
    c. children develop increasingly elaborate cognitive maps as a result of exposure to varied environmental experiences.
    d. culturally-relevant knowledge domains are acquired through social interaction with more skilled partners.

21. According to _____ theory, children build on innate concepts by theorizing about everyday events and then testing their explanations against experience, revising them when they cannot adequately account for new information. (p. 253)
    a. theory
    b. naïve
    c. formal operational
    d. bioecological

22. How did Piaget's view of children's private speech differ from that of Vygotsky? (p. 257)
    a. Piaget thought that private speech resulted from children's inability to take the perspective of others, while Vygotsky reasoned that children use private speech for self-guidance.
    b. Piaget viewed private speech as the foundation for all complex mental activities, while Vygotsky regarded private speech as nonsocial, senseless utterances.
    c. Vygotsky concluded that private speech is ineffective and uncommunicative, while Piaget did not study this phenomenon.
    d. Vygotsky stressed the importance of private speech during early childhood, whereas Piaget discussed the utility of private speech over the course of the lifespan.

23. Scaffolding is: (p. 258)
    a. a concept that calls attention to adult and child contributions to a cooperative dialogue without specifying the precise features of communication.
    b. the process whereby participants who begin a task with different understandings arrive at a shared understanding.
    c. a range of tasks that a child cannot yet perform alone but can do with the assistance of more skilled partners.
    d. a changing quality of social support over the course of a teaching session in which the adult adjusts the assistance provided to fit the child's current level of performance.

24. Vygotskian classrooms promote: (p. 260)
    a. children's self-paced discovery through spontaneous interaction with the environment.
    b. passive student participation in teacher-led activities.
    c. highly structured, large group lessons teaching concrete concepts and skills.
    d. assisted discovery in which teachers guide children's learning.

25. Questioning, summarizing, clarifying, and predicting are cognitive strategies used in: (pp. 261–262)
    a. private speech.
    b. reciprocal teaching.
    c. cooperative learning.
    d. guided participation.

CHAPTER 7
COGNITIVE DEVELOPMENT:
AN INFORMATION-PROCESSING PERSPECTIVE

BRIEF CHAPTER SUMMARY

The information-processing approach views the mind as a complex, symbol-manipulating system through which information flows, much like a computer. Two general models of adult information processing have influenced research on children's cognition. The store model assumes that information is held, or stored, in three parts of the system for processing: the sensory register; working, or short-term, memory; and long-term memory. While the sensory register and working memory are limited in capacity, long-term memory, our permanent knowledge base, is limitless. Connectionist, or artificial neural network, models use computer simulations to imitate the workings of neurons in the brain. Connectionists have succeeded in depicting changes in children's performance on a variety of tasks and believe that the human cognitive system is a general processing device that gradually attains domain-specific competencies as it is exposed to relevant learning opportunities.

Several developmental models of information processing have attracted widespread attention. To create an overall vision of development, Case's neo-Piagetian perspective uses Piaget's theory as a starting point, reinterpreting it within an information-processing framework. Compared with Piaget, Case acknowledges greater domain-specific change, attributing this to the complexity of tasks and children's experiences. Siegler's model of strategy choice suggests that children generate a variety of strategies for solving challenging problems; with experience, some strategies are selected and survive, whereas others die off. As with physical characteristics, variation and selection characterize children's mental strategies, yielding adaptive problem-solving techniques.

Attention is fundamental to human thinking, since it determines the information that will be considered in any task. Attention improves greatly during early and middle childhood, becoming more selective, adaptable, and planful. Gains in cognitive inhibition lead to the expansion of processing capacity and underlie children's greater selectivity of attention. Development of attentional (and memory) strategies occur in the following four phases: production deficiency, control deficiency, utilization deficiency, and effective strategy use.

As attention improves, so do memory strategies. Researchers have studied the development of three strategies that enhance memory for new information—rehearsal, organization, and elaboration. Recognition, the simplest form of retrieval, is a fairly automatic process that is highly accurate by the preschool years. In contrast, recall, or generating a mental representation of an absent stimulus, is more difficult and shows much greater improvement with age, as older children make use of a wider range of retrieval cues.

When people are given complex, meaningful material to remember, condensations, additions, and distortions appear, indicating that we select and interpret much information we encounter in our daily lives. Fuzzy-trace theory suggests that when we first encode information, we reconstruct it automatically, creating both a vague, fuzzy version, called a gist, that preserves the essential content without details and is useful for reasoning, and a verbatim version adapted to answering questions about specifics. With age, children's gist memory improves.

Gains in the quantity and structure of the knowledge base enhance memory performance by making new, related information easier to store and retrieve. Like adults, young children remember familiar experiences in terms of scripts. Autobiographical memory, representations of one-time events that are personally meaningful, expands over the preschool years. Children's metacognitive knowledge changes from a passive to an active, constructive view of mental functioning in middle childhood as the awareness of cognitive capacities, strategies for processing information, and task variables expands. Cognitive self-regulation develops slowly during childhood and adolescence. Recently, information-processing researchers have turned their attention to children's academic learning.

A major strength of the information-processing approach is its explicitness and precision in breaking down complex cognitive performance into its separate elements so each can be studied. However, by analyzing cognition into its components, information processing has had difficulty putting them back together into a broad, comprehensive theory of development. Also, computer models of cognitive processing do not reflect the richness of real-life learning experiences. A final shortcoming is the slowness of information-processing research to respond to the growing interest in the biological bases of cognitive development.

LEARNING OBJECTIVES

After reading this chapter, you should be able to:

7.1   Summarize the basic tenants of the information-processing approach to cognitive development. (p. 270)

7.2   Discuss general models of information processing, including the store model and the connectionist model. (pp. 270–274)

7.3   Describe two developmental theories of information processing, including Case's neo-Piagetian theory and Siegler's model of strategy choice. (pp. 274–277)

7.4   Discuss the development of attention across childhood, with particular emphasis on changes in selectivity, adaptability, and planfulness. (pp. 278–282)

7.5   Discuss developmental strategies for storing new information, including rehearsal, organization, and elaboration. (pp. 282–285)

7.6   Describe the strategies that children learn for retrieving information from long-term memory, with particular attention to recognition, recall, and reconstruction. (pp. 285–288)

7.7   Explain the association between knowledge and memory. (pp. 288–289)

7.8   Discuss children's use of scripts to remember familiar events, and explain how scripts may act as the developmental link between episodic and semantic memory. (p. 289)

7.9   Discuss theories of infantile amnesia, and describe the development of autobiographical memory. (pp. 289–293)

7.10 Summarize changes in metacognitive knowledge across childhood. (pp. 294–295)

7.11 Trace the development of cognitive self-regulation from childhood into adolescence. (p. 296)

7.12 Explain how the information-processing approach has been applied in educational settings to improve children's learning in reading, mathematics, and scientific reasoning. (pp. 298–305)

7.13 Summarize strengths and limitations of the information-processing approach. (pp. 305–306)

STUDY QUESTIONS

The Information-Processing Approach

1. Most information-processing theorists view the mind as a complex, symbol-manipulating system through which information flows, much like a _____. (p. 270)

General Models of Information Processing

The Store Model

1. According to the *store model,* individuals store information in three parts of the mental system for processing. Name and describe each of these parts. (p. 271)

   A. _____

      _____

   B. _____

      _____

   C. _____

      _____

2. As information flows through the information-processing system, it can be operated on and transformed using _____, thereby increasing the efficiency of thinking and the chances that we will retain the information for later use. (p. 271)

3. What is the *central executive*? (p. 272)

_____

_____

4. True or False: Long-term memory has a limitless capacity. (p. 272)

5. According to the store model, what two aspects of the cognitive system increase with age? (p. 272)

A. _____

B. _____

6. _____, a measure of working memory, refers to the longest sequence of items that a person can recall. (p. 272)

7. Speed of information processing on cognitive tasks (increases / decreases) with age. (p. 272)

Connectionism

1. Explain the *connectionist model* of information processing. (p. 273)

_____

_____

_____

2. An artificial neural network includes a(n) _____ layer, which encodes the task; one or more _____ layers, which represents information; and a(n) _____ layer, which generates a response. (p. 273)

3. What is another name for artificial neural networks? (p. 273)

_____

4. True or False: The connections between information-processing units are programmed to change with experience. (p. 273)

5. True or False: Once initial learning takes place, the neural connections change rapidly, leading children to consistently display correct responses almost immediately after learning occurs. (p. 274)

6. The connectionist model (supports / refutes) assumptions of the core knowledge perspective. (p. 274)

Developmental Theories of Information Processing

Case's Neo-Piagetian Theory

1. Case's neo-Piagetian theory accepts Piaget's stages but views change within each stage, as well as movement from one stage to the next, as due to increases in _____. Each major stage involves a distinct type of _____ structure. (p. 274)

2. Discuss the three factors responsible for gains in working memory capacity from infancy to adolescence. (pp. 274–275)

   A. _____
   _____

   B. _____
   _____

   C. _____
   _____

3. Summarize Case's information-processing account of horizontal décalage. (p. 275)

   _____
   _____
   _____

4. True or False: Case acknowledges greater domain-specific change than did Piaget, making his theory better able to account for unevenness in cognitive development. (p. 275)

Siegler's Model of Strategy Choice

1. Siegler's model of strategy choice applies an _____ perspective to children's cognitive development. Explain this approach. (p. 276)

   _____

   _____

   _____

2. Siegler found that strategy use follows an _____ pattern in which children generate a variety of strategies to solve a given problem, several of which may overlap at any given time; then they gradually select strategies on the basis of two adaptive criteria: *speed* and _____. (p. 276)

3. Cite two ways that children can move from less to more efficient problem-solving strategies. (pp. 276–277)

   A. _____

   B. _____

4. True or False: Siegler's model reveals that no child thinks in just one way. (p. 277)

**From Research to Practice: Speech-Gesture Mismatches—
Using the Hand to Read the Mind**

1. What are speech-gesture mismatches? (p. 278)

   _____

   _____

   _____

2. Explain the implications of speech-gesture mismatches for academic learning. (p. 278)

   _____

   _____

   _____

3. True or False: Research shows that at times, children's gestures capture their progress better than does their speech. (p. 278)

Selectivity and Adaptability

1. As toddlers become increasingly capable of goal-directed behavior, their attention to novelty (increases / decreases) and sustained attention (improves / declines). (p. 279)

2. True or False: Selective attention improves sharply between 6 and 9 years of age. (p. 279)

3. Discuss changes in older children's adaptability and flexibility of attention. (p. 279)

_____

_____

_____

4. What is *cognitive inhibition*? (p. 279)

_____

_____

5. How does cognitive inhibition foster performance on cognitive tasks? (p. 279)

_____

_____

_____

6. Researchers believe that maturation of the _____ lobe regions of the brain are largely responsible for gains in cognitive inhibition. (pp. 279–280)

7. List and describe the four-phase sequence of attentional strategy development. (p. 280)

A. _____

_____

B. _____

_____

C. _____

_____

D. _____

_____

8. Cite two reasons that application of a new strategy may not lead to gains in young children's task performance. (p. 280)

A. _____

B. _____

Planning

1. What is *planning*? (p. 280)

_____

_____

2. Explain how the development of planning illustrates how attention becomes coordinated with other cognitive processes. (p. 281)

_____

_____

_____

3. Explain how children acquire planning skills. (p. 281)

_____

_____

_____

4. How can parents foster their children's development of planning? (p. 281)

_____

_____

_____

Biology and Environment: Children with Attention-Deficit Hyperactivity Disorder

1. Describe characteristics typical of children with attention-deficit hyperactivity disorder (ADHD). (pp. 282–283)

_____

_____

_____

2. True or False: The intelligence of ADHD children is normal, and they show no signs of serious emotional disturbance. (pp. 282–283)

3. Discuss hereditary and environmental contributions to ADHD. (pp. 282–283)

Hereditary: _____

_____

_____

Environmental: _____

_____

_____

4. Discuss three ways to treat ADHD, noting which method is the most common and which method is the most effective. (pp. 282–283)

A. _____

_____

B. _____

_____

C. _____

_____

Memory

Strategies for Storing Information

1. List and describe three memory strategies that emerge during childhood. (pp. 282–283)

A. _____

_____

B. _____

_____

C. _____

_____

2. Preschoolers (do / do not) use semantic organization—grouping objects or words into meaningful categories. (p. 283)

3. True or False: Once children discover elaboration, they find it so effective that it tends to replace other memory strategies. (p. 284)

4. Discuss the impact of culture and schooling on children's development of memory strategies. (pp. 284–285)

    _____

    _____

    _____

Retrieving Information

1. Name three ways in which information can be retrieved from memory. (p. 285)

    A. _____

    B. _____

    C. _____

2. Explain the difference between *recognition* and *recall*. (p. 285)

    Recognition: _____

    _____

    Recall: _____

    _____

3. (Recall / Recognition) shows much greater improvement with age. Why is this the case? (p. 286)

    _____

    _____

4. Describe *reconstruction memory*. (p. 286)

    _____

    _____

    _____

5. Research on reconstruction shows that much of the information that children and adults recall is (accurate / inaccurate). Briefly elaborate on your response. (p. 286)

_____

_____

_____

6. Describe the two types of encoding outlined in *fuzzy-trace theory*. (p. 287)

A. _____

_____

B. _____

_____

7. True or False: Fuzzy-trace theorists assume that all reconstructions are transformations of verbatim memory. (p. 287)

8. With age, children rely more on (verbatim memory / fuzzy, reconstructed gists). (p. 287)

9. (Fuzzy traces / Verbatim memories) are less likely to be forgotten, thereby serving as enduring retrieval cues. (p. 288)

The Knowledge Base and Memory Performance

1. Discuss the relationship between knowledge and memory. (p. 288)

_____

_____

_____

Scripts: Basic Building Blocks of Structured Knowledge

1. _____ *memory* is the vast, intricately organized knowledge system in long-term memory. (p. 289)

2. What is *episodic memory*? (p. 289)

_____

_____

3. Preschoolers remember familiar events in terms of _____—general representations of what occurs and when it occurs in a particular situation. Discuss the utility of this strategy. (p. 289)

_____

_____

_____

Autobiographical Memory

1. What is *autobiographical memory*? (p. 289)

_____

_____

2. The inability of older children and adults to remember experiences that happened before 3 years of age is known as _____ *amnesia*. (p. 290)

3. Summarize two psychological hypotheses of infantile amnesia. (p. 290)

   A. _____

   _____

   B. _____

   _____

4. Cite two developmental milestones that lead to the offset of infantile amnesia. (p. 290)

   A. _____

   B. _____

5. Explain the two styles, elaborative and repetitive, which are used by adults to elicit children's autobiographical narratives, and note which style leads to better memory of events over time. (p. 291)

   Elaborative: _____

   _____

   Repetitive: _____

   _____

Social Issues: Health—Children's Eyewitness Testimony

1. True or False: Children as young as age 3 are frequently asked to provide testimony in court cases involving child abuse and neglect. (pp. 292–293)

2. Summarize age differences in children's ability to provide accurate testimony. (pp. 292–293)

   _____

   _____

   _____

   _____

3. Discuss five reasons why younger children are more prone to memory errors. (pp. 292–293)

   A. _____

   B. _____

   C. _____

   D. _____

   E. _____

4. True or False: When adults lead children by suggesting incorrect information, they increase the likelihood of incorrect reporting among preschool and school-age children alike. (pp. 292–293)

5. True or False: Special interviewing methods involving the use of anatomically correct dolls have been successful in prompting more accurate recall of sexual abuse experiences, particularly among preschoolers. (pp. 292–293)

6. Discuss three interventions that can be used to assist child witnesses. (pp. 292–293)

   A. _____

   _____

   B. _____

   _____

   C. _____

   _____

1. Define *metacognition*. (p. 294)

    _____

    _____

2. _____ is a coherent understanding of people as mental
    beings, which children revise as they encounter new evidence. (p. 294)

Metacognitive Knowledge

1. True or False: Without strong situational cues, such as a challenging task or a thoughtful
    expression, preschoolers deny that a person is thinking. (p. 294)

2. Describe the difference between young children's understanding of cognitive capacities and that
    of older children. (p. 294)

    Younger children: _____

    _____

    Older children: _____

    _____

3. True or False: School-age children are more conscious of mental strategies than are preschoolers.
    (pp. 294–295)

4. Discuss how knowledge of task variables changes with age. (p. 295)

    _____

    _____

    _____

Cognitive Self-Regulation

1. Define *cognitive self-regulation*. (p. 296)

    _____

    _____

2. Children's difficulties with self-regulation on complex tasks are evident in their _____ monitoring—sensitivity to how well they understand a spoken or written message. (p. 296)

3. Explain how cognitive self-regulation relates to academic success. (p. 296)

_____

_____

_____

4. Discuss ways that parents and teachers can foster self-regulation. (p. 296)

_____

_____

_____

Applications of Information Processing to Academic Learning

Reading

1. True or False: Preschoolers have an understanding of written language long before they learn to read and write. (p. 298)

2. What is *emergent literacy*? (p. 298)

_____

_____

3. How does Siegler's strategy-choice model help to explain children's literacy development in middle childhood? (p. 299)

_____

_____

_____

4. The two sides in the great debate about how to teach beginning reading are the _____ approach and the _____ approach. Contrast these two perspectives. (p. 299)

_____

_____

_____

_____

5. True or False: Research clearly demonstrates that the basic-skills approach is superior to the whole-language approach. (p. 299)

6. Why might combining phonics with whole-language be the most effective strategy? (p. 299)

_____

_____

_____

_____

Social Issues: Education—Teaching First Graders to Read: Instruction that Works

1. Based on findings from Pressley's research on effective reading instruction, identify five teaching characteristics that distinguish the most effective teachers from the least effective teachers. (p. 300)

   A. _____

   B. _____

   C. _____

   D. _____

   E. _____

2. True or False: None of the most effective teachers preferred either a basic-skills approach or a whole-language approach; instead, they combined the two approaches. (p. 300)

Mathematics

1. Between 14 and 16 months, toddlers display a beginning grasp of _____, or order relationships between quantities, such as 3 is more than 2 and 2 is more than 1. (p. 301)

2. Between ages 4 and 5, children grasp the principle of _____— the understanding that the last number in a counting sequence indicates the quantity of items in the set. (p. 301)

3. True or False: Cross-cultural research suggests that basic arithmetic knowledge emerges universally around the world. (p. 301)

4. Discuss the two-sided argument about how to teach basic math skills, noting what approach is most beneficial to student learning. (p. 302)

_____

_____

_____

_____

Cultural Influences: Asian Children's Understanding of Multidigit Addition and Subtraction

1. Contrast American students' understanding of multidigit addition and subtraction with that of Asian students. (p. 303)

   American students: _____

   _____

   _____

   Asian students: _____

   _____

   _____

2. Discuss five factors that contribute to the sharp skill advantage of Asian students over American pupils in multidigit addition and subtraction. (p. 303)

   A. _____

   _____

   B. _____

   _____

   C. _____

   _____

   D. _____

   _____

   E. _____

   _____

Scientific Reasoning

1. What is *scientific reasoning*? (p. 302)

   _____

   _____

   _____

2. Summarize improvements in scientific reasoning from childhood into adolescence and adulthood. (p. 304)

   _____

   _____

   _____

3. Describe the relationship between metacognitive understanding and scientific reasoning ability. (p. 304)

   _____

   _____

   _____

Evaluation of the Information-Processing Approach

1. Cite three strengths of the information processing approach. (p. 305)

   A. _____

   _____

   B. _____

   _____

   C. _____

   _____

2. Discuss four limitations of the information processing approach. (pp. 305–306)

   A. _____

   _____

B. _____

_____

C. _____

_____

D. _____

_____

ASK YOURSELF . . .

Review: Summarize evidence indicating that both the basic capacity of the information-processing system and the effectiveness of strategy use increase with age. (p. 277)

_____

_____

_____

_____

_____

Review: What is a connectionist, or artificial neural network, model? Why do connectionists claim that children's development is continuous rather than stagelike? What evidence leads connectionists to view the information-processing system as a general processing device that attains domain-specific competence through relevant experiences? (p. 277)

_____

_____

_____

_____

_____

Apply: Five-year-old Kayla used several strategies when solving conservation of number problems involving rows of pennies. On the first one, she said, "The rows aren't the same." On the second one, she said, "The rows have the same number because you didn't add any." On the third one, she said, " I counted the pennies. The rows have the same number." Why is it beneficial for Kayla to experiment with strategies? Which strategy is she likely to select over time, and why? (p. 277)

_____

_____

_____

_____

_____

Connect: Explain how Case's neo-Piagetian theory offers a more precise account of the mechanisms of cognitive development than does Piaget's theory? (p. 277)

_____

_____

_____

_____

_____

Review: What aspect of brain development supports gains in cognitive inhibition? How does cognitive inhibition increase processing capacity? (p. 281)

_____

_____

_____

_____

_____

Review: Cite advances in information processing that contribute to improved planning in middle childhood? What can adults do to promote children's planning skills? (p. 281)

_____

_____

_____

_____

_____

Apply: Seven-year-old Jonah played his piano pieces from beginning to end instead of granting extra practice to the hard sections. Around age 8, he devoted more time to sections he knew least well, but his performance did not improve for several months. What explains Jonah's gradual strategy development and improvement in performance? (p. 281)

_____

_____

_____

_____

_____

Review: What factors contribute to the offset of infantile amnesia after age 3? How can parents foster a rich, detailed autobiographical memory in young children? (p. 291)

_____

_____

_____

_____

_____

Review: According to fuzzy-trace theory, why do we encode information in gist form? Describe the development of gist and verbatim representation, and explain how gist representations contribute to improved reasoning and recall with age. (p. 291)

_____

_____

_____

_____

_____

Apply: When asked what happens at kindergarten, 5-year-old Ali replies, "First, you have circle time and center time. Sometimes you listen to a story. Next is snack and outdoor play." But Ali can't remember what she did during center time two days ago. Explain Ali's memory performance. Why is this type of reconstructive memory useful? (p. 291)

_____

_____

_____

_____

_____

Connect: Using what you have learned about development of gist and autobiographical memory, explain why preschoolers' eyewitness testimony is usually less accurate than that of older children. What situational factors combine with reconstructive processing to heighten children's suggestibility? (p. 291)

_____

_____

_____

_____

_____

Review: What evidence indicates that the preschooler views the mind as a passive container of information, whereas school-age children view it as an active, constructive agent. (p. 296)

_____

_____

_____

_____

_____

Review: Explain why cognitive self-regulation develops gradually in childhood and adolescence. (p. 296)

_____

_____

_____

_____

_____

Apply: While doing her homework, 9-year-old Melody makes many careless mistakes. Although her parents constantly tell her to look over her work, her performance hasn't improved. What can they do to help Melody? (p. 296)

_____

_____

_____

_____

_____

Review: Cite evidence indicating that reading and mathematics achievement in elementary school build on a rich foundation of informally acquired knowledge during the preschool years. (p. 306)

_____

_____

_____

_____

_____

Review: Why are gains in processing capacity and metacognition especially important for the development of scientific reasoning? What can teachers do to promote the development of scientific reasoning? (p. 306)

_____

_____

_____

_____

_____

Apply: Review Heidi's reasoning about the impact of several variables on the bounce of tennis balls on page 302. What features of her thinking suggest that she is beginning to reason scientifically? (p. 306)

_____

_____

_____

_____

_____

Connect: Using mechanisms of cognitive development discussed in this chapter, explain why teaching both basic skills and the understanding of concepts and strategies is vital for children's solid mastery of reading and mathematics in middle childhood. (p. 306)

_____

_____

_____

_____

_____

SUGGESTED STUDENT READINGS

Barkley, R. A. (1998). *Attention-deficit hyperactivity disorder: A handbook for diagnosis and treatment (2nd ed.).* New York: The Guilford Press. For those interested in working with school-age children, this book presents current literature on the diagnosis, assessment, and treatment of ADHD.

Ferrari, M. (Ed.). (2002). *The pursuit of excellence through education: The educational psychology series.* Mahwah, NJ: Lawrence Erlbaum Associates. A collection of chapters focusing on the unique role of self-regulation in academic achievement. This book also highlights how motivation contributes to and supports children and adolescents' self-regulatory processes.

Neuman, S. B., Copple, C., & Bredekamp, S. (2001). *Learning to read and write: Developmentally appropriate practices for young children.* Washington, DC: National Association of Young Children. Written primarily for parents and caregivers, this book presents developmentally appropriate practices for fostering early literacy development in young children. Also included are guidelines and suggestions for ensuring that all children learn to read and write by the end of the third grade.

Bjorklund, D. F. (2000). *Children's thinking (3rd ed.).* Belmont, CA: Wadsworth. Offers an overview of major research findings in areas such as the development of perception, memory, conceptual understanding, language, and problem solving. Also discusses theories of cognitive development, including Piagetian, information-processing, sociocultural, and connectionist approaches.

PUZZLE 7.1

Across

5. _____ deficiency: failure to produce a mental strategy when it could be helpful

7. _____-_____ memory: the part of the mental system that contains our permanent knowledge base

8. _____ strategies: learned procedures that operate on and transform information

9. _____ strategy use refers to consistent use of a mental strategy that leads to improvement in performance.

10. ___-_____ theory reinterprets Piaget's stages within an information-processing framework.

12. _____ deficiency: consistent use of a mental strategy, with little or no improvement in performance

13. The longest sequence of items a person can recall is known as memory _____.

16. Cognitive _____: the ability to control internal and external distracting stimuli

17. _____ memory: conscious part of the mental system, where we work on a limited amount of information to ensure that it will be retained

18. _____ register: the first part of the mental system, where sights and sounds are represented directly but held only briefly

Down

1. _____ conceptual structures: networks of concepts and relations that permit children to think about a wide range of situations in more advanced ways

2. A childhood disorder involving inattention, impulsivity, and excessive motor activity (abbr.)

3. Central _____: the part of working memory that directs the flow of information by coordinating information coming from the environment with information already in the system

4. According to the _____ model, information is held in three parts of the mental system for processing: the sensory register, short-term memory, and longterm memory

6. _____ models focus on the most basic information-processing units and their connections

11. Model of _____ choice: Siegler's evolutionary theory; states that variation and selection characterize children's mental strategies

14. Thinking out a sequence of acts ahead of time and allocating attention accordingly to reach a goal

15. _____ deficiency: failure to execute a mental strategy effectively

PUZZLE 7.2

Across

2. Principle specifying the order relationships among quantities
4. Cognitive self-_____: continually monitoring progress toward a goal, checking outcomes, and redirecting unsuccessful efforts
8. _____ memory: memory for personally experienced events
9. Type of memory that involves generating a mental representation of an absent stimulus
12. Principle specifying that the last number in a counting sequence indicates the quantity of items in the set
15. Infantile _____: inability of older children and adults to remember experiences that happened before age 3.
16. A fuzzy representation of information that preserves essential content without details
17. Type of memory that involves noticing whether a stimulus is identical or similar to one previously experienced
18. _____ memory: representations of special, one-time events that are long-lasting and particularly meaningful in terms of the life story that each of us creates
20. _____ memory: vast, intricately organized knowledge system in long-term memory
21. _____ literacy: young children's active efforts to construct literacy knowledge through informal experiences

Down

1. _____-_____ approach: approach to beginning reading; emphasizes training in phonics
3. Memory strategy of creating a relationship between two or more pieces of information that are not members of the same category
5. Type of memory in which complex, meaningful material is reinterpreted in terms of existing knowledge
6. Awareness and understanding of various aspects of thought
7. _____-_____ approach: approach to beginning reading; parallels natural language and keeps reading materials whole and meaningful
10. Memory strategy of grouping together related information
11. _____-_____ theory: proposes two types of encoding, one that automatically reconstructs information into a gist and a second that is verbatim
13. Memory strategy of repeating information
14. General representations of what occurs and when it occurs in a particular situation
19. Theory of _____: understanding of people as mental beings

PRACTICE TEST

1. In information processing, procedures that operate on and transform information, increasing the efficiency of thinking and the chances that information will be retained, are called: (p. 271)
   a. schemas.
   b. organizational processes.
   c. representational strategies.
   d. mental strategies.

2. Which of the following is the conscious part of our mental system, where we actively work on a limited amount of information? (p. 271)
   a. perceptual register
   b. sensory register
   c. short-term memory
   d. long-term memory

3. According to the connectionist model: (p. 273)
   a. infants are born with innate, special-purpose knowledge systems that are unaffected by environmental experiences.
   b. information is held in three pares of the mental system for processing: the sensory register, short-term memory, and long-term memory.
   c. computer simulations can be used to imitate the workings of neurons in the brain; if the network's responses resemble those of people, they are assumed to represent a good model of human learning.
   d. children's mental strategies are characterized by variation and selection, yielding adaptive problem-solving techniques and an overlapping waves pattern of cognitive development.

4. According to the information processing perspective proposed by Robbie Case, advances in cognitive development result from: (p. 275)
   a. automation of cognitive schemas, which frees up space in working memory, thus allowing children to focus on combining old schemas and creating new ones.
   b. gains in long-term memory and increasingly efficient retrieval processes.
   c. generation and selection of increasingly efficient mental strategies.
   d. children's interactions with adults.

5. Siegler's model of strategy choice applies a(n) _____ perspective to children's cognition. (p. 276)
   a. evolutionary
   b. connectionist
   c. ecological
   d. sociocultural

6. According to Siegler's model of strategy choice: (p. 277)
    a. children are usually able to generate only one strategy for solving a challenging problem.
    b. children move from less to more efficient strategies as a result of brain growth spurts.
    c. no child thinks in just one way, even on the same task.
    d. once children learn more adaptive strategies, they immediately apply this new knowledge on a variety of cognitive tasks.

7. Selective attention depends on _____—the ability to control internal and external distracting stimuli. (p. 279)
    a. cognitive self-regulation
    b. cognitive inhibition
    c. cognitive monitoring
    d. metacognition

8. The failure to use an attentional strategy in situations in which it could be helpful is indicative of a(n): (p. 280)
    a. utilization deficiency
    b. production deficiency
    c. control deficiency
    d. location deficiency

9. Across early and middle childhood, attention becomes more: (p. 280)
    a. planful.
    b. fleeting.
    c. disorderly.
    d. effortful.

10. Three strategies that enhance memory for new information include: (p. 282)
    a. assimilation, accommodation, and planning.
    b. cognitive inhibition, cognitive self-regulation, and metacognition.
    c. rehearsal, organization, and elaboration.
    d. recognition, recall, and reconstruction.

11. When trying to remember the words *book* and *monkey*, Jordan creates a mental image of a monkey reading a book. This is an example of: (p. 284)
    a. organization.
    b. rehearsal.
    c. elaboration.
    d. planning.

12. _____ memory requires that the child generate a mental image of an absent stimulus. (p. 285)
   a. Recognition
   b. Recall
   c. Retrospective
   d. Reflective

13. Research on long-term retrieval shows that: (p. 286)
   a. people usually copy material into the storage system and faithfully reproduce it at retrieval.
   b. people often re-interpret complex, meaningful material in terms of existing knowledge.
   c. when individuals reconstruct material, they can easily distinguish the reconstructed version from the original information.
   d. children do not engage in reconstructive processing because they lack sufficient prior experience.

14. Which of the following is true in relation to fuzzy-trace theory? (p. 287)
   a. Fuzzy-trace theorists suggest that individuals cannot possibly retain a literal, verbatim version of new information, and thus, they create a vague, fuzzy version called a gist.
   b. Fuzzy-trace theorists believe that both verbatim and gist memories are both present and are stored separately so they can be used for different purposes.
   c. Individuals have a bias toward verbatim memory because it requires less working memory capacity than does gist.
   d. With age, children rely less on fuzzy, reconstructed gists and more on verbatim memory.

15. Preschoolers remember familiar events in terms of _____, or general descriptions of what occurs and when it occurs in a particular situation. (p. 289)
   a. schemas
   b. scripts
   c. plots
   d. recasts

16. Which of the following is true with regard to the development of autobiographical memory? (p. 291)
   a. Infants as young as 6 months begin to form autobiographical memories.
   b. Boys are more advanced in the development of autobiographical memories than are girls.
   c. Asian children produce autobiographical narratives with more talk about thoughts, emotions, and preferences than do American children.
   d. Preschoolers whose parents use an elaborative style for eliciting autobiographical narratives produce more coherent, detailed personal stories than do children whose parents use a repetitive style.

17. Preschoolers' awareness and understanding of various aspects of thought is known as: (p. 294)
    a. egocentrism.
    b. reflective thought.
    c. metacognition.
    d. intersubjectivity.

18. Which of the following most accurately describes preschoolers' theory of mind? (p. 295)
    a. Preschoolers understand that people have an internal mental life but view the mind as a passive container of information.
    b. Preschoolers focus on the process of thinking but fail to recognize the outcomes of thought.
    c. Preschoolers view the mind as an active, constructive agent.
    d. Preschoolers do not yet show an understanding of mental activities.

19. Parents can foster children's cognitive self-regulation by: (p. 296)
    a. simply providing feedback as to whether responses are correct or incorrect.
    b. suggesting effective strategies and emphasizing the value of self-correction.
    c. allowing children to discover appropriate skills without questioning their actions.
    d. telling children what to do but letting them figure out on their own why particular strategies are effective.

20. Which of the following is true? (p. 298)
    a. Preschoolers do not understand much about written language until they learn to read and write.
    b. Preschoolers have a great deal of understanding about written language long before they learn to read and write.
    c. Since written language lacks meaning for preschool-age children, they typically do not attend to it.
    d. Preschoolers demonstrate a simultaneous understanding of the names of letters and their corresponding sounds.

21. The _____ approach to beginning reading instruction emphasizes training in phonics and use of simplified reading materials. (p. 299)
    a. whole-language
    b. basic-skills
    c. dynamic systems
    d. sequential

22. Between ages 4 and 5, children grasp the principle of _____; that is, they understand that the last number in a counting sequence indicates the quantity of items in the set. (p. 301)
    a. cardinality
    b. ordinality
    c. addition
    d. centration

23. Math instruction is most effective when it focuses on: (pp. 301–302)
    a. drill and repetition.
    b. automatic retrieval of math facts.
    c. formal computational techniques.
    d. both computational strategies and conceptual understanding.

24. Scientific reasoning ability: (p. 304)
    a. is fully developed by middle childhood.
    b. develops independently of formal schooling.
    c. requires sophisticated metacognitive knowledge.
    d. starts to develop in adolescence, when individuals receive direct instruction in complex problem-solving and strategy use.

25. The greatest drawback of the information-processing perspective is that it: (p. 305)
    a. fails to account for the continuity of human thinking from infancy into adulthood.
    b. regards infants and toddlers as passive beings who are acted on by their environment rather than acknowledging them as active, inquiring beings.
    c. explains cognitive development in terms of discrete stages.
    d. analyzes cognition in terms of its components, but has difficulty putting the components back together into a comprehensive theory.

CHAPTER 8
INTELLIGENCE

BRIEF CHAPTER SUMMARY

The psychometric approach to cognitive development is the basis for the variety of intelligence tests used to assess individual differences in children's mental abilities. Researchers interested in intelligence testing seek to determine what factors, or dimensions, make up intelligence, and how they change with age. They are interested in how intelligence can be measured so that scores are useful for predicting future academic achievement, career attainment, and other aspects of intellectual success.

Factor analysis emerged as a statistical method to identify the underlying mental abilities that contribute to successful intelligence test performance. However, factor analysts have been criticized for devoting too much attention to identifying factors and too little to clarifying the cognitive processes that underlie them. To overcome the limitations of factor analysis, some researchers combine psychometric and information-processing approaches and conduct componential analyses of children's test scores. Sternberg's triarchic theory of intelligence extends these efforts by emphasizing the complexity of human mental skills and the limitations of current tests in assessing that complexity. Gardner's theory of multiple intelligences identifies eight distinct domains of ability, each defined by unique processing operations.

A variety of tests are currently available to assess children's intelligence. Accurately measuring the intelligence of infants is an especially challenging task. IQs obtained after age 6 show substantial correlational stability. IQ is an effective predictor of academic achievement, occupational attainment, and certain aspects of psychological adjustment.

The relationship of socioeconomic status to intellectual development has sparked the IQ nature–nurture debate. Heritability estimates support a moderate role for heredity in accounting for individual differences in IQ. However, they cannot be used to explain ethnic and socioeconomic differences in test scores. Language customs, lack of familiarity with test content, and reactions to testing conditions can lead test scores to underestimate minority children's intelligence. Shared and nonshared environmental influences also contribute to individual differences in intelligence. In addition, family attitudes toward intellectual success and academic performance are powerful predictors of academic success.

Research on early intervention programs indicates that although immediate IQ gains wash out with time, lasting benefits occur in school adjustment. To induce larger and longer-lasting cognitive gains, intervention must start earlier, last longer, and be more intensive.

Recognition that intelligence tests do not sample the entire range of human mental skills has led to an expanded conception of giftedness, which includes creativity. High creativity is usually manifested as talent; individuals usually demonstrate it in only one or a few related fields.

LEARNING OBJECTIVES

After reading this chapter, you should be able to:

8.1 Describe the psychometric approach to cognitive development. (p. 312)

8.2. Discuss differing definitions of intelligence, including those of Binet and the factor analysts, as well as recent advances in defining intelligence, focusing on Sternberg's triarchic theory and approaches combining psychometric and information processing perspectives. (pp. 312–320)

8.3. Cite commonly used intelligence tests for infants and children, and discuss the utility of infant tests for predicting later intelligence. (pp. 320–323)

8.4 Describe the computation and distribution of IQ scores. (p. 323)

8.5 Discuss the stability of IQ scores, and note the ability of intelligence tests to predict academic achievement, occupational attainment, and psychological adjustment. (pp. 323–328)

8.6. Summarize ethnic and socioeconomic variations in IQ, including differences in both general intelligence and specific mental abilities. (pp. 328–330)

8.7. Discuss evidence indicating that both heredity and environment contribute to intelligence. (pp. 330–334)

8.8. Describe cultural influences on intelligence test performance, and discuss efforts to reduce cultural bias in intelligence testing. (pp. 334–339)

8.9 Summarize the impact of shared and nonshared environmental influences on IQ. (pp. 339–342)

8.10 Discuss the impact of early intervention on intellectual development. (pp. 342–345)

8.11. Summarize theories of the development of creativity, including the psychometric view and the multifaceted approach known as investment theory. (pp. 345–349)

STUDY QUESTIONS

1. The _____ *approach* is a product-oriented approach to cognitive development that focuses on the construction of tests to assess mental abilities. (p. 312)

Alfred Binet: A Holistic View

1. For what purpose were Binet and Simon asked to construct a test of intelligence? (p. 313)

    _____

2. Binet and Simon's intelligence test was designed to assess (sensory responsiveness and reaction time / verbal and nonverbal reasoning). (p. 313)

3. Binet and Simon's test was the first _____ approach to test construction – items varied in difficulty and each was classified according to the age at which a typical child could first pass it. (p. 313)

4. What is the name of the American version of Binet's test? (p. 313)

    _____

The Factor Analysts: A Multifaceted View

1. Briefly explain the statistical procedure known as *factor analysis*. (p. 313)

    _____

    _____

    _____

2. Describe Spearman's *two-factor theory of intelligence*. (p. 313)

    _____

    _____

    _____

    _____

3. Louis Thurstone concluded that intelligence consists of seven distinct _____ *mental abilities*: verbal meaning, perceptual speed, reasoning, number, rote memory, word fluency, and spatial visualization. (p. 313)

4. Current theorists and test designers reconcile Spearman's and Thurstone's views by proposing _____ *models* of mental abilities, with "g" at the highest level, followed by specialized factors assumed to represent a child's strengths and weaknesses. (p. 314)

5. Distinguish between *fluid* and *crystallized intelligence*. (p. 314)

    Fluid: _____

    _____

    Crystallized: _____

    _____

6. (Fluid / Crystallized) intelligence depends on culture and learning opportunities, whereas (fluid / crystallized) intelligence is believed to depend largely on conditions in the brain. (p. 315)

7. Describe John Carroll's *three-stratum theory of intelligence*. (p. 315)

    _____

    _____

    _____

8. True or False: Most recently developed tests of intelligence measure all of Carroll's factors. (p. 316)

Recent Advances in Defining Intelligence

Combining Psychometric and Information-Processing Approaches

1. When investigators conduct _____ *analyses* of children's test scores, they look for relationships between aspects of information processing and children's performance. (p. 316)

2. True or False: Studies show that speed of information-processing, as measured by reaction time on cognitive tasks, is related to general intelligence, as well as to gains in mental test performance over time. (p. 316)

3. Awareness of problem-solving strategies and organizational and planning skills (are / are not) good predictors of general intelligence. (pp. 316–317)

4. Cite one limitation of the componential approach to defining intelligence. (p. 317)

    _____

    _____

Sternberg's Triarchic Theory

1. Match each of the subtheories of Sternberg's triarchic theory of intelligence with the appropriate description. (p. 317)

_____ Ability to process information in novel situations	1. Componential subtheory
_____ Ability to adapt information-processing skills to fit with personal desires and the demands of one's everyday worlds	2. Experiential subtheory
	3. Contextual subtheory
_____ Information-processing skills that underlie intelligent behavior, including strategy application, knowledge acquisition, metacognition, and self-regulation	

2. Explain how Sternberg's theory is relevant to the controversy surrounding cultural bias in intelligence testing. (pp. 317–318)

_____

_____

_____

Gardner's Theory of Multiple Intelligences

1. True or False: Gardner's theory emphasizes the importance of "g," or general mental ability. (p. 318)

2. List the eight intelligences included in Gardner's *theory of multiple intelligences*. (p. 318)

A. _____

B. _____

C. _____

D. _____

E. _____

F. _____

G. _____

H. _____

3. True or False: Neurological evidence supports the independence of Gardner's eight intelligences. (p. 319)

1. What is *social intelligence*? (pp. 320–321)

   _____

   _____

2. Describe the characteristics of *emotional intelligence*. (pp. 320–321)

   _____

   _____

   _____

   _____

3. True or False: Recent evidence suggests that measures of emotional intelligence are excellent predictors of future life success beyond the influence of IQ. (pp. 320–321)

1. Distinguish between group and individually administered intelligence tests, and cite the advantages of each. (pp. 320–321)

   Group administered: _____

   _____

   Advantages: _____

   _____

   Individually administered: _____

   _____

   Advantages: _____

   _____

2. Match the following intelligence tests with the appropriate descriptions: (p. 322)

_____ Appropriate for individuals age 6–16

_____ Appropriate for individuals between 2 years of age and adulthood

_____ Assesses two broad intellectual factors: verbal and performance

_____ Assesses four broad intellectual factors: verbal reasoning, quantitative reasoning, abstract/visual reasoning, and short-term memory

_____ First test to be standardized on samples representing the total population of the United States, including ethnic minorities

1. Stanford-Binet Intelligence Scale
2. Wechsler Intelligence Scale for Children-III (WISC-III)

Infant Intelligence Tests

1. Most infant intelligence tests measure _____ and _____ responses. (p. 323)

2. One commonly used infant test is the _____ _____ *of Infant Development*, designed for children between 1 month and 3-and-one-half years. (p. 323)

3. Infant tests emphasizing perceptual and motor behavior are (poor / good) predictors of intelligence during childhood. (p. 323)

4. Traditional infant tests are somewhat better at making long-term predictions for very (low- / high-) scoring babies. (p. 323)

5. True or False: Speed of habituation/recovery to visual stimuli is among the best infant correlates of childhood intelligence. (p. 323)

The Computation and Distribution of IQ Scores

1. The _____ _____ (IQ) indicates the extent to which the raw score deviates from the typical performance of same-age individuals. (p. 323)

2. Performances at each age level form a _____, or bell-shaped, curve in which most people fall near the center and progressively fewer fall out toward the extremes. (p. 323)

3. Describe two important features of the normal curve. (p. 323)

   A. _____

   _____

   B. _____

   _____

4. Most intelligence tests convert their raw scores such that the mean is set at _____ and the standard deviation is set at _____. (p. 323)

What and How Well Do Intelligence Tests Predict?

Stability of IQ Scores

1. Cite two generalizations about the stability of IQ that have emerged from studies examining the correlational stability of IQ scores across repeated testings. (p. 324)

   A. _____

   B. _____

2. Summarize three explanations for why preschool IQ scores predict less well than do later IQ scores. (p. 324)

   A. _____

   _____

   B. _____

   _____

   C. _____

   _____

3. True or False: Longitudinal research shows that the majority of children show substantial IQ fluctuations over childhood and adolescence. (p. 325)

4. Describe the characteristics of children whose IQ scores change the most across childhood and adolescence. (p. 325)

Gainers: _____

_____

Decliners: _____

_____

5. Explain the *environmental cumulative deficit hypothesis*. (p. 325)

_____

_____

_____

IQ as a Predictor of Academic Achievement

1. Correlations between IQ and achievement test scores are typically around (.2 / .5 / .9). (p. 325)

2. Describe two theories explaining why IQ is a good predictor of scholastic performance. (p. 325)

A. _____

_____

B. _____

_____

Cultural Influences: Does Schooling Influence IQ?

1. Discuss at least three research findings showing that schooling has a profound effect on IQ. (p. 326)

A. _____

_____

B. _____

_____

C. _____

_____

2. List three ways in which schooling is thought to influence IQ. (p. 326)

A. _____

_____

B. _____

_____

C. _____

_____

IQ as a Predictor of Occupational Attainment

1. True or False: The relationship between IQ and adult occupational attainment is much weaker than that between IQ and academic achievement. (p. 327)

2. Discuss at least two factors other than IQ that contribute to occupational attainment. (p. 327)

A. _____

_____

B. _____

_____

3. Once a person enters an occupation, _____ *intelligence*—mental abilities apparent in the real world but not in testing situations—predict on-the-job performance at least as well or better than IQ. (p. 327)

IQ as a Predictor of Psychological Adjustment

1. Describe research evidence regarding the relationship between childhood aggressiveness and IQ. (p. 328)

_____

_____

_____

2. True or False: Adjustment disorders such as anxiety, social withdrawal, and depression are unrelated to mental test scores. (p. 328)

Ethnic and Socioeconomic Variations in IQ

1. Researchers assess a family's social position and economic well-being using an index called _____. List three variables included in this measure. (p. 328)

   A. _____

   B. _____

   C. _____

Differences in General Intelligence

1. True or False: On average, African-American children score 15 points below Caucasian-American children on IQ tests. (p. 329)

2. True or False: There is little variability in IQ *within* each ethnic group. (p. 329)

3. Ethnicity and SES account for approximately (one-quarter / one-half / three-quarters) of the total variation in IQ. (p. 329)

Differences in Specific Mental Abilities

1. Distinguish the two types of intelligence elaborated in Jenson's Level I-Level II theory, providing examples of each. (p. 329)

   Level I: _____

   _____

   Examples: _____

   Level II: _____

   _____

   Examples: _____

2. According to Jenson, black-white and SES differences in IQ are due to Level (I / II) abilities. (pp. 329–330)

Explaining Individual and Group Differences in IQ

Genetic Influences

1. Behavioral geneticists conduct _____ *studies* to examine the contributions of heredity and environment to complex human characteristics such as intelligence. (p. 330)

2. True or False: The greater the genetic similarity between family members, the more they resemble one another in IQ. (p. 331)

3. Discuss evidence from twin studies supporting the importance of heredity in IQ. (p. 332)

_____

_____

_____

_____

4. Recent research in Western industrialized nations shows that approximately (one-quarter / one-half / three-quarters) of the variation in IQ is due to individual differences in heredity. (p. 332)

5. Explain why using within-group heritabilities to explain between-group differences is like comparing different seeds in different soil. (p. 332)

_____

_____

_____

6. Describe evidence from adoption research indicating that both heredity and environment affect IQ scores. (p. 333)

Heredity: _____

_____

_____

Environment: _____

_____

_____

7. True or False: When African-American children are placed in economically advantaged white homes during the first year of life, they show significantly higher mean IQ scores than those of children growing up in low-income black communities. (p. 333)

Biology and Environment: The Flynn Effect—The Massive Generational Gains in IQ

1. What is the *Flynn effect*? (p. 335)

    _____

    _____

    _____

2. In relation to the Flynn effect, the largest gains occurred on (fluid- /crystallized-) ability tests. (p. 335)

3. The Flynn effect is (biological / environmental). Briefly explain your response. (p. 335)

    _____

    _____

    _____

Ethnicity: Genetic or Cultural Groupings

1. DNA analyses reveal wide genetic variations (between / within) races and minimal genetic variation (between / within) them. (p. 334)

2. True or False: Many commonly used racial labels, assumed to have genetic meaning, are actually arbitrary. (p. 334)

Test Bias

1. Explain what is meant by the term *test bias*. (p. 334)

    _____

    _____

    _____

2. Compare traditional language customs in middle-SES white homes, low-SES black homes, and homes of Hispanic immigrants. (p. 336)

Middle-SES white homes: _____

_____

_____

Low-SES black homes: _____

_____

_____

Homes of Hispanic immigrants: _____

_____

_____

3. True or False: Research indicates that ethnic minority children perform better on tests that are modified to focus on spatial and performance tasks rather than verbal and fact-oriented tasks. (pp. 336–337)

4. Describe evidence indicating that intelligence test performance is influenced by learning opportunities. (p. 337)

_____

_____

_____

_____

5. How might fixed instructions and lack of feedback undermine minority students' performance on intelligence tests? (p. 337)

_____

_____

Reducing Test Bias

1. Since IQ scores may lead to incorrect labeling of minority children as slow learners, causing them to be assigned to remedial classes, test scores need to be combined with assessments of the children's _____ *behavior*—their ability to cope with the demands of their everyday environments. (p. 337)

2. Describe *dynamic testing*, noting three ways in which it can be distinguished from traditional testing approaches. (p. 337)

Description: _____

_____

A. _____

_____

B. _____

_____

C. _____

_____

3. True or False: Dynamic testing is far more effective in predicting academic achievement than are traditional tests. (p. 338)

From Research to Practice: Authentic Assessment

1. Explain the nature of *authentic assessment* and provide some examples of authentic assessment techniques. (p. 339)

Description: _____

_____

_____

Techniques: _____

_____

_____

2. True or False: Research shows that SES, ethnicity, and gender strongly affect the relationship between classroom experiences and achievement on authentic assessment measures. (p. 339)

Home Environment and IQ

1. Describe the two broad types of home influences, providing an example of each. (pp. 338–339)

   A. _____

   _____

   Example: _____

   B. _____

   _____

   Example: _____

2. The _____ is a
   checklist for gathering information about the quality of children's home lives through
   observation and parental interviews. (p. 340)

1. Based on research using the HOME checklist, summarize characteristics of the home
   environment that are associated with mental development in infancy, preschool, and middle
   childhood. (p. 340)

   Infancy: _____

   _____

   _____

   Preschool: _____

   _____

   _____

   Middle childhood: _____

   _____

   _____

4. True or False: The relationship between HOME scores and IQ declines in middle childhood.
   (p. 340)

5. Summarize research findings on the relationship between parental expectations and children's academic achievement. (p. 341)

_____

_____

_____

_____

6. Kinship studies suggest that (shared / nonshared) environmental factors have a more powerful influence, particularly during the adolescent years. (p. 341)

7. Give three examples of nonshared environmental influences. (pp. 341–342)

A. _____

B. _____

C. _____

Early Intervention and Intellectual Development

1. Cite two assumptions on which early intervention programs are based. (p. 342)

A. _____

B. _____

2. Describe three components of a typical Head Start program. (p. 342)

A. _____

_____

B. _____

_____

C. _____

_____

Benefits of Early Intervention

1. Describe the long-term impact of preschool intervention on low-SES children's development, comparing outcomes of university-based programs with those of Head Start programs. (p. 343)

   University-based programs: _____

   _____

   _____

   Head Start programs: _____

   _____

   _____

Social Issues: Education—The Carolina Abecedarian Project: A Model of Early Intervention

---

1. Summarize the early intervention services provided to treatment group infants in the Carolina Abecedarian Project. (p. 344)

   _____

   _____

   _____

2. True or False: Compared to children in the control group, treatment group children showed an IQ advantage by 12 months of age, and they retained this advantage into the adolescent years. (p. 344)

3. Findings from the Carolina Abecedarian Project showed that intervening during (infancy and early childhood / middle childhood) produced the greatest impact on children's IQ and academic achievement. (p. 344)

The Future of Early Intervention

1. Explain the *two-generation approach* to early intervention. (p. 345)

   _____

   _____

   _____

Development of Creativity

1. Define *creativity*. (p. 345)

_____

_____

The Psychometric View

1. Distinguish between convergent and divergent thinking. (p. 346)

Convergent: _____

_____

Divergent: _____

_____

2. Creativity is assessed using (convergent / divergent) thinking tasks. Give at least one example of such a task. (p. 346)

_____

_____

A Multifaceted View

1. Explain the *investment theory of creativity*. (p. 346)

_____

_____

_____

2. List and describe at least four high-level cognitive skills involved in creative work. (p. 347)

A. _____

_____

B. _____

_____

C. _____

_____

D. _____

_____

3. _____ refers to outstanding performance in a particular field. (p. 347)

4. Creativity is (moderately / strongly) correlated with IQ. (p. 347)

5. List four personality characteristics that are crucial to the development of creativity. (p. 348)

A. _____

B. _____

C. _____

D. _____

6. Motivation for creativity must be (task- / goal-) focused. Briefly explain your response. (p. 348)

_____

_____

_____

7. Describe typical characteristics of the parent-child relationship in families with a gifted child. (p. 348)

_____

_____

_____

8. True or False: Gifted youths experience more emotional and social difficulties than do peers, including low self-esteem and depression. (p. 348)

9. Cite classroom characteristics found to facilitate the development of creativity. (p. 348)

_____

_____

_____

ASK YOURSELF . . .

Review: Citing the work of the factor analysts, explain why a single IQ score might not adequately represent human mental functioning. (p. 319)

_____

_____

_____

_____

_____

Review: Using Sternberg's triarchic theory and Gardner's theory of multiple intelligences, discuss the limitations of current mental tests in assessing the complexity of human intelligence. (p. 319)

_____

_____

_____

_____

_____

Apply: Eight-year-old Regina, an immigrant from Mexico, couldn't answer test items asking for word definitions and general information. But she figured out which number comes next in a complex series and solved puzzles easily. How does Regina score in crystallized and fluid intelligence, and what might explain the difference? (p. 319)

_____

_____

_____

_____

_____

Connect: Cite similarities between Gardner's theory of multiple intelligences and the core knowledge view of the mind (see Chapter 6, pages 251–256). What questions raised about this view also apply to Gardner's theory? (p. 319)

_____

_____

_____

_____

_____

Review: Explain how infant intelligence tests differ from childhood intelligence tests in content and correlational stability. (p. 330)

_____

_____

_____

_____

_____

Review: Discuss factors that might lead a child's IQ to show large gains or declines during childhood and adolescence. (p. 330)

_____

_____

_____

_____

_____

Apply: Seven-year-old Scott's parents are concerned about Scott's average IQ because they want Scott to go to college and enter a high-status occupation. What factors besides IQ are likely to contribute to Scott's life success? (p. 330)

_____

_____

_____

_____

_____

Connect: Describe the bidirectional relationship between IQ and schooling. (p. 330)

_____

_____

_____

_____

_____

Review: Summarize ethnic differences in IQ. Why can't heritability estimates explain these differences? According to research, what environmental factors contribute to ethnic variations in test scores? (p. 342)

_____

_____

_____

_____

_____

Review: IQ correlations for fraternal twins and siblings decline from childhood to adolescence. What does this suggest about the impact of shared and nonshared environmental influences on IQ? (p. 342)

_____

_____

_____

_____

_____

Apply: Desiree, an African-American child, was quiet and withdrawn while taking an intelligence test. Later she remarked, "I can't understand why that lady asked me all of those questions, like what a ball and a stove are for. She must _know_ what a ball and a stove are for!" Explain Desiree's reaction. Why is her IQ score likely to underestimate her intelligence? (p. 342)

_____

_____

_____

_____

_____

Connect: Explain how dynamic testing is consistent with Vygotsky's concepts of the zone of proximal development and scaffolding. (See Chapter 6, pages 258–259.) (p. 342)

_____

_____

_____

_____

_____

Review: Summarize the benefits of early intervention programs, such as Head Start, for poverty-stricken children. What program characteristics might contribute to those benefits? (p. 349)

_____

_____

_____

_____

_____

Review: How do psychometric measures of creativity differ from psychometric measures of intelligence? Why are psychometric measures poor predictors of creative accomplishment? (p. 349)

_____

_____

_____

_____

_____

Apply: Senator Smith heard that IQ and achievement gains resulting from Head Start do not last, so he plans to vote against funding for the program. Write a letter to Senator Smith explaining why he should support Head Start. (p. 349)

_____

_____

_____

_____

_____

Apply: What can parents and schools do to foster the cognitive, personality, motivational, and environmental resources that contribute to creativity? (p. 349)

_____

_____

_____

_____

_____

Connect: Using what you learned about brain development in Chapter 5 (see pages 181–186), explain why intensive intervention for poverty-stricken children starting in infancy and continuing through early childhood has a greater impact on IQ than does intervention starting later. (p. 349)

_____

_____

_____

_____

_____

SUGGESTED STUDENT READINGS

Colangelo, N., & Assouline, S. G. (Eds.). (2001). *Talent development IV: Proceedings from the 1998 Henry B. and Jocelyn Wallace National Research Symposium on Talent Development.* Scottsdale, AZ: Great Potential Press. Presents an extensive overview of current research on the development of gifted children. In addition, leading experts discuss ways to enhance children's talent.

Reynolds, A. J. (2000). *Success in early intervention: The Chicago child-parent centers.* Lincoln, NE: University of Nebraska Press. Presents an overview of the Child-Parent Center (CPC) program in Chicago, the second oldest federally funded early intervention program in the United States. The author emphasizes the unique features of this program, including mandatory parental involvement and a single, sustained educational system which extends from preschool to third grade. Also includes follow-up data from a study on the long-term outcomes of the CPC program.

Shonkoff, J. P., & Meisels, S. J. (Eds.). (2001). *Handbook of early childhood intervention (2nd ed.).* New York: Cambridge University Press. For those interested in the health, development, and overall well-being of young children and their families, this book presents a multidisciplinary approach to early intervention by drawing on research from the fields of psychology, education, child development, social work, child psychiatry, and social policy.

Sternberg, R. J. (Ed.). (2000). *Handbook of intelligence.* New York: Cambridge University Press. A collection of chapters examining the development and assessment of intelligence. Other topics include group and cultural differences in intelligence, biological influences, and the relationship between intelligence and information processing.

PUZZLE 8.1

Across

1. Product-oriented approach to cognitive development that focuses on the construction of tests to assess mental abilities

7. _____ mental abilities: in Thurstone's theory of intelligence, seven distinct mental abilities identified through factor analysis

9. _____-_____ Intelligence Scale: modern descendent of Binet's first successful intelligence test for children (2 words)

10. A score that permits an individual's performance on an intelligence test to be compared to the typical performance of same-age individuals is known as an intelligence _____.

11. In Spearman's theory, the _____ factor is a common factor representing abstract reasoning power that underlies a variety of test items.

12. _____ analysis: statistical procedure that combines scores from many separate test items into a few factors, which substitute for the separate scores

13. Gardner's theory of _____ intelligences identifies eight independent intelligences.

14. In Cattell's theory, a form of intelligence that involves the ability to see relationships among stimuli

16. _____ intelligence: set of abilities involving the perception, expression, understanding, and management of emotions

Down

2. In Spearman's theory, the _____ factor is unique to a particular task.

3. In Cattell's theory, a form of intelligence that consists of accumulated knowledge and skills and depends on culture and learning opportunities

4. _____-_____ theory of intelligence: Carroll's theory which represents the structure of intelligence as a pyramid (2 words)

5. _____ intelligence: mental abilities apparent in the real world but not in testing situations

6. Sternberg's _____ theory of intelligence states that information-processing skills, prior experience with tasks, and contextual factors combine to influence intelligent behavior.

8. _____ analysis: researchers look for relationships between aspects of information-processing and children's intelligence test performance

15. _____-III: individually administered IQ test measuring general intelligence and a variety of verbal and performance skills (abbr.)

PUZZLE 8.2

Across

1. Thinking that involves generation of a single correct answer to a problem
5. Assessment approach that measures intellectual progress by examining students' real performance in school over time
6. Outstanding performance in a particular field
8. Checklist for gathering information about the quality of children's home lives (abbr.)
9. Thinking that involves the generation of multiple and unusual possibilities when faced with a task or problem
10. _____ effect: large gains in IQ that have occurred over successive generations, from 1930 to present
12. _____ theory of intelligence: investing in novel projects depends on intellectual, personality, motivational, and environmental resources
14. Ability to produce work that is original yet appropriate
16. Project _____ _____: federal program that provides low-income children with a year or two of preschool, along with nutritional and medical services (2 words)

Down

2. _____ cumulative deficit hypothesis: age-related declines in IQ among ethnic minority and other children who live in poverty result from the cumulative effects of underprivileged rearing conditions.
3. Environmental influences that pervade the general atmosphere of the home, and consequently, similarly affect all children living in it
4. _____ effect: loss of IQ and achievement gains resulting from early intervention within a few years after the program ends
7. Jenson's _____I-_____ II theory states that ethnic and SES differences in IQ are due to genetic differences in abstract reasoning and problem solving abilities.
11. Environmental influences that make siblings living in the same home different from one another
13. _____ testing: individualized teaching is introduced into the testing situation to see what the child can attain with social support
15. A measure of a family's social position and economic well-being (abbr.)

PRACTICE TEST

1. The _____ approach to cognitive development focuses on the construction of tests to assess mental abilities. (pp. 311–312)
   a. componential
   b. factor analytic
   c. psychoanalytic
   d. psychometric

2. For what purpose was Binet asked to construct what would become the first successful test of intelligence? (p. 313)
   a. for assigning students to special education classes.
   b. for identifying gifted students.
   c. to assess the relationship between home environment and IQ.
   d. to evaluate reaction times of military personnel.

3. In Cattell's theory, which of the following refers to a form of intelligence that consists of accumulated knowledge and skills and depends on culture and learning opportunities. (p. 314)
   a. primary mental abilities
   b. general factor ("g")
   c. crystallized intelligence
   d. fluid intelligence

4. In componential analysis: (p. 316)
   a. scores from many separate test items are combined into a few factors which substitute for the separate scores.
   b. researchers look for relationships between aspects of information processing and children's intelligence test performance.
   c. researchers explore components of the home environment that affect mental test performance.
   d. individual items from children's intelligence tests are examined for cultural bias.

5. In Sternberg's triarchic theory of intelligence, which subtheory states that highly intelligent individuals process information more skillfully in novel situations than do less intelligent individuals? (p. 317)
   a. componential subtheory
   b. experiential subtheory
   c. contextual subtheory
   d. pragmatical subtheory

6. According to Gardner's theory of multiple intelligences,: (p. 318)
   a. intelligence is composed of a common underlying general factor, called "g," as well as several specific factors representing abilities unique to a particular task.
   b. intelligence consists of seven distinct primary mental abilities.
   c. individuals possess eight independent intelligences that are based on distinct sets of processing operations applied in culturally valued activities.
   d. intelligence consists of two factors: crystallized intelligence and fluid intelligence.

7. Both the WISC-III and the WPPSI-R measure: (p. 322)
   a. general intelligence, as well as four intelligence factors including verbal reasoning, quantitative reasoning, abstract/visual reasoning, and short-term memory.
   b. verbal and performance abilities.
   c. information-processing capacity.
   d. sensorimotor skills.

8. Which of the following is true of infant intelligence tests? (p. 323)
   a. Infant intelligence tests which measure perceptual and motor responses are the best available correlates of childhood intelligence.
   b. Infant intelligence tests typically measure the same skill and ability areas measured by adult intelligence tests.
   c. Infant tests provide a more accurate measure of intelligence than do tests used in childhood and adolescence.
   d. Infant intelligence tests are largely used for screening—helping to identify infants who are likely to have developmental problems.

9. Most intelligence tests have a mean, or average score, of _____. (p. 323)
   a. 50
   b. 85
   c. 100
   d. 125

10. At what age are mental test scores first stably predictive of later IQ? (p. 324)
    a. infancy
    b. preschool
    c. middle childhood
    d. adolescence

11. Which of the following is true? (p. 325)
    a. IQ is moderately correlated with academic achievement.
    b. IQ is far less predictive of occupational attainment than of academic achievement.

c. School-age children with higher IQs are more likely than agemates to be rejected by peers.

d. Mental test scores are strongly related to many adjustment disorders, including anxiety, social withdrawal, and depression.

12. Jenson's _____ theory emphasizes two types of intelligence, the first of which emphasizes short-term and rote memory, and the second of which involves abstract reasoning and problem solving. (p. 329)
   a. two-factor
   b. Level I-Level II
   c. bimodal
   d. triarchic

13. Kinship studies reveal that: (p. 330)
   a. heredity is the sole determinant of IQ.
   b. environment is the primary determinant of IQ.
   c. both heredity and environment contribute significantly to IQ.
   d. individuals possess many different independent intelligences rather than one general intelligence.

14. Research on African-American children adopted into middle-SES white homes during the first year of life suggests that: (p. 333)
   a. enriched environments lead to little or no gain in IQ but substantial gains in academic achievement.
   b. genetic factors are largely responsible for the lower IQ scores of African-American children.
   c. environmental factors are largely responsible for the lower IQ scores of African-American children.
   d. enriched family environments overcome the effects of all other cultural influences, resulting in lasting improvement in IQ scores.

15. Which of the following is true with regard to test bias? (p. 337)
   a. When tests are based on spatial and performance tasks rather than verbal, fact-oriented tasks, ethnic minority children obtain significantly higher scores.
   b. Low-income minority children often show a significant advantage on spatial reasoning tasks as a result of growing up in object-oriented rather than people-oriented homes.
   c. African-American children show improved performance when the testing situation is modified such that they get to know the examiner and they are given frequent praise.
   d. Most recently developed intelligence tests have almost entirely eliminated culturally-biased test items.

16. The _____ testing approach introduces teaching into the testing situation to see what kids can attain with social support. (p. 337)
    a. dynamic
    b. microgenetic
    c. standardized
    d. individualized

17. An example of a nonshared environmental influence is: (pp. 338–339)
    a. availability of books in the home.
    b. modeling by parents of intellectual activities.
    c. birth order.
    d. type of neighborhood.

18. Which of the following is true? (p. 340)
    a. Home Observation for Measurement of the Environment (HOME) scores are unrelated to IQ in infancy and early childhood.
    b. The HOME-IQ relationship declines in middle childhood as children spend more time in settings outside the home.
    c. The HOME-IQ relationship is strongest during the adolescent years.
    d. The HOME-IQ correlation is the same for both adopted and biological children.

19. Project Head Start is an early intervention program targeting: (p. 342)
    a. low-income children.
    b. children with physical disabilities.
    c. children with cognitive delays.
    d. gifted children.

20. Longitudinal studies have found that children who attend Head Start Programs: (p. 342)
    a. do not evidence any gains in IQ or academic achievement when compared to a control group of similar children who did not attend Head Start.
    b. evidence higher IQ and academic achievement during early elementary school when compared to a control group of similar children who did not attend Head Start but show declining test scores after that time.
    c. exhibit permanent gains in IQ and academic achievement.
    d. are just as likely as other low-SES children to be placed in a special education program or to be retained in grade.

21. One way to prevent the washout effects which often occur following participation in early intervention programs is to: (p. 343)
    a. begin intervention programs after children enter elementary school.
    b. begin intervention programs in infancy.
    c. shorten the time spent in early intervention programs.
    d. exclude parents from participating in early intervention programs.

22. _____ thinking involves the generation of multiple and unusual possibilities when faced with a task or problem. (p. 346)
    a. divergent
    b. convergent
    c. pluralistic
    d. psychometric

23. Talent: (p. 347)
    a. requires only limited knowledge.
    b. is usually demonstrated by a given individual in only one or a few related fields.
    c. must be motivated by extrinsic rewards.
    d. is almost perfectly correlated with IQ.

24. Gifted children: (p. 348)
    a. spend as much time interacting with peers as do nongifted agemates.
    b. report higher levels of emotional and social difficulties.
    c. tend to have parents who are driven and overly ambitious.
    d. often have higher self-esteem than ordinary peers.

25. Gifted education programs based on _____ are especially useful for identifying talented low-SES, ethnic minority children. (p. 349)
    a. Gardner's theory of multiple intelligences
    b. Spearman's general factor ("g")
    c. Jenson's Level I-Level II theory
    d. Carroll's three-stratum theory of intelligence

CHAPTER 9
LANGUAGE DEVELOPMENT

BRIEF CHAPTER SUMMARY

Language—the most awesome of universal human achievements—develops with extraordinary speed during early childhood. In mastering language, children acquire four components—phonology, semantics, grammar, and pragmatics—that they combine into a flexible communication system.

Three theories provide different accounts of how children develop language. According to the behaviorist perspective, language is learned through operant conditioning and imitation. In contrast, Chomsky's nativist view regards children as biologically equipped with a language acquisition device that supports rapid early mastery of the structure of language. Interactionist theories offer a compromise between these two views, stressing that innate abilities, a strong desire to interact with others, and social environment combine to promote language development.

Infants are specially prepared for language learning. During the first year of life, inborn capabilities, cognitive and social milestones, and environmental supports pave the way for verbal communication. Neonates have a built-in capacity to detect a wide variety of sound categories in human speech. By the second half of the first year, infants become increasingly sensitive to the phonemes, words, and phrase structure of their native tongue. Research reveals that caregiver–child interaction contributes greatly to the transition to language.

Phonological development is a complex process that depends on the child's ability to attend to sound sequences, produce sounds, and combine them into understandable words and phrases. Pronunciation improves greatly as the vocal tract matures and preschoolers engage in active problem-solving.

Semantic development takes place with extraordinary speed as preschoolers fast-map thousands of words into their vocabularies. Children's language comprehension develops ahead of production. Complex genetic and environmental influences contribute to the age at which the first word is spoken. Lexical contrast theory is a controversial account of how semantic development takes place. Preschoolers draw on many sources of information to deduce word meanings.

Between 1½ and 2½ years, children combine two words to express a variety of meanings. As children move beyond two-word utterances, a grammatical explosion takes place. In first combining words, children are preoccupied with figuring out the meanings of words and in getting their thoughts across to others. By age 6, children have mastered most of the grammar of their native tongue. Certain complex forms, however, continue to be refined in middle childhood.

Besides phonology, vocabulary, and grammar, children must learn to use language effectively in social contexts. During early and middle childhood, children acquire a variety of pragmatic devices that permit them to engage in more sustained and effective conversation with others. Parents the world over realize the importance of socially appropriate communication and tutor children in social routines from an early age. Although preschoolers show the beginnings of metalinguistic awareness, major advances do not take place until middle childhood. Historically, Americans have held negative attitudes toward childhood bilingualism. However, children fluent in two languages score higher in analytical reasoning, concept formation, cognitive flexibility, and metalinguistic awareness.

LEARNING OBJECTIVES

After reading this chapter, you should be able to:

9.1   Describe the four components of language. (pp. 354–355)

9.2   Describe three major theories of language development, indicating the extent to which each emphasizes biological and environmental influences. (pp. 355–363)

9.3   Describe how infants prepare for language, and explain how adults support their emerging linguistic capacities. (pp. 363–366)

9.4   Discuss the course of phonological development. (pp. 368–369)

9.5   Summarize the course of semantic development. (pp. 369–376)

9.6   Describe individual and cultural differences in early language development, noting the factors which influence these differences. (pp. 371–372)

9.7   Discuss ideas about how semantic development takes place, including the influence of memory, as well as strategies for word learning. (pp. 374–376)

9.8   Summarize the course of grammatical development from toddlerhood to middle childhood. (pp. 376–381)

9.9   Discuss ideas about how grammatical development takes place, including strategies for the acquisition of grammar, as well as environmental support for grammatical development. (pp. 376–381)

9.10 Trace the development of conversational skills and sociolinguistic understanding. (pp. 382–385)

9.11 Describe the course of metalinguistic awareness. (pp. 385–387)

9.12 Discuss the impact of bilingualism on linguistic and cognitive development. (pp. 387–389)

STUDY QUESTIONS

Components of Language

1. Match each of the following components of language with the appropriate description: (pp. 354–355)

    _____ Component of language concerned with syntax and morphology

    _____ Component of language concerned with the rules governing the structure and sequencing of speech sounds

    _____ Component of language concerned with how to engage in effective and appropriate communication with others

    _____ Component of language concerned with understanding the meaning of words and word combinations

    1. Phonology
    2. Semantics
    3. Grammar
    4. Pragmatics

Theories of Language Development

The Behaviorist Perspective

1. The behaviorist perspective suggests that language, like any other behavior, is acquired through (classical / operant) conditioning. (p. 355)

2. True or False: The behaviorist perspective is currently the most prominent theory of language development. (p. 355)

3. Cite two arguments against the behaviorist perspective of language development. (p. 355)

    A. _____

    _____

    B. _____

    _____

The Nativist Perspective

1. Discuss Chomsky's nativist perspective of language acquisition, noting how this approach differs from the behaviorist perspective. Be sure to explain the language acquisition device in your response. (pp. 356–357)

_____

_____

_____

_____

2. Research on language acquisition in dolphins and chimpanzees (does / does not) support Chomsky's assumption that language is a uniquely human accomplishment. Cite research evidence supporting your response. (pp. 357–358)

_____

_____

_____

_____

3. Name the two language-specific areas of the brain, and cite the function of each. (pp. 359–360)

   A. _____

   _____

   B. _____

   _____

4. Language processing and grammatical functions are usually concentrated in the (right / left) cerebral hemisphere. (p. 360)

5. True or False: Research supports the idea that there is a sensitive period for language development. (p. 360)

6. Discuss four challenges to Chomsky's theory. (pp. 360–361)

   A. _____

   _____

B. _____

_____

C. _____

_____

D. _____

_____

Cultural Influences: Children Invent Language— Homesign and Hawaiian Creole English

1. Susan Goldin-Meadow has found that deaf preschoolers whose parents discourage manual signing and address them verbally will spontaneously produce a gestural communication system known as _____, which is similar in basic structure to hearing children's verbal language. (pp. 356–357)

2. True or False: The gestural vocabularies of deaf children contain distinct forms for nouns and verbs which are combined into novel sentences that conform to grammatical rules. (pp. 356–357)

3. Hearing children reach language milestones (earlier / later) than do children who acquire homesign. (pp. 356–357)

4. What are *Creole* languages? (pp. 356–357)

_____

_____

5. Cite two arguments in support of Bickerton's contention that Creole languages are based on innate mechanisms. (pp. 356–357)

A. _____

_____

B. _____

_____

Biology and Environment: Language Development in Children with Williams Syndrome

1. Describe the symptoms of Williams Syndrome. (p. 362)

   _____

   _____

   _____

2. Children with Williams Syndrome have (fewer / more) advanced language skills than do children with Down syndrome. (p. 362)

3. Summarize areas of strength and weakness in the linguistic abilities of children and adolescents with Williams Syndrome, and discuss why these children show such an uneven language profile. (p. 362)

   Strengths: _____

   _____

   Weaknesses: _____

   _____

   Reason for uneven profile: _____

   _____

   _____

4. Findings from studies of language development in children with Williams Syndrome (support / refute) Chomsky's concept of a language acquisition device (LAD). (p. 362)

The Interactionist Perspective

1. Summarize the interactionist perspective of language development. (p. 361)

   _____

   _____

   _____

2. Although several interactionist theories exist, all stress the _____ *context* of language learning. (p. 361)

3. True or False: The interactionist perspective predicts individual differences in language learning. (p. 361)

Prelinguistic Development: Getting Ready to Talk

Receptivity to Language

1. A _____ is the smallest sound unit that can signal a change in meaning. (p. 363)

2. Phonemes (are / are not) the same across all languages. (p. 363)

3. What is *categorical speech perception*? (p. 363)

   _____

   _____

4. True or False: Within the first few days after birth, infants distinguish and prefer the overall sound pattern of their native language to that of other languages. (p. 363)

5. Describe the characteristics of *child-directed speech*. (p. 364)

   _____

   _____

   _____

6. True or False: From birth, infants prefer to listen to child-directed speech over other kinds of adult talk. (p. 364)

First Speech Sounds

1. Distinguish between *cooing* and *babbling*. (p. 365)

   Cooing: _____

   Babbling: _____

2. True or False: The timing of early babbling seems to be due to maturation, since babies everywhere (even those who are deaf) start babbling at about the same age and produce a similar range of early sounds. (p. 365)

3. How do cooing and babbling help to prepare infants for language? (p. 365)

_____

_____

_____

Becoming a Communicator

1. Describe the notion of *joint attention*, and discuss its impact on early language development. (p. 365)

_____

_____

_____

2. True or False: Turn-taking games such as pat-a-cake and peekaboo contribute to the infant's acquisition of language skills. (p. 365)

3. Explain the difference between *protodeclarative* and *protoimperative* preverbal gestures. (p. 365)

Protodeclarative: _____

_____

Protoimperative: _____

_____

4. True or False: Cross-cultural research confirms that adult molding of infant communication is essential if children are to acquire language within the normal time frame of development. (p. 366)

From Research to Practice: Parent-Child Interaction—Impact on Language and Cognitive Development of Deaf Children

1. True or False: Deaf children with hearing parents experience fewer delays in language and complex make-believe play than do deaf children with deaf parents. (p. 367)

2. How do the parent–child communication patterns of hearing parents and deaf children differ from those of deaf parents and deaf children? (p. 367)

_____

_____

_____

_____

3. Hearing parents lack experience with _____ communication, which enables deaf parents to respond readily to a deaf child's needs. Elaborate on your response. (p. 367)

_____

_____

_____

Phonological Development

The Early Phase

1. Explain how early phonological and semantic development are related. (p. 368)

_____

_____

_____

Appearance of Phonological Strategies

1. Trace the general pattern of phonological strategy development. (p. 369)

_____

_____

_____

_____

2. True or False: Phonological development occurs at the same rate for children in all cultures around the world. (pp. 368–369)

Later Phonological Development

1. Phonological development is largely complete by age _____. (p. 369)

2. List two aspects of phonological development that are not mastered until later childhood or adolescence. (p. 369)

A. _____

B. _____

Semantic Development

1. On average, children say their first word at _____ months of age. (p. 369)

2. In language development, _____ refers to the words and word combinations that children *use*, whereas _____ refers to the words and word combinations that children *understand*. (p. 370)

3. Why does language comprehension develop ahead of language production? (p. 370)

_____

_____

_____

The Early Phase

1. Briefly describe the nature of toddlers' first words (for example, to which subjects do these words commonly refer?) (p. 371)

_____

_____

_____

2. Although young toddlers add to their vocabulary slowly, a spurt in vocabulary often takes place between _____ and _____ months of age. (p. 371)

3. Explain how children use the process of *fast-mapping* to quickly build their vocabularies. (p. 371)

_____

_____

_____

4. True or False: Girls are slightly ahead of boys in early vocabulary growth. (p. 371)

5. Distinguish between referential and expressive styles of early language learning, noting which style is associated with faster vocabulary development. (p. 371)

Referential: _____

_____

Expressive: _____

_____

Style associated with faster vocabulary development: _____

6. What are the three most common types of words in young children's vocabularies? (p. 372)

A. _____   B. _____

C. _____

7. Many children have more (action / object) words in their beginning vocabulary. Why is this the case? (p. 372)

_____

_____

_____

8. What are *state words,* and what are some examples? (p. 372)

Definition: _____

_____

Examples: _____

9. _____ is an early vocabulary error in which a word is applied too narrowly, to a smaller number of objects and events than is appropriate. Conversely, _____ is an early vocabulary error in which a word is applied too broadly, to a wider collection of objects and events than is appropriate. (p. 373)

10. Provide an example of underextension and an example of overextension. (p. 373)

Underextension: _____

Overextension: _____

Later Semantic Development

1. True or False: The rate of vocabulary growth during the school years exceeds that of early childhood. (p. 374)

2. Describe changes in children's word definitions between the beginning and end of middle childhood. (p. 374)

_____

_____

_____

3. The capacity for _____ *reasoning* permits adolescents to master sarcasm and irony. (p. 374)

Ideas About How Semantic Development Takes Place

1. Explain the *phonological store,* and discuss how it is related to semantic development. (p. 374)

_____

_____

_____

2. Discuss the two principles assumed to govern vocabulary growth according to *lexical contrast theory*. (p. 375)

A. _____

_____

B. _____

_____

3. The principle of _____ refers to an assumption by children in the early stages of vocabulary growth that words refer to entirely separate (nonoverlapping) categories. (p. 375)

4. What is *syntactic bootstrapping*? (p. 375)

_____

_____

5. True or False: Children are able to effectively use social cues to identify word meanings. (p. 375)

Grammatical Development

First Word Combinations

1. Explain the nature of *telegraphic speech*. (p. 376)

_____

_____

_____

From Simple Sentences to Complex Speech

1. At what age do English-speaking children begin to use three-word sentences that follow a subject-verb-object word order? (p. 377)

_____

2. *Grammatical* _____ are small markers that change the meaning of sentences, as in "Suzy*'s*" dog" and "he *is* playing." (p. 377)

3. When children apply regular grammatical rules to words that are exceptions—for example, saying "I runned fast" instead of "I ran fast"—they are making an error called _____. (p. 378)

4. Why do children use some correct irregular forms before they start to overregularize? (p. 378)

_____

_____

Development of Complex Grammatical Forms

1. List and describe the three types of negation in the order in which they develop. (pp. 378–379)

   A. _____
   _____

   B. _____
   _____

   C. _____
   _____

2. Summarize the sequence in which children learn to ask questions. (p. 379)

   _____
   _____
   _____
   _____

Later Grammatical Development

1. Discuss two gains in grammatical construction that emerge during the school years. (pp. 379–380)

   A. _____
   _____

   B. _____
   _____

Ideas About How Grammatical Development Takes Place

1. Evidence that grammatical development is an extended rather than a sudden process (supports / refutes) Chomsky's strict nativist perspective. (p. 380)

2. Define *semantic bootstrapping*. (p. 380)

   _____
   _____

3. Other than semantic bootstrapping, discuss three additional theories about how children master grammar. (pp. 380–381)

   A. _____

   _____

   B. _____

   _____

   C. _____

   _____

4. Explain how adults use *expansions* and *recasts* to support children's grammatical development. (p. 381)

   _____

   _____

   _____

Pragmatic Development

Acquiring Conversational Skills

1. At the beginning of early childhood, children (are / are not) capable of effective communication, such as initiating conversation, responding appropriately to another's comments, and conversational turn-taking. (p. 382)

2. _____ is a conversational strategy in which the speaker not only comments on what has just been said but also adds a request to get the other person to respond again. (p. 382)

3. _____ is a conversational strategy in which a change of topic is initiated gradually by modifying the focus of the discussion. (p. 382)

4. What is *illocutionary intent*? (p. 382)

   _____

   _____

5. Discuss one strategy that parents can use to help children learn advanced conversational skills. (p. 382)

_____

_____

6. True or False: Having an older sibling facilitates the acquisition of pragmatic language. (p. 382)

Communicating Clearly

1. What are *referential communication skills*? (p. 383)

_____

_____

2. Describe the situations in which preschoolers' referential communication is less mature. (p. 383)

_____

_____

_____

Sociolinguistic Understanding

1. Language adaptations to social expectations are called _____. (p. 384)

2. Explain how the importance of speech register adjustments is reflected in how parents teach social routines. (p. 384)

_____

_____

_____

Development of Metalinguistic Awareness

1. What is *metalinguistic awareness*? (p. 385)

_____

_____

2. At what age do metalinguistic skills fully develop? (p. 385)

_____

3. Provide two examples of children's developing metalinguistic awareness. (p. 385)

A. _____

B. _____

Bilingualism: Learning Two Languages in Childhood

1. _____ million American school-age children speak a language other than English at home. (p. 387)

2. Cite two ways in which children can become bilingual, and discuss children's development in each instance. (pp. 387–388)

A. _____

_____

_____

_____

B. _____

_____

_____

_____

3. Research shows that bilingualism has (positive / negative) consequences for development. Discuss your response. (p. 388)

_____

_____

_____

Social Issues: Education – Bilingual Education

1. Discuss the current controversy surrounding the education of American ethnic minority children with limited English proficiency, and describe educational outcomes associated with each perspective. (p. 389)

_____

_____

_____

_____

_____

_____

2. _____ refers to inadequate proficiency in both one's native and second languages. (p. 389)

ASK YOURSELF . . .

Review: Summarize outcomes of attempts to teach language to animals. Are results consistent with the nativist assumption that human children are uniquely endowed with an LAD? Explain. (p. 363)

_____

_____

_____

_____

_____

Review: How does the interactionist perspective on language development differ from behaviorist and nativist views? Why is it attractive to so many contemporary researchers? (p. 363)

_____

_____

_____

_____

_____

Apply: Describe evidence that supports the existence of a sensitive period for second-language learning. What practical implications do these findings have for teaching children a second language in school? (p. 363)

_____

_____

_____

_____

_____

Connect: Cite research in this chapter and in Chapter 5 indicating that with age, areas of the cortex become increasingly specialized for language. Relate these findings to the concept of brain plasticity. (p. 363)

_____

_____

_____

_____

_____

Review: Cite findings indicating that both infant capacities and the language environment contribute to prelinguistic development. (p. 366)

_____

_____

_____

_____

_____

Apply: Fran frequently corrects her 17-month-old son Jeremy's attempts to talk and refuses to respond to his gestures, fearing he won't use words. How might Fran be contributing to Jeremy's slow language progress? What should she do to encourage his language development? (p. 366)

_____

_____

_____

_____

_____

Connect: Explain how parents' use of child-directed speech illustrates Vygotsky's zone of proximal development. (See Chapter 6, page 258.) (p. 366)

_____

_____

_____

_____

_____

Review: Using your knowledge of phonological and semantic development, explain why "Mama" and "Dada" are usually among children's first words. (p. 376)

_____

_____

_____

_____

_____

Review: Cite examples of how semantic development parallels advances in children's thinking. (p. 376)

_____

_____

_____

_____

_____

Apply: Katy's first words included "see," "give," and "thank you," and her vocabulary grew slowly during the second year. What style of language learning did she display, and what factors might have contributed to it? (p. 376)

_____

_____

_____

_____

_____

Connect: Explain how children's strategies for word learning support the interactionist perspective on language development. (p. 376)

_____

_____

_____

_____

_____

Review: Do young children use a consistent grammar in their telegraphic speech? Cite evidence to support your answer. (p. 381)

_____

_____

_____

_____

_____

Review: Cite examples of how both semantic and structural complexity underlie English-speaking children's mastery of grammatical morphemes. (p. 381)

_____

_____

_____

_____

_____

Apply: Three-year-old Jason's mother explained that the family would take a vacation in Miami. The next morning Jason announced, "I gotted my bags packed. When are we going to Your-ami?" What do Jason's errors reveal about his approach to mastering grammar? (p. 381)

_____

_____

_____

_____

_____

Connect: Explain why similarities between children's and artificial neural networks' mastery of grammatical structures are at odds with a nativist view of grammatical development. (p. 381)

_____

_____

_____

_____

_____

Review: Summarize findings indicating that patient, sensitive interactions with adults foster preschoolers' conversational skills as well as general language progress. (p. 385)

_____

_____

_____

_____

_____

Apply: What pragmatic skills are reflected in Erin's utterances in the opening of this chapter? How did Erin's parents and brother encourage her pragmatic development? (p. 385)

_____

_____

_____

_____

_____

Connect: Cite examples of cognitive advances that contribute to the development of referential communication. (p. 385)

_____

_____

_____

_____

_____

Review: Explain why metalinguistic awareness expands greatly in middle childhood. What might account for bilingual children's advanced metalinguistic skills? (p. 388)

_____

_____

_____

_____

_____

Apply: Reread the examples of Erin's language at the beginning of this chapter. Were Dorothy and Oscar wise to teach Erin both English and Spanish? Does Erin's mixing of the two languages indicate confusion? Justify your answers with research findings. (p. 388)

_____

_____

_____

_____

_____

SUGGESTED STUDENT READINGS

Bloom, P. (2000). *How children learn the meanings of words.* Cambridge, MA: The MIT Press. Examines the dynamic cognitive processes involved in the acquisition of word meaning. The author argues that learning new words, even simple nouns, requires complex interactions between the child's conceptual, social, and linguistic capacities.

MacWhimey, B. (Ed.). (1999). *The emergence of language.* Mahwah, NJ: Erlbaum. Presents a series of accounts of language acquisition including neural network theory, dynamic systems, linguistic functionalism, construction grammar, optimality theory, and statistically driven learning.

Piper, T. (1998). *Language and learning: The home and school years (2nd ed.).* Upper Saddle River, NJ: Prentice-Hall. Discusses how children learn language, how it is taught, and how the two are sometimes at odds. Traces language acquisition from birth through the school years, using experiences of a number of different children to illustrate stages and sequences of development.

PUZZLE 9.1

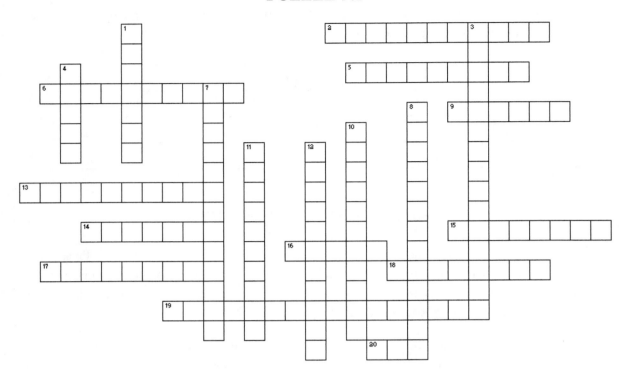

Across

2. Connecting a word with an underlying concept after only a brief encounter (2 words)
5. Component of language concerned with the rules governing the structure and sequence of speech sounds
6. Component of language concerned with how to engage in effective and appropriate communication with others
9. Pleasant vowel-like noises made by infants beginning around 2 months of age
13. _____ style: toddlers use language mainly to talk about people's feelings and needs
14. The smallest unit of sound that can signal a change in meaning
15. Repetition of consonant-vowel combinations in long strings, beginning around 4 months of age
16. _____ attention: two conversational partners attend to the same object or event
17. Component of language concerned with understanding the meaning of words and word combinations
18. _____'s area: area of the brain responsible for interpreting language
19. Preverbal gesture in which infants make an assertion about an object by touching it, holding it up, or pointing to it
20. In Chomsky's theory, an innate system that permits children to speak in a rule-oriented fashion as soon as they learn enough words (abbr.)

Down

1. Component of language concerned with syntax and morphology
3. Preverbal gesture in which infants point, reach, and make sounds to get another person to do something
4. _____'s area: area of the brain that controls the production of language
7. In language development, the words and word combinations that children understand
8. _____-_____ speech: form of speech marked by high-pitched, exaggerated expression, clear pronunciations, distinct pauses between speech segments, and repetition of new words (2 words)
10. _____ style: toddlers use language mainly to label objects
11. In language development, the words and word combinations that children use
12. The tendency to perceive as identical a range of sounds that belong to the same phonetic class is known as _____ speech perception.

PUZZLE 9.2

Across

1. _____ store: part of working memory that permits us to retain speech-based information
4. _____ communication skills involve the ability to produce clear verbal messages and to recognize when the meaning of others' messages is unclear.
5. Early vocabulary error in which a word is applied too broadly, to a wider collection of objects and events than is appropriate
8. _____ speech: children's two-word utterances that leave out smaller and less important words
10. Early vocabulary error in which a word is applied too narrowly, to a smaller number of objects and events than is appropriate
13. Adult responses that elaborate on a child's utterance, increasing its complexity
14. The ability to think about language as a system is referred to as _____ awareness.
16. _____ bootstrapping: figuring out word meanings by observing how words are used in the structure of sentences
17. _____ contrast theory assumes that the principles of conventionality and contrast govern semantic development.

Down

2. Application of regular grammatical rules to words that are exceptions
3. _____ bootstrapping: relying on word meanings to figure out sentence structure
6. Principle of _____ exclusivity: assumption by children in the early stages of vocabulary growth that words refer to entirely separate categories
7. Grammatical _____: small markers that change the meaning of sentences
9. Illocutionary _____ is what a speaker means to say, even if the form of the utterance is not perfectly consistent with it.
11. Conversational strategy in which the speaker not only comments on what has just been said but also adds a request to get the partner to respond again
12. Language adaptations to social expectations are called speech _____.
15. Adult responses that restructure a child's grammatically incorrect speech into correct form
16. Conversational strategy in which a change of topic is initiated gradually by modifying the focus of discussion

PRACTICE TEST

1. The component of language concerned with understanding the meaning of words and word combinations is: (p. 354)
   a. phonology.
   b. semantics.
   c. grammar.
   d. pragmatics.

2. According to Skinner's behaviorist perspective, language is acquired through: (p. 355)
   a. classical conditioning.
   b. operant conditioning.
   c. scaffolding.
   d. natural development of the language areas of the brain.

3. In Chomsky's theory, the _____ is a biologically-based system that permits children, no matter what language they hear, to speak in a rule-oriented fashion as soon as they have learned enough words. (p. 356)
   a. language acquisition device
   b. bio-linguistic mechanism
   c. linguistic processing device
   d. zone of proximal development

4. Which of the following provides evidence that children are biologically primed to acquire language? (pp. 356–357)
   a. Human languages around the world have vastly different grammatical forms.
   b. Children show a gradual mastery of language, with development taking place well into middle childhood.
   c. Children with Williams Syndrome show certain weaknesses in language development that are consistent with the cognitive impairments associated with the disorder.
   d. Children show a remarkable ability to invent new language systems, such as homesign and Hawaiian Creole English.

5. Which area of the brain is responsible for interpreting language? (p. 359)
   a. Chomsky's area
   b. Broca's area
   c. Wernicke's area
   d. parietal lobe

6. The case of Genie, a child reared in a linguistically and emotionally impoverished environment until she was 13 1/2 years old, supports the hypothesis that: (p. 360)
   a. there is a sensitive period for language development.
   b. damage to Wernicke's area may occur if a child is reared in a poor environment.
   c. language development does not have unique biological properties.
   d. children do not spontaneously develop gestural communication systems in the absence of verbal communication.

7. The tendency to perceive as identical a range of sounds that belong to the same phonemic class is called: (p. 363)
   a. underextension.
   b. syntactic bootstrapping.
   c. lexical contrast.
   d. categorical speech perception.

8. Child-directed speech: (p. 364)
   a. is calming to infants because of its low-pitched, monotonous tone.
   b. is used deliberately by parents in an effort to teach infants to talk.
   c. is effective for keeping children's attention and easing their task of understanding.
   d. is unrelated to children's development of language comprehension.

9. One-year-old Paige sees some cookies sitting out on the table. She begins pointing and reaching toward the cookies and making noise in an effort to get her mother to give her the cookies. This is an example of: (p. 365)
   a. a protodeclarative gesture.
   b. a protoimperative gesture.
   c. referential communication.
   d. joint attention.

10. Which of the following is true with regard to phonological development? (p. 368)
    a. Children's first words are influenced by the small number of sounds they can produce.
    b. Early phonological and semantic development are unrelated.
    c. Children around the world produce very different phonological errors, depending on the language that they speak.
    d. Phonological development is complete by age 3.

11. Young children are able to build their vocabularies extremely quickly because they can connect a new word to an underlying concept after only a brief encounter—a process called: (p. 371)
    a. word linking.
    b. conceptual bootstrapping.
    c. fast-mapping.
    d. syntactic mapping.

12. A toddler whose early vocabulary consists mainly of words referring to objects is using a(n) _____ style. (p. 371)
    a. expressive
    b. referential
    c. concrete
    d. attributional

13. Children's knowledge of categorical relationships would lead us to predict that they would be most likely to overextend the word *doggie* to: (p. 373)
    a. other furry, four-legged animals.
    b. all other animals.
    c. any living thing.
    d. nearly anything; their errors are random.

14. When asked to define the word *knife*, Jerome replies, "Something you cut with. A saw is like a knife. It could also be a weapon." Jerome is probably: (p. 374)
    a. a preschooler.
    b. a first grader.
    c. a sixth grader.
    d. a high school student.

15. Lexical contrast theory: (p. 375)
    a. assumes that language production develops ahead of language comprehension.
    b. suggests that children use syntactic bootstrapping to deduce word meanings.
    c. assumes that words refer to entirely separate, nonoverlapping entities.
    d. assumes that vocabulary growth is governed by the principles of conventionality and contrast.

16. When children use two-word utterances that leave out smaller, less important words, such as by saying "more cookie," this is referred to as: (p. 376)
    a. babbling.
    b. underextension.
    c. telegraphic speech.
    d. referential style.

17. Grammatical morphemes: (p. 377)
    a. are applied consistently by children once they first appear.
    b. are acquired in a regular sequence by young English-speaking children.
    c. are similar in all languages around the world.
    d. are acquired in their regular form first, followed by their irregular form.

18. A child who extends grammatical rules to words that are exceptions, such as by saying "I runned fast" instead of "I ran fast," is making an error known as: (p. 378)
    a. overextension.
    b. overregularization.
    c. lexical contrast.
    d. shading.

19. In the development of complex grammatical forms: (p. 379)
    a. children begin to use negation at the end of the preschool years.
    b. denial, as a type of negation, appears before nonexistence.
    c. questions first appear in the early elementary school years and develop in a haphazard sequence.
    d. children learn correct question form for yes/no questions before they learn the correct form for *wh-* questions.

20. Young Colleen says, "I go school, too." Her mother replies, "Yes, you are going to school, too." Her mother's response would be classified as: (p. 381)
    a. repetition and correction.
    b. correction and reflection.
    c. rejection and restatement.
    d. expansion and recast.

21. Pragmatic development involves: (p. 382)
    a. learning to use language effectively in social contexts.
    b. learning the rules governing the structure and sequence of speech sounds.
    c. learning to understand the meaning of words and word combinations.
    d. learning the rules by which words are arranged into sentences.

22. _____ is a conversational strategy in which the speaker not only comments on what has just been said but also adds a request to get the partner to respond again. (p. 382)
    a. Illocutionary intent
    b. Shading
    c. Turnabout
    d. Recasting

23. Language adaptations to social expectations are called: (p. 384)
    a. phonological stores.
    b. speech registers.
    c. phonemes.
    d. morphemes.

24. Metalinguistic awareness: (p. 385)
    a. is fully developed by the time children enter elementary school.
    b. does not emerge until middle childhood.
    c. is a good predictor of vocabulary and grammatical development during the preschool years.
    d. is unrelated to other areas of language development.

25. Which of the following statements is true? (p. 388)
    a. When bilingual parents try to teach their children both languages during early childhood, the children often experience severe problems in language development.
    b. Parents and teachers should be concerned if bilingual children start mixing the two languages.
    c. Recent research refutes the notion of a sensitive period for second language learning.
    d. Bilingual children show advances in cognitive development.

CHAPTER 10
EMOTIONAL DEVELOPMENT

BRIEF CHAPTER SUMMARY

Although the emotional side of development was overshadowed by cognition for several decades, new excitement surrounds the study of emotions today. The functionalist approach emphasizes that the broad function of emotions is to prompt action in the service of personal goals. It regards emotions as central forces in all aspects of human activity—cognitive processing, social behavior, and even physical health. In addition, emotions are viewed as important in the emergence of self-awareness, which fosters self-conscious emotions. As children adapt to their physical and social world, they gradually gain voluntary control over their emotions.

The development of emotional expression is a gradual process that begins in infancy and continues into adolescence. Changes in happiness, anger, sadness, and fear reflect infants' developing cognitive capacities and serve social as well as survival functions. Signs of almost all the basic emotions are present in early infancy, and they soon become clear, well-organized signals. At the end of the second year, self-conscious emotions emerge. Emotional self-regulation originates in infancy, and during the preschool years, children start to conform to the emotional display rules of their culture. Parenting practices and the child's temperament affect the development of emotional self-regulation. The ability to meaningfully interpret others' emotional expressions emerges at the end of the first year. Around this time, infants start to engage in social referencing. Although the roots of empathy are present early in development, true empathy requires children to understand that the self is distinct from other people.

Heredity influences early temperament, but child-rearing experiences affect whether a child's emotional style is sustained or modified over time. Nonetheless, long-term predictions about temperament are best achieved after the second year of life, when styles of responding are better established. According to ethological theory, infants are biologically prepared to contribute to the attachment bond with the caregiver, which evolved to promote survival. Caregiving that is responsive to babies' needs supports the development of secure attachment, whereas insensitive caregiving is linked to attachment insecurity. Family circumstances, parents' internal working models, culture, and infants' health and temperament also contribute to the quality of attachment. Although some findings indicate that secure attachment in infancy causes improved cognitive, emotional, and social competence during later years, continuity of caregiving may be responsible for these outcomes.

Today the majority of American mothers with children younger than age 2 are employed. Infant child care is associated with a slight risk of attachment insecurity. Quality of care is the determining factor in the effect of child care on young children's emotional security.

LEARNING OBJECTIVES

After reading this chapter, you should be able to:

10.1 Describe the functionalist approach to emotional development, noting how emotions are related to cognitive processing. (pp. 394–397)

10.2 Describe changes in the expression of happiness, anger, sadness, and fear across infancy and toddlerhood. (pp. 397–400)

10.3 Discuss the development of self-conscious emotions, emotional self-regulation, and conformity to emotional display rules, including cognitive, linguistic, parental, and cultural influences. (pp. 400–404)

10.4 Discuss changes in emotional understanding from infancy into adolescence, including the roles of cognitive development and social experience. (pp. 404–406)

10.5 Distinguish between empathy and sympathy, and describe the development of empathy from infancy into adolescence, noting factors that influence individual differences. (pp. 407–408)

10.6 Compare and contrast Thomas and Chess's model of temperament with that of Rothbart. (pp. 408–411)

10.7 Explain how temperament is measured, and discuss the stability of temperament over time. (pp. 411–414)

10.8 Summarize genetic and environmental influences on temperament, and describe the goodness-of-fit model. (pp. 414–417)

10.9 Describe the unique features of the ethological theory of attachment in comparison to psychoanalytic and drive-reduction (behaviorist) views. (pp. 417–419)

10.10 Describe the Strange Situation and Attachment Q-Sort procedures for measuring attachment, and discuss the four attachment patterns that have been identified using these techniques. (pp. 419–421)

10.11 Discuss the factors that affect attachment security, including opportunity for attachment, quality of caregiving, infant characteristics, family circumstances, and parents' internal working models. (pp. 422–425)

10.12 Discuss fathers' attachment relationships with their infants, and explain the role of early attachment quality in later development. (pp. 425–427)

10.13 Discuss the effects of maternal employment and child care on attachment security and psychological development. (pp. 428–431)

STUDY QUESTIONS

The Functions of Emotions

1. A(n) _____ expresses your readiness to establish, maintain, or change your relation to the environment on a matter of importance to you. (p. 394)

2. The _____ approach emphasizes that the broad function of emotions is to prompt action in the service of personal goals. (p. 394)

3. Cite three ways in which an event can become personally relevant, thereby prompting an emotional reaction. (p. 394)

A. _____

_____

B. _____

_____

C. _____

_____

Emotions and Cognitive Processing

1. True or False: Emotions have a profound impact on cognitive processing. (p. 394)

2. Explain how emotions such as anxiety can affect memory and performance. (p. 394)

_____

_____

_____

3. Most functionalist theorists view the relationship between emotion and cognition as
_____—a dynamic interplay that is evident in the first half-year of
life. (pp. 394–395)

Emotions and Social Behavior

1. True or False: Emotional reactions of others regulate children's social behavior. (p. 395)

2. In research, how have infants reacted when the exchange of emotional signals between mother
and infant is disrupted by having the mother assume an unreactive pose or a depressed emotional
state? (p. 395)

_____

_____

_____

Emotions and Health

1. Describe how studies of children adopted from Romanian orphanages illustrate the relationship
between emotions and health. (p. 395)

_____

_____

_____

2. True or False: Positive parenting practices are largely ineffective in reducing stress reactivity in
emotionally traumatized children. (p. 395)

Other Features of the Functionalist Approach

1. According to the functionalist approach, emotions are important in the emergence of self-
_____. (p. 397)

2. As children learn the circumstances in which it is acceptable to communicate feelings in their
culture, emotions are expressed (more / less) frequently. (p. 397)

Biology and Environment: Maternal Depression and Child Development

1. Approximately _____ to _____ percent of women experience chronic depression—mild to
severe feelings of sadness, distress, and withdrawal that continue for months or years. (p. 396)

2. Depression that emerges or strengthens after childbirth but fails to subside as the new mother adjusts to hormonal changes in her body and gains confidence in caring for her baby is called _____ depression. (p. 396)

3. Discuss how the experience of postpartum depression affects the mother's interactions with her infant. (p. 396)

_____

_____

_____

4. Explain the ways in which persistent maternal depression and associated parenting behaviors may impact the development of the infant. (p. 396)

_____

_____

_____

_____

5. To prevent maternal depression from interfering with the parent-child relationship and harming children, _____ is vital. (p. 396)

Development of Emotional Expression

1. _____ offer the most reliable cues as to which emotions infants are experiencing. (p. 397)

2. True or False: Cross-cultural research indicates that when looking at photographs of facial gestures, people around the world do not typically associate them with the same emotions. (p. 397)

3. Discuss the controversy concerning whether infants come into the world with the ability to express a wide variety of emotions. (p. 398)

_____

_____

_____

_____

4. True or False: By the middle of the first year, emotional expressions are well organized and specific. (p. 398)

Happiness

1. What is a *social smile*, and when does it develop? (p. 398)

_____

_____

_____

2. By 2 to 3 months of age, infants smile and coo when they discover a contingency between their behavior and an event. Shortly thereafter, babies smile most when interacting with _____. (p. 398)

3. Laughter, which appears around _____ to _____ months, reflects (faster / slower) processing of information than does smiling. (p. 399)

4. How do expressions of happiness change between early infancy and the middle of the first year? (p. 399)

_____

_____

Anger and Sadness

1. The frequency and intensity of infants' angry reactions (increases/decreases) with age. Explain why this occurs and how it is adaptive. (p. 399)

_____

_____

_____

_____

2. Expressions of sadness are (more / less) frequent than expressions of anger. (p. 399)

3. Name two circumstances in which infants commonly experience sadness. (p. 399)

Fear

1. Fear reactions (increase/decrease) during the second half of the first year. (p. 399)

2. The most frequent expression of fear in infants is _____ anxiety. (p. 399)

3. True or False: To minimize stranger anxiety, an unfamiliar adult should immediately pick up the infant and talk to him or her. (pp. 399–400)

4. Once wariness develops, infants use the familiar caregiver as a(n) _____ from which to confidently explore the environment and to which the infant can return for emotional support. (p. 400)

5. What factors influence the decline of fear reactions in toddlerhood? (p. 400)

_____

_____

Self-Conscious Emotions

1. What are *self-conscious emotions*? (p. 400)

_____

_____

2. Cite several examples of self-conscious emotions. (p. 400)

_____

3. Besides self-awareness, what ingredient is required in order for children to experience self-conscious emotions? (p. 400)

_____

4. True or False: The situations in which adults encourage children's expressions of self-conscious emotions are very similar from culture to culture. (p. 400)

5. Self-conscious emotions of 3-year-olds are clearly linked to self-_____. (p. 400)

6. Distinguish between guilt and shame, noting how each is related to development. (p. 401)

Guilt: _____

_____

Shame: _____

_____

7. True or False: School-age children experience self-conscious emotions in the absence of adult monitoring and encouragement. (p. 401)

Emotional Self-Regulation

1. Define *emotional self-regulation*. (p. 401)

   _____

   _____

2. Babies depend on _____ for help in adjusting their emotional reactions. (p. 401)

3. Rapid development of the _____ cortex increases the baby's tolerance for stimulation. (p. 401)

4. Explain how a caregiver's responses to an infant's emotional cues impact the infant's development of self-regulation. (pp. 401–402)

   _____

   _____

5. By the end of the second year, gains in representation and language lead to new ways of regulating emotion. Explain how this occurs.(p. 402)

   _____

   _____

   _____

6. List 3 ways in which children engage in active efforts to control their emotions during early childhood. (p. 402)

   A. _____

   B. _____

   C. _____

7. Discuss the impact of parenting on children's development of emotional self-regulation. (p. 402)

   _____

   _____

   _____

8. Discuss changes in children's management of emotions across middle childhood and adolescence. (p. 402)

_____

_____

_____

9. Compared with preschoolers, school-age children and adolescents more often use _____ strategies to manage emotion, a change resulting from an improved ability to reflect on their thoughts and feelings. (p. 403)

10. When the development of emotional self-regulation has gone well, young people acquire a sense of emotional _____—a feeling of being in control of their emotional experience. (p. 403)

Acquiring Emotional Display Rules

1. What are *emotional display rules*? (p. 403)

_____

_____

2. Not until age _____ can children pose an expression they do not feel. These expressions are usually limited to (positive / negative) feelings. (p. 403)

3. Cultures that stress (individualistic / collective) needs place particular emphasis on emotional display rules. Cite one example of this. (p. 403)

_____

_____

4. Explain how children's understanding of emotional display rules changes as they reach middle childhood. (p. 404)

_____

_____

_____

Understanding and Responding to the Emotions of Others

1. Early on, babies detect others' emotions through a fairly automatic process of *emotional* _____. (p. 404)

Social Referencing

1. Define *social referencing*, and explain the functions it serves for infants and toddlers. (p. 404)

   _____

   _____

   _____

2. True or False: Mothers are much more effective sources of emotional information for babies than are fathers. (p. 404)

3. True or False: By the middle of the second year, children appreciate that others' emotional reactions may differ from their own. (p. 405)

Emotional Understanding in Childhood

1. By age _____ to _____, children can correctly judge the causes of many basic emotional reactions. (p. 405)

2. True or False: Preschoolers realize that thoughts and feelings are interconnected. (p. 405)

3. True or False: When explaining emotion, preschoolers are likely to emphasize internal states to a greater extent than external factors. (pp. 405–406)

4. An improved ability to consider conflicting cues when explaining others' emotions develops during (early childhood / middle childhood / adolescence). (p. 406)

5. Preschoolers (do / do not) recognize that people can experience more than one emotion at a time. (p. 406)

6. Both _____ development and experience foster emotional understanding. (p. 406)

7. What types of social experiences contribute to children's emotional understanding? (p. 406)

   _____

   _____

   _____

Empathy and Symapthy

1. Distinguish between *empathy* and *sympathy*. (p. 407)

    Empathy: _____

    _____

    Sympathy: _____

    _____

2. Empathy is an important motivator of _____ behavior, or actions that benefit another person without any expected reward for the self. (p. 407)

3. True empathy requires children to understand that the _____ is distinct from others. (p. 407)

4. Empathic responding (increases / decreases) over the elementary school years. What factors contribute to this change? (p. 407)

    _____

5. What changes occur in empathic responding during late childhood and adolescence? (p. 407)

    _____

6. Discuss the impact of parenting on children's development of empathy and sympathy. (p. 408)

    _____

    _____

    _____

Temperament and Development

1. Define *temperament*. (p. 408)

    _____

    _____

2. Cite two important findings from the New York longitudinal study of temperament. (pp. 408–410)

    A. _____

    B. _____

The Structure of Temperament

1. List and describe the three styles of temperament that emerged from the work of Thomas and Chess. (pp. 410–411)

   A. _____

   _____

   B. _____

   _____

   C. _____

   _____

2. True or False: All children fit into one of the three categories of temperament described above. (p. 411)

3. Of the three types, the _____ pattern places children at highest risk for adjustment problems. (p. 411)

4. List the three underlying components of temperament represented in Rothbart's model. (p. 411)

   A. _____

   _____

   B. _____

   _____

   C. _____

   _____

Measuring Temperament

1. Cite three methods used to assess temperament. (p. 411)

   A. _____

   B. _____

   C. _____

2. Discuss the advantages and disadvantages of using parent reports to assess children's temperament. (p. 411)

Advantages: _____

_____

_____

Disadvantages: _____

_____

_____

3. Parental ratings are (strongly / moderately) related to observational measures of children's behavior. (p. 411)

4. Most physiological assessments of temperament have focused on _____ children, who react negatively to and withdraw from novel stimuli, and _____ children, who display positive emotion to and approach novel stimuli. (pp. 411–412)

Stability of Temperament

1. True or False: Temperamental stability from one age period to the next is generally low to moderate. (p. 412)

2. Long-term predictions about early temperament are best achieved after the _____ year of life, when styles of responding are better established. (p. 413)

3. True or False: Many children show little or no change in biologically-based temperamental traits, suggesting that such traits cannot be modified through environmental experiences. (pp. 413–414)

Genetic and Environmental Influences

1. Describe the findings from twin studies relating to the biological bases of temperament. (p. 414)

_____

_____

_____

_____

2. Adoption studies report (low / modest / high) correlations for temperament and personality for both biological and nonbiological siblings. This suggests that (shared / nonshared) environmental factors are especially salient in personality development. (p. 414)

3. Explain how nonshared environmental influences operate to affect temperament and personality. (p. 414)

_____

_____

4. Consistent ethnic differences in infant temperament (do / do not) exist. (p. 415)

5. Discuss differences in temperament between American and Asian infants, noting the influence of parenting on such differences. (p. 415)

_____

_____

_____

_____

Temperament as a Predictor of Children's Behavior

1. Distinguish temperamental characteristics associated with learning and cognitive performance from those associated with poor school achievement. (p. 415)

Learning and cognitive performance: _____

_____

Poor school performance: _____

_____

2. Describe the association between temperament and social behavior. (p. 415)

_____

_____

_____

Temperament and Child Rearing: The Goodness-of-Fit Model

1. Describe the *goodness-of-fit* model. (p. 416)

   _____

   _____

   _____

2. The goodness-of-fit model helps explain why Western middle-SES children with _____ temperaments are at high risk for later behavior problems. (p. 416)

3. Provide two examples of how the goodness-of-fit model is culturally dependent. (p. 416)

   A. _____

   _____

   B. _____

   _____

4. What type of parenting is beneficial to difficult and shy children? (p. 416)

   _____

   _____

5. True or False: While reserved, inactive toddlers benefit from highly stimulating maternal behavior, the same parental behavior has a negative impact on active children. (p. 416)

Biology and Environment: Biological Basis of Shyness and Sociability

1. Kagan, a researcher who studies shyness and sociability in children, believes that individual differences in arousal of the _____, an inner brain structure that controls avoidance reactions, contributes to these contrasting temperamental styles. (pp. 412–413)

2. Discuss four physiological correlates of approach-withdrawal behavior. (pp. 412–413)

   A. _____

   B. _____

C. _____

D. _____

3. Heritability research indicates that genes contribute (modestly / substantially) to shyness and sociability. (pp. 412–413)

4. Explain how child-rearing practices affect the chances that an emotionally reactive baby will become a fearful child. (pp. 412–413)

_____

_____

_____

Development of Attachment

1. Define *attachment*. (p. 417)

_____

_____

2. True or False: Both psychoanalytic and behaviorist theories emphasize feeding as the central context in which infants and caregivers build a close emotional bond. (p. 417)

3. How did research on rhesus monkeys challenge the idea that attachment depends on hunger satisfaction? (p. 417)

_____

_____

4. In addition to the challenges mentioned above in question #3, cite two additional problems with psychoanalytic and drive reduction theories of attachment. (p. 417)

A. _____

_____

B. _____

_____

Bowlby's Ethological Theory

1. True or False: The ethological theory of attachment is the most widely accepted view of the infants' emotional tie to the caregiver. (p. 417)

2. What did Lorenz's studies of imprinting in baby geese contribute to Bowlby's theory of attachment? (p. 418)

_____

_____

_____

3. According to Bowlby, the attachment bond has strong (biological / environmental) roots. It can best be understood within a framework in which survival of the fittest is of utmost importance. (p. 418)

4. Match each phase of attachment with the appropriate description. (p. 418–419)

_____ Attachment to the familiar caregiver is evident, and infants display separation anxiety

_____ Infants are not yet attached to their mother and do not mind being left with an unfamiliar adult

_____ Separation anxiety declines as children gain an understanding of the parent's comings and goings and can predict his/her return

_____ Infants start to respond differentially to a familiar caregiver than to a stranger

1. The preattachment phase
2. The attachment-in-the-making phase
3. The phase of "clear-cut" attachment
4. Formation of a reciprocal relationship

5. According to Bowlby, children develop an *internal working model* based on their experiences during the four phases of attachment. Define and explain this term. (p. 419)

_____

_____

_____

Measuring the Security of Attachment

1. The _____ technique, designed by Mary Ainsworth, is the most widely used technique for measuring the quality of attachment between 1 and 2 years of age. (p. 419)

2. What assumptions underlie the use of the Strange Situation? (p. 419)

_____

_____

3. The Strange Situation takes the baby through eight short episodes in which brief
   _____ and _____ with the parent occur. (p. 419)

4. Match each of the following attachment classifications with the appropriate description.
   (pp. 419–420)

_____ Before separation, these infants seek closeness
to the parent and fail to explore. When she returns,
they display angry behaviors, may continue to cry
after being picked up, and cannot be easily
comforted.

_____ Before separation, these infants use the parent as a
base from which to explore. They are upset by the
parent's absence, and they seek contact and are easily
comforted when she returns.

_____ Before separation, these infants seem unresponsive to
the parent. When she leaves, they react to the stranger
in much the same way as to the parent. Upon her return,
they are slow to greet her.

_____ When the parent returns, these infants show confused,
contradictory behaviors, such as looking away while
being held.

1. Secure
2. Avoidant
3. Resistant
4. Disorganized/Disoriented

5. The Attachment _____ is used as an alternative to the Strange Situation for
   measuring attachment. Briefly describe this method. (p. 420)

   _____

   _____

   _____

Stability of Attachment

1. True or False: Insecurely attached infants maintain their attachment status more often than do
   securely attached infants. (p. 421)

2. Overall, many children show (short-term / long-term) instability in attachment quality. (p. 421)

Cultural Variations

1. German infants show considerably more _____ attachment than American babies, while an unusually high number of Japanese infants display _____ attachment. (p. 421)

2. True or False: The secure pattern is the most common attachment classification in all societies studied to date. (p. 421)

3. Explain what researchers found when the Attachment Q-sort was used to assess conceptions of the ideal child among mothers from diverse cultures? (p. 421)

   _____

Factors That Affect Attachment Security

1. List four important influences that affect attachment security. (p. 422)

   A. _____

   B. _____

   C. _____

   D. _____

2. True or False: Research on adopted children indicates that children can develop a first attachment bond as late as 4 to 6 years of age. (p. 422)

3. Describe several adjustment problems evidenced by children and adolescents who lacked the opportunity to develop attachment bonds during infancy and early childhood. (p. 422)

   _____

   _____

   _____

4. Describe differences in caregiving experienced by securely attached and insecurely attached infants. (p. 422)

   Securely attached: _____

   _____

Insecurely Attached: _____

_____

5. A special form of communication known as interactional _____ appears to separate the experiences of securely and insecurely attached infants. Describe this pattern of communication. (p. 422)

_____

_____

_____

6. How does the child care experienced by securely attached infants differ from that experienced by avoidant and resistant infants? (p. 423)

_____

_____

_____

_____

7. Among maltreated infants, _____ attachment is especially high. (p. 423)

8. True or False: Researchers have concluded that infant temperament exerts an extremely powerful influence on attachment security, as evidenced by the fact that infants display an attachment quality that is consistent across familiar adult caregivers. (p. 423)

9. A major reason that temperament and other child characteristics do not show strong relationships with attachment quality may be that their influence depends on _____. (p. 424)

10. Explain how family circumstances, such as job loss, a failing marriage, or financial difficulties, can affect infant attachment. (p. 424)

_____

_____

_____

11. True or False: The quality of maternal working models shows little or no relationship with attachment in infancy and early childhood. (p. 424)

12. True or False: The way parents *view* their childhood experiences is more influential than the actual experiences themselves in determining how parents rear their own children. (p. 425)

Multiple Attachments: The Father's Special Role

1. True or False: Throughout infancy and early childhood, infants direct their attachment behaviors to a single person, typically the mother. (p. 425)

2. Describe how mothers and fathers differ in the way they related to and interact with their infants, and discuss how these patterns are changing due to the revised work status of women. (p. 425)

_____

_____

_____

_____

3. Employed mothers tend to engage in (more / less) playful stimulation of their babies than do unemployed mothers. (p. 426)

4. List two conditions associated with increased paternal involvement with caregiving. (p. 426)

A. _____

B. _____

Attachment and Later Development

1. Discuss research findings on the link between infant-mother attachment and cognitive, emotional, and social development. (p. 426)

_____

_____

_____

_____

2. True or False: Research consistently shows that secure infants show more favorable development than insecure infants. (p. 426)

3. _____ attachment is consistently related to high hostility and aggression in early and middle childhood. (p. 426)

4. Lamb suggests that continuity of caregiving determines whether attachment is linked to later development. Briefly explain this relationship. (pp. 426–427)

_____

_____

_____

Attachment, Parental Employment, and Child Care

1. Today, over _____ percent of American mothers with a child under age 2 are employed. (p. 428)

2. Discuss the link between child care quality and child outcomes. (pp. 428–429)

_____

_____

_____

3. True or False: Research suggests that over 75 percent of children under age 2 who are placed in child care homes or centers receive high quality care that is characteristic of positive caregiving. (p. 430)

4. List and describe five signs of high-quality care, based on the standards for developmentally appropriate practice. (p. 431)

A. _____

_____

B. _____

_____

C. _____

_____

D. _____

_____

E. _____

_____

Cultural Influences: Father-Infant Relationships Among the Aka

1. Describe Aka fathers' involvement with their babies, noting how the relationship between Aka husbands and wives encourages fathers' participation in child-rearing. (p. 427)

_____

_____

_____

_____

Social Issues: Does Child Care in Infancy Threaten Attachment Security and Later Adjustment?

1. True or False: American infants placed in full-time child care before 12 months of age are more likely than home-reared infants to display insecure attachments. (pp. 428–429)

2. Discuss several reasons why we must be cautious about concluding that child care is harmful to infants' attachment security. (pp. 428–429)

_____

_____

_____

_____

3. Cite two factors that influence the impact of child care experiences on attachment security. (pp. 428–429)

   A. _____

   B. _____

4. True or False: Research suggests that early, extensive child care has a far stronger impact on preschoolers' problem behavior than does parenting. (pp. 428–429)

ASK YOURSELF . . .

Review: Cite a research-based example of the impact of emotions on children's (1) cognitive processing, (2) social behavior, and (3) physical health. (p. 397)

_____

_____

_____

_____

_____

Apply: Jeannine's husband recently moved out. Lonely, depressed, and anxious about finances, Jeannine spends most of her days caring for 3-month-old Jacob. How might Jeannine's state of mind affect Jacob's emotional development? What can be done to help Jacob? (p. 397)

_____

_____

_____

_____

_____

Review: Why do many infants show stranger anxiety in the second half of the first year? What factors can increase or decrease wariness of strangers? (p. 404)

_____

_____

_____

_____

_____

Review: Explain how parenting, language, and temperament contribute to the development of emotional self-regulation. (p. 404)

_____

_____

_____

_____

_____

Apply: At age 14 months, Reggie built a block tower and gleefully knocked it down. At 2 years of age, Reggie called to his mother and pointed proudly to his tall block tower. What explains this change in Reggie's emotional behavior? (p. 404)

_____

_____

_____

_____

_____

Connect: How do children of depressed mothers fare in regulating emotion? (See page 396.) What implications does their self-regulation competence have for handling cognitive and social challenges? (p. 404)

_____

_____

_____

_____

_____

Review: What do preschoolers understand about emotion, and how do cognition and social experience contribute to their understanding? (p. 408)

_____

_____

_____

_____

Review: How does empathy change from infancy to adolescence? (p. 408)

_____

_____

_____

_____

Apply: While running, 15-month-old Ellen fell down. She looked at her mother, who smiled and exclaimed, "Oh, wasn't that a funny tumble!" How is Ellen likely to respond emotionally, and why? (p. 408)

_____

_____

_____

_____

_____

Connect: Explain why good emotional self-regulation is vital for empathy to result in sympathy and prosocial behavior. How can parents promote emotional self-regulation, empathy, and sympathy at the same time? (p. 408)

_____

_____

_____

_____

_____

Review: Why is the stability of temperament only low to moderate? (p. 417)

_____

_____

_____

_____

_____

Review: How do genetic and environmental factors work together to promote a child's temperament? Cite examples from research on shyness, nonshared environmental influences, and cultural variations. (p. 417)

_____

_____

_____

_____

_____

Apply: Eighteen-month-old, highly active Jake, who climbed out of his high chair, had a temper tantrum when his father made him sit at the table until the meal was finished. Using the concept of goodness-of-fit, suggest another way of handling Jake. (p. 417)

_____

_____

_____

_____

_____

Connect: Compared with their agemates, shy, inhibited 2-year-olds are less likely to respond with sympathetic, prosocial behavior to an unfamiliar, upset person (Young, et al., 1999). Using the distinction between empathy and sympathy on page 407, explain why. (p. 417)

_____

_____

_____

_____

_____

Review: What factors explain stability in attachment quality for some children and change for others? Are the same factors involved in the link between infant–mother attachment and later development? Explain. (p. 427)

_____

_____

_____

_____

_____

Review: What contributions do quality of caregiving and infant characteristics make to attachment security? Which influence is more powerful, and why? (p. 427)

_____

_____

_____

_____

_____

Apply: In evaluating her childhood attachment experiences, Monica recalls her mother as tense and distant. Is Monica's newborn daughter likely to develop an insecure infant–mother attachment? Explain, drawing on research into adults' internal working models. (p. 427)

_____

_____

_____

_____

_____

Connect: Review research on emotional self-regulation on pages 401–403. How do the caregiving experiences of securely attached infants promote the development of emotional self-regulation? (p. 427)

_____

_____

_____

_____

_____

Review: Cite evidence that high-quality infant and toddler child care supports development, whereas poor quality care undermines it. (p. 430)

_____

_____

_____

_____

_____

Apply: Randi and Mike are worried that placing their 6-month-old baby, Lucinda, in child care may disrupt the development of attachment. List steps that Randi and Mike can take to ensure that Lucinda's experiences—at home and in child care—support attachment security. (p. 430)

_____

_____

_____

_____

_____

SUGGESTED STUDENT READINGS

Brandstaetter, H., & Eliasz, A. (Eds.). (2001). *Persons, situations and emotions: An ecological approach.* New York: Oxford University Press. An edited book detailing the dynamic interaction between temperament and personality traits and their contribution to the development of mood and emotions.

Bronson, M. B. (2000). *Self-regulation in early childhood: Nature and nurture.* New York: The Guilford Press. A collection of chapters examining the development of self-regulation through the first 8 years of life. Also includes practical advice for parents and educators for enhancing self-regulatory skills througout infancy and early childhood.

Crittenden, P. M., & Claussen, A. H. (Eds.). (2000). *The organization of attachment relationships: Maturation, culture, and context.* New York: Cambridge University Press. Investigates the role of culture, maturation, and developmental context in relation to attachment theory. Topics include: cultural variations in attachment styles, the influence of attachment style on adolescent behavior, risks to attacment security, such as maternal depression, child abuse, and institutionalization, and factors affecting attachment status in twins.

Taylor, R. D., & Wang, M. C. (Eds.). (1997). *Social and emotional adjustment and family relations in ethnic minority families.* Mahwah, NJ: Eribaum. Collection of essays addressing issues related to the intersection of family relationships and several contexts for social and emotional development of ethnic minority adolescents.

PUZZLE 10.1

Across

5. Attachment style characterizing infants who respond in a confused, contradictory fashion when reunited with the parent (a.k.a. disoriented attachment)

9. Attachment _____: method for assessing the quality of the attachment bond in which the parent sorts a set of descriptors of attachment-related behaviors based on how well they describe the child

11. Attachment style characterizing infants who are distressed at parental separation and easily comforted upon parental return

15. Emotions that can be directly inferred from facial expressions

16. Attachment style characterizing infants who are not distressed by parental separation and who avoid the parent when she returns

17. Procedure involving brief separations from and reunions with the parent that assesses the quality of the attachment bond (2 words)

Down

1. _____ working model: set of expectations derived from early caregiving experiences

2. An expression of readiness to establish, maintain, or change one's relation to the environment on a matter of personal importance

3. Feelings of concern or sorrow for another's plight

4. ___-____ emotions involve injury to or enhancement of the sense of self.

6. Emotional self-_____: strategies for adjusting our emotional state to a comfortable level of intensity

7. The strong affectional tie that humans feel toward special people in their lives

8. _____ theory of attachment: views the infant's emotional tie to the caregiver as an evolved response that promotes survival

10. _____ anxiety refers to an infant's distressed reaction to the departure of a familiar caregiver.

12. Attachment style characterizing infants who remain close to the parent prior to separation and display angry behavior upon reunion

13. Ability to understand another's emotional state and feel with that person

14. _____, or altruistic, behavior: actions that benefit another without any expected reward for the self

PUZZLE 10.2

Across

4. Developmentally _____ practice: NAEYC standards specifying program characteristics that meet developmental and individual needs of young children of varying ages
6. Stable, individual differences in quality and intensity of emotional reaction, activity level, and emotional self-regulation
7. _____ approach: emotions serve to prompt action in the service of personal goals
8. The _____ smile is evoked by the stimulus of the human face.
9. Temperament style characterized by inactivity, mild, low-key reactions to environmental stimuli, negative mood, and slow adjustment to new experiences
11. Social _____ involves reliance upon another's emotional reaction to appraise an uncertain situation.
13. A child who reacts negatively to and withdraws from novel stimuli
14. Interactional _____: sensitively-tuned emotional dance in which caregiver responds to infant signals in a well-timed, appropriate fashion and both partners match emotional states

15. A child who displays positive emotion to and approaches novel stimuli
16. _____ anxiety: infant's expression of fear in response to unfamiliar adults

Down

1. Model of attachment which states that an effective match between child-rearing practices and a child's temperament leads to favorable adjustment
2. Emotional _____ rules specify when, where, and how it is culturally appropriate to express emotions.
3. Infants use the caregiver as a secure _____ from which to explore, returning for emotional support.
5. Temperament style characterized by irregular daily routines, slow acceptance of new experiences, and negative, intense reactions
10. _____ caregiving involves prompt, consistent, and appropriate responding to infant signals.
12. Temperament style characterized by establishment of regular routines in infancy, general cheerfulness, and easy adaptation to new experiences

PRACTICE TEST

1. According to functionalist theory, emotions: (p. 394)
   a. prompt action in the service of personal goals.
   b. interfere with the development of self-efficacy.
   c. have an entirely biological basis.
   d. have little impact on physical health.

2. Emotions that can be directly inferred from facial expressions are referred to as: (p. 398)
   a. social emotions.
   b. self-conscious emotions.
   c. basic emotions.
   d. referential emotions.

3. Research on happiness indicates that: (p. 398)
   a. infants do not begin to smile until around 3 months of age.
   b. by 3 months of age, infants smile more often when they see a dynamic, eye-catching object than when they interact with people.
   c. smiling reflects faster processing of information than does laughing.
   d. infants smile and laugh when they achieve new skills.

4. Angry expressions: (p. 399)
   a. first emerge at 8 to 10 months of age.
   b. increase in frequency and intensity from 4 to 6 months into the second year.
   c. decrease in frequency and intensity after the middle of the first year.
   d. rarely occur during infancy and early childhood.

5. Stranger anxiety: (pp. 399–400)
   a. is a universal phenomenon demonstrated by children in all cultures.
   b. is lessened if the parent remains nearby.
   c. is diminished if the unfamiliar adult immediately picks up the infant.
   d. is a relatively uncommon fear among children.

6. Which of the following are characterized as self-conscious emotions? (p. 400)
   a. happiness and sadness
   b. fear and anger
   c. interest and surprise
   d. shame and embarrassment

7. The capacity to adjust one's emotional state to a comfortable level of intensity is known as: (p. 401)
   a. affective monitoring.
   b. emotional self-regulation.
   c. emotional self-control.
   d. emotive self-referencing.

8. Which of the following is true? (p. 403)
   a. Parenting practices in the first few months of life often promote the well-known sex difference in emotional expression (i.e., girls as more emotionally expressive than boys).
   b. Between 18 months and 2 years of age, infants develop the ability to pose an emotion that they do not feel.
   c. Individualistic cultures place greater emphasis on emotional display rules than do collectivist cultures.
   d. Children of all ages find it more difficult to act pleased than to act angry or sad.

9. When an unfamiliar adult offers Heather a toy, she hesitates and looks at her mother, who smiles and nods. Heather then reaches out and takes the toy. This is an example of: (p. 404)
   a. self-control.
   b. social referencing.
   c. emotional contagion.
   d. compliance.

10. Empathy: (p. 407)
   a. always promotes sympathetic, prosocial responding.
   b. is equally likely in all children, regardless of parental influence.
   c. leads to personal distress and self-focused responding in some children.
   d. is expressed more often by abused children than by their non-abused agemates.

11. A child who has irregular daily routines, is slow to accept new experiences, and tends to react negatively and intensely would best fit into which of the following categories of temperament? (p. 411)
   a. easy
   b. difficult
   c. slow-to-warm-up
   d. apathetic

12. In the measurement of temperament: (p. 411)
    a. parent reports have been found to be the most reliable, unbiased source of information.
    b. parent reports are only weakly related to laboratory observations of children's behavior.
    c. laboratory observations are the most reliable measure for all children, regardless of temperament.
    d. physiological assessments have been successful in differentiating children with different temperament styles.

13. Research on the stability of temperament shows that: (p. 412)
    a. temperament is highly stable from infancy to adulthood.
    b. temperament is moderately stable from one age period to the next.
    c. temperament is not at all stable from one age period to the next.
    d. temperament stabilizes in late childhood and is consistent after that time.

14. Studies on genetic and environmental influences on temperament show that: (p. 414)
    a. identical twins are no more similar than fraternal twins across a wide range of temperamental traits.
    b. twin resemblance for temperament and personality is higher than for intelligence.
    c. siblings growing up in the same family show a high degree of resemblance in temperament and personality, suggesting that shared environmental factors make an important contribution.
    d. unique, non-shared experiences are especially salient in the development of personality.

15. The notion that an effective match between child-rearing practices and a child's temperament will lead to favorable outcomes is known as: (p. 416)
    a. secure base.
    b. goodness-of-fit.
    c. interactional synchrony.
    d. sensitive caregiving.

16. The most widely accepted view of attachment is the _____ theory. (p. 417)
    a. behaviorist
    b. psychoanalytic
    c. ethological
    d. drive-reduction

17. According to Bowlby, during which phase of attachment development do infants display separation anxiety, becoming upset when the caregiver leaves? (p. 418)
    a. the preattachment phase
    b. the attachment-in-the-making phase
    c. the phase of "clear-cut" attachment
    d. the formation of a reciprocal relationship phase

18. Based on their experiences during Bowlby's four phases of attachment development, children construct a(n) _____, or a set of expectations about the availability of attachment figures, their likelihood of providing support during times of stress, and the self's interactions with those figures. (p. 419)
    a. attachment schema
    b. secure attachment
    c. secure base
    d. internal working model

19. When placed in the Strange Situation, infants who seek closeness to their mother before separation but display angry behavior when she returns are classified as having which pattern of attachment? (pp. 419–420)
    a. secure
    b. avoidant
    c. resistant
    d. disorganized/disoriented

20. Which of the following is a measure of attachment quality in which parents are asked to sort a set of descriptors of attachment-related behaviors on the basis of how well they describe the child? (p. 420)
    a. Child Attachment Inventory
    b. Attachment Q-Sort
    c. Strange Situation
    d. Individual Attachment Quality Checklist

21. Which is the most stable pattern of attachment, with nearly 70% of children retaining this classification over the second year? (p. 421)
    a. secure
    b. avoidant
    c. resistant
    d. disorganized/disoriented

22. Research on the relationship between caregiving and attachment style shows that: (p. 422)
    a. sensitive caregiving distinguishes securely from insecurely attached infants.
    b. secure attachment is associated with almost 100% interactional synchrony between mother and infant.
    c. resistant infants tend to have mothers who are minimally involved in caregiving and unresponsive to infant signals.
    d. children who experience abuse and neglect are no more likely than other children to develop insecure attachments.

23. Fathers: (p. 426)
    a. are less involved in caregiving, and therefore, often have insecure attachments with their infants.
    b. experience less anxiety than do mothers about daily separations from their child.
    c. tend to encourage more exciting, physical play with infants than do mothers.
    d. are more likely than mothers to provide toys, talk to their infants, and initiate conversational games such as pat-a-cake and peek-a-boo.

24. _____ determines whether attachment security is liked to later development. (p. 426)
    a. Continuity of caregiving
    b. Individual temperament
    c. Quality of caregiving during infancy
    d. Strength of the child's internal working model

25. Studies examining child care in the United States show that: (pp. 428–429)
    a. infants and young children exposed to poor quality child care, regardless of whether they come from middle- or low-SES homes, score lower on measures of cognitive and social skills.
    b. even high-quality child care is ineffective at reducing the negative impact of a stressed, poverty-stricken life.
    c. stringent federal guidelines ensure that the majority of American children are placed in high-quality child care facilities.
    d. the NAEYC's standards for developmentally appropriate practice have little or no relationship to children's actual experiences in child care centers.

CHAPTER 11
SELF AND SOCIAL UNDERSTANDING

BRIEF CHAPTER SUMMARY

The development of social cognition deals with how children's understanding of themselves, other people, and relationships between people changes with age. Virtually all investigators agree that the self has two distinct aspects: the I-self and the me-self. By the end of the second year, self-recognition is well established. The emergence of representational and language capacities permits toddlers to construct a categorical self as they classify themselves and others on the basis of salient characteristics. Early in the preschool years, children become aware of an inner self of private thoughts and imaginings. Around age 4, they have formed a sophisticated theory of mind in which they understand the relationship of belief and desire to behavior. Research suggests that language, cognitive abilities, make-believe play, and social experiences contribute to young children's theory of mind.

Self-concept evolves from an appreciation of typical emotions, attitudes, and observable characteristics to an emphasis on personality traits. At the same time, self-esteem differentiates, becomes hierarchically organized, and declines in the early school years. Cultural forces and child-rearing practices profoundly affect self-esteem. Similarly, adult communication patterns affect children's attributions for success and failure in achievement contexts and their willingness to persist at challenging tasks. Erikson first recognized identity—the construction of a solid self-definition consisting of self-chosen values and goals—as the major personality achievement of adolescence. Four identity statuses describe the degree of progress adolescents have made toward forming a mature identity. Children's understanding of other people has much in common with their developing understanding of themselves. Around age 4, children move beyond the fusion of intention with behavior and appreciate intention as an internal mental state that is distinct from other mental states and from outcomes of actions.

Like self-concept, person perception shifts in middle childhood from a focus on concrete activities and behaviors to an emphasis on personality traits. By the early school years, children absorb prevailing attitudes toward social groups and link physical characteristics with social status. During adolescence, inferences about others' psychological characteristics are drawn together into organized character sketches. Perspective taking begins with a limited awareness of others' thoughts and feelings and evolves into advanced recursive and societal perspective-taking capacities. The ability to understand the viewpoints of others contributes to diverse social skills.

With age, children become better at resolving conflict through social problem solving. Training in social problem solving leads to improved peer relations and academic performance.

LEARNING OBJECTIVES

After reading this chapter, you should be able to:

11.1 Summarize trends in the development of social cognition, and explain how social cognition differs from nonsocial cognition. (pp. 435–436)

11.2 Describe the emergence of self-awareness in infancy and toddlerhood and explain how it influences early emotional and social development. (pp. 436–439)

11.3 Distinguish between the categorical and remembered selves. (p. 439)

11.4 Trace the development of young children's theory of mind, noting its consequences for belief-desire reasoning, and summarize the factors that contribute to young children's theory of mind. (pp. 439–442)

11.5 Discuss the development of self-concept from early childhood through adolescence, and note cognitive, social, and cultural influences on self-concept development. (pp. 444–446)

11.6 Summarize changes in self-esteem from early childhood through adolescence, including the impact of social comparison, cultural influences, and child-rearing practices. (pp. 447–452)

11.7 Describe the emergence of achievement-related attributions, distinguishing mastery-oriented and learned-helpless attributional styles, and summarize the factors that influence achievement-related attributions. (pp. 452–456)

11.8 Describe Marcia's four identity statuses, noting how each is related to psychological adjustment, and describe factors that influence identity development. (pp. 456–462)

11.9 Discuss gains in children's understanding of intention and person perception, including their developing understanding of ethnicity and social class. (pp. 462–465)

11.10 Trace the development of perspective taking from early childhood into adolescence, and explain the role of perspective taking skills in children's social behavior. (pp. 465–468)

11.11 Discuss the development of social problem solving, and cite ways to intervene with children who have weak social problem solving skills. (pp. 468–471)

STUDY QUESTIONS

1. Define *social cognition*. (pp. 435–436)

   _____

   _____

   _____

2. Cite four trends in children's development of social cognition. (p. 436)

   A. _____

   B. _____

   C. _____

   D. _____

3. True or False: Social cognition develops more slowly than nonsocial cognition. (p. 436)

4. List three features of social experience that probably help children make early sense of its complexity. (p. 436)

   A. _____

   B. _____

   C. _____

Emergence of Self and Development of Self-Concept

1. The earliest aspect of the self to emerge is the _____-self, a sense of self as knower and actor. Cite four realizations that are included in this aspect of self. (p. 436)

   A. _____

   B. _____

   C. _____

   D. _____

2. A second aspect of the self, the _____-self, is a sense of the self as an object of knowledge and evaluation. List three qualities that make up this component of self. (p. 437)

A. _____

B. _____

C. _____

Self-Awareness

1. Explain how the I-self emerges during the first few months of life. (p. 437)

   _____

   _____

   _____

   _____

2. Around age 2, _____-recognition—perception of the self as a physically distinctive being—is well established. (p. 438)

3. True or False: The development of self is fostered by sensitive caregiving. (p. 438)

4. Describe four ways in which self-awareness is associated with early emotional and social development. (p. 438)

A. _____

   _____

B. _____

   _____

C. _____

   _____

D. _____

   _____

The Categorical and Remembered Selves

1. Distinguish between the categorical and remembered selves. (p. 439)

Categorical: _____

_____

Remembered: _____

_____

Cultural Influences: Personal Storytelling—Implications for Early Self-Concept

1. Based on the ethnographic research of Peggy Miller, discuss differences in storytelling practices between Chinese and Irish-American parents and explain how these differences influence children's self-images. (p. 440)

_____

_____

_____

_____

The Inner Self: Young Children's Theory of Mind

1. Explain the *inner self*. (p. 439)

_____

_____

2. Distinguish between the *belief theory of mind* and the *belief–desire theory of mind*, noting the age at which each emerges. (p. 440)

Belief theory of mind: _____

_____

_____

Belief–desire theory of mind: _____

_____

_____

3. An illustration of belief-desire reasoning comes from games that test whether preschoolers know that _____ *beliefs*—ones that do not accurately represent reality—can guide people's actions. (p. 441)

4. Discuss four consequences of belief-desire reasoning for children's social development. (p. 441)

   A. _____

   _____

   B. _____

   _____

   C. _____

   _____

   D. _____

   _____

5. Discuss four factors that contribute to the development of children's theory of mind. (pp. 441–442)

   A. _____

   _____

   B. _____

   _____

   C. _____

   _____

   D. _____

   _____

Biology and Environment: "Mindblindness" and Autism

1. Describe the characteristics associated with infantile autism. (p. 443)

   _____

   _____

   _____

2. Researchers agree that infantile autism stems from abnormal _____ functioning, usually due to genetic or prenatal environmental causes. (p. 443)

3. Describe three hypotheses regarding the specific causes of autism. (p. 443)

   A. _____

   _____

   B. _____

   _____

   C. _____

   _____

Self-Concept

1. What is a *self-concept*? (p. 444)

   _____

   _____

2. Describe the quality of preschoolers' self-descriptions. (p. 444)

   _____

   _____

   _____

3. Explain how self-concept changes in middle childhood. (p. 444)

   _____

   _____

   _____

4. Discuss how the capacity to make social comparisons impacts children's self-concept during middle childhood. (p. 444)

   _____

   _____

   _____

5. True or False: Young adolescents often provide contradictory self-descriptions, for example, describing themselves as both shy and outgoing. (pp. 444–445)

6. Compared to school-age children, teenagers place (more / less) emphasis on social virtues, such as being friendly, considerate, kind, and cooperative. Why is this the case? (p. 445)

_____

_____

_____

Cognitive, Social, and Cultural Influences on Self-Concept

1. Cognitive development affects the changing _____ of the self, while both cognitive capacities and feedback from others produce changes in the _____ of the self. (p. 445)

2. George Herbert Mead referred to the self as a _____—a blend of what we imagine important people in our lives think of us. (p. 445)

3. Discuss the relationship between perspective-taking skills and self-concept development. (pp. 445–446)

_____

_____

_____

_____

4. True or False: Beginning in middle childhood, peers become more important than parents in children's self-definitions. (p. 446)

5. True or False: Self-concept development follows the same pattern in all societies. (p. 446)

Self-Esteem: The Evaluative Side of Self-Concept

1. Define *self-esteem*. (p. 447)

_____

_____

2. Research shows that preschoolers (do / do not) have several different self-esteems. (p. 448)

3. List four self-esteems that children form by the age of 6 to 7. (p. 448)

A. _____

B. _____

C. _____

D. _____

4. As children begin to combine their separate self-evaluations into a general psychological image of themselves, self-esteem takes on a _____ structure. (p. 448)

5. True or False: Separate self-evaluations contribute equally to general self-esteem. Briefly explain your response. (p. 448)

_____

_____

_____

6. Cite three new dimensions of self-esteem that emerge during adolescence. (pp. 448–449)

A. _____

B. _____

C. _____

7. Self-esteem (rises / drops) during the early elementary school years. Explain why this is the case. (p. 449)

_____

_____

_____

8. Except for temporary declines associated with _____, most individuals experience a rise in self-esteem during adolescence. (p. 449)

Influences on Self-Esteem

1. Chinese and Japanese children score (lower / higher) in self-esteem than do American children. Briefly explain why this is the case. (p. 450)

    _____

    _____

    _____

2. True or False: African-American children and adolescents have a higher self-esteem than do Caucasian-American children and adolescents. (p. 450)

3. Describe the child-rearing practices associated with high self-esteem for children and adolescents. (p. 451)

    _____

    _____

    _____

4. When parental support is _____, adolescents display false self-behavior, leading to a devaluation of their true selves that often results in low self-esteem, depression, and pessimism about the future. (p. 451)

From Research to Practice: How Should Parents Boost Their Children's Self-Esteem?

1. Over the past two decades, the self-esteem of children and adolescents has (increased / decreased). (pp. 450–451)

2. True or False: Children and adolescents with highly inflated self-esteem often exhibit serious adjustment problems. Briefly explain your response. (pp. 450–451)

    _____

    _____

    _____

3. Cross-cultural research shows that self-esteem is the (producer / product) of real accomplishment. (pp. 450–451)

Achievement-Related Attributions

1. _____ are common, everyday explanations for the causes of behavior. (p. 452)

2. Into what two broad categories do we group the causes of our own and others' behavior? (p. 452)

    A. _____

    B. _____

3. Define *achievement motivation*. (p. 452)

    _____

    _____

4. Around age _____, children begin making attributions about their successes and failures. (p. 452)

5. True or False: When making self-evaluations, preschoolers tend to rate their own ability as extremely low and often overestimate task difficulty. (p. 452)

6. True or False: Preschoolers readily internalize adult evaluations. (p. 452)

7. Distinguish between *mastery-oriented attributions* and *learned helplessness*, noting the differences between children who possess these attributional styles. (p. 453)

    Mastery-oriented attributions: _____

    _____

    _____

    Learned helplessness: _____

    _____

    _____

8. Differentiate between an *incremental view of ability* and an *entity view of ability*. (p. 453)

    Incremental view: _____

    _____

    Entity view: _____

    _____

9. Mastery-oriented children focus on _____ goals—increasing ability through effort and seeking information on how to do so, while learned-helpless children focus on _____ goals—obtaining positive and avoiding negative evaluations of their fragile sense of ability. (p. 453)

10. True or False: Over time, the ability of learned-helpless children no longer predicts their performance. Explain your response. (p. 453)

_____

_____

_____

11. Discuss the role of parent communication in accounting for children's development of learned-helpless attributions. (p. 454)

_____

_____

_____

12. Differentiate teacher behaviors that lead students to develop mastery-oriented attributions from those that lead students to develop learned-helpless attributions. (p. 454)

Mastery-oriented: _____

_____

Learned-helpless: _____

_____

13. True or False: Girls and low-income ethnic minority children are especially vulnerable to learned helplessness. (p. 454)

14. _____ is an intervention that encourages learned-helpless children to believe that they can overcome failure by exerting more effort. Describe this technique. (p. 454)

_____

_____

_____

Constructing an Identity

1. Discuss Erikson's notion of an *identity crisis*. (p. 456)

   _____

   _____

   _____

2. Current theorists (do / do not) agree with Erikson that the process of identity development constitutes a "crisis." (p. 456)

3. Match each of the following identity statuses with the appropriate description. (p. 457)

   _____ Committed to values and goals without taking
   time to explore alternatives

   _____ Have not yet made definite commitments and are
   still exploring alternatives

   _____ Committed to self-chosen values and goals after
   having already explored alternatives

   _____ Lack clear direction; are not committed to values
   and goals and are not actively seeking them

   1. Identity achievement
   2. Moratorium
   3. Identity foreclosure
   4. Identity diffusion

4. Most adolescents start out at "lower" statuses, such as _____ and _____, but by the time they reach their twenties, they have moved toward "higher" statuses, including _____ and _____. (p. 457)

5. True or False: Most adolescent girls follow a different path to identity formation than do boys: They postpone the task of establishing an identity, focusing instead on intimacy development. (p. 457)

6. True or False: Research supports the conclusion that identity achievement and moratorium are healthy routes to a mature self-definition, whereas identity foreclosure and identity diffusion are maladaptive. Elaborate on your answer. (p. 458)

   _____

   _____

   _____

   _____

7. Match the following identity statuses with the appropriate description of associated personality, familial, school, community, and larger cultural factors. Descriptions may apply to more than one identity status. (p. 457)

_____ Assume that absolute truth is always attainable
_____ Lack confidence in the prospect of ever knowing anything with certainty
_____ Appreciate that they can use rational criteria to choose among alternatives
_____ Feel attached to parents but are also free to voice their own opinions
_____ Have close bonds with parents but lack healthy separation
_____ Report the lowest levels of warm, open communication at home
_____ Fostered by classrooms that promote high-level thinking, as well as extracurricular and community activities that permit teens to take on responsible roles

1. Identity achievement
2. Moratorium
3. Identity foreclosure
4. Identity diffusion

Social Issues: Health—Adolescent Suicide: Annihilation of the Self

1. True or False: Suicide is currently the third leading cause of death among young people in the United States. (pp. 458–459)

2. True or False: Adolescent suicide rates are roughly equivalent in all industrialized countries. (pp. 458–459)

3. Discuss sex differences in suicidal behavior, noting whether boys or girls are more likely to kill themselves. (pp. 458–459)

_____

_____

_____

4. Compared with the white majority, nonwhite ethnic minority adolescents have (lower / higher) suicide rates. (pp. 458–459)

5. True or False: Gay, lesbian, and bisexual youth are three times more likely to attempt suicide than are other adolescents. (pp. 458–459)

6. List five warning signs of suicide. (pp. 458–459)

   A. _____

   B. _____

   C. _____

   D. _____

   E. _____

7. Describe two types of young people who tend to commit suicide. (pp. 458–459)

   A. _____

   _____

   B. _____

   _____

8. Discuss cognitive changes that contribute to the rise in suicide among adolescents. (pp. 458–459)

   _____

   _____

9. What types of treatments are available for depressed and suicidal adolescents? (pp. 458–459)

   _____

   _____

   _____

10. True or False: Teenage suicides often take place in clusters. Elaborate on your response. (pp. 458–459)

   _____

   _____

   _____

1. What is an *ethnic identity*? (p. 461)

    _____

    _____

2. Explain why ethnic minority adolescents often experience unique problems in developing a sense of identity. (p. 461)

    _____

    _____

    _____

3. Many minority high school students are _____ or _____ on ethnic identity issues. (p. 461)

4. List four ways in which minority adolescents can be helped to resolve identity conflicts constructively. (p. 461)

    A. _____

    B. _____

    C. _____

    D. _____

5. What is a *bicultural identity*, and how does it benefit minority adolescents? (p. 461)

    _____

    _____

    _____

Thinking About Other People

Understanding Intentions

1. Children begin to talk about intention by age _____—announcing behaviors that they are about to perform. (p. 462)

2. True or False: A 3-year-old believes that if statements and actions do not match, then the behavior was not intended. (p. 462)

3. Around age _____, children begin to appreciate intention as an internal mental state that is distinct from other mental states, as well as from the outcomes of behavior. (p. 462)

4. Between ages 5 and 9, children increasingly rely on a _____-_____ *consistency rule* to evaluate the sincerity of people's statements about their intentions. (p. 463)

Person Perception

1. What is *person perception*? (p. 463)

_____

_____

2. Before age _____, children's descriptions of others focus on commonly experienced emotions and attitudes, concrete activities, and behaviors. (p. 463)

3. Explain how children's descriptions of others change across late childhood and adolescence. (p. 463)

_____

_____

_____

4. True or False: Most 3- to 4-year-olds have formed basic concepts of race and ethnicity. (p. 463)

5. Indicators of social class are (more / less) accessible to young children than are indicators of race and ethnicity. (pp. 463–464)

6. Explain how children absorb prevailing societal attitudes toward social groups. (p. 464)

_____

_____

_____

7. Prejudice (increases / declines) in middle childhood. Explain why this is the case. (p. 464)

_____

_____

_____

8. Discuss three factors that influence childhood prejudice. (pp. 464–465)

A. _____

_____

B. _____

_____

C. _____

_____

Perspective Taking

1. What is *perspective taking*? (p. 465)

_____

_____

2. Name and describe Selman's five stages of perspective taking. (p. 466)

A. _____

_____

B. _____

_____

C. _____

_____

D. _____

_____

E. _____

_____

3. At what age do children understand that a person's prior knowledge affects that person's ability to understand new information? (p. 466) _____

4. _____ *thought*, the form of perspective taking that involves thinking about what another person is thinking, improves from middle childhood to adolescence. (p. 467)

5. Children in (individualistic / collectivist) cultures tend to do better on perspective taking tasks. (p. 468)

6. Explain the link between perspective-taking skills and social behavior. (p. 468)

_____

_____

_____

_____

7. True or False: Good perspective taking always results in prosocial behavior. Briefly explain your response. (p. 468)

_____

_____

_____

Thinking About Relations Between People: Understanding Conflict

1. List the six steps in Crick and Dodge's social problem-solving model. (p. 469)

A. _____

B. _____

C. _____

D. _____

E. _____

F. _____

2. Discuss how social problem solving affects peer relations. (p. 469)

_____

_____

_____

_____

3. Differentiate the social problem strategies of younger children and children with poor peer relations from those of older children and children with good peer relations. (p. 470)

Younger children and children with poor peer relations: _____

_____

_____

Older children and children with good peer relations: _____

_____

_____

4. Summarize the components of a social problem-solving training program for intervening with children who have weak social problem-solving skills. (pp. 470–471)

_____

_____

_____

_____

_____

ASK YOURSELF. . .

Review: What factors contribute to the development of a belief-desire theory of mind, and why is each influential? (p. 446)

_____

_____

_____

_____

_____

Review: Describe major changes in self-concept from early childhood to adolescence. What factors lead self-descriptions to change in these ways? (p. 446)

_____

_____

_____

_____

_____

Apply: List indicators of healthy self-development in the first 2 years, and suggest ways that parents can promote a sturdy sense of self in infants and toddlers. (p. 446)

_____

_____

_____

_____

_____

Connect: Recall from Chapter 6 (see page 237) that between 4 and 8 years, children figure out who is really behind the activities of Santa Claus and the Tooth Fairy, and they realize that magicians use trickery. How might these understandings relate to their developing theory of mind? (p. 446)

_____

_____

_____

_____

_____

Review: Describe and explain changes in the structure and level of self-esteem from early childhood to adolescence. (p. 456)

_____

_____

_____

_____

_____

Review: Describe mastery-oriented and learned-helpless children's differing views of ability. What impact do those views have on achievement motivation? (p. 456)

_____

_____

_____

_____

_____

Apply: Should parents promote children's self-esteem by telling them they're "smart" and "wonderful?" Is it harmful if children do not feel good about everything they do? Why or why not? How would you recommend that parents foster children's self-esteem? (p. 456)

_____

_____

_____

_____

_____

Connect: Why is the rise in self-esteem during the 1980s and 1990s, depicted in Figure 11.6, called a *cohort effect?* (See Chapter 2, page 58). (p. 456)

_____

_____

_____

_____

_____

Review: Explain how the four identity statuses are linked to psychological adjustment. (p. 462)

_____

_____

_____

_____

_____

Review: Cite personal and contextual factors that contribute to identity development. (p. 462)

_____

_____

_____

_____

_____

Apply: Frank and Vera worry that their 18-year-old son Jules will waste time at college because he is unsure about his major and his career goals. Explain why Jules's uncertainty might be advantageous for his identity development. (p. 462)

_____

_____

_____

_____

_____

Connect: Return to pages 444–445 and 448 to review changes in self-concept and self-esteem at adolescence. How might these changes pave the way for constructing an identity? (p. 462)

_____

_____

_____

_____

_____

Review: Describe changes in children's understanding of intention over the preschool years. (p. 468)

_____

_____

_____

_____

_____

Review: What factors account for variations in perspective-taking skills among children of the same age? How does perspective taking contribute to social development? (p. 468)

_____

_____

_____

_____

_____

Apply: Ten-year-old Marla is convinced that her classmate, Bernadette, who gets poor grades, is lazy. In contrast, Jane thinks Bernadette tries but can't concentrate because her parents are getting a divorce. Why is Marla more likely than Jane to harbor social prejudices? (p. 468)

_____

_____

_____

_____

_____

Connect: Children pass *false-belief* tasks around age 4, long before they understand that people's *preexisting beliefs* affect their viewpoints, between ages 6 and 8. Why is the latter understanding more difficult? (Hint: Note the difference between false-belief and perspective-taking tasks, described on page 465). (p. 468)

_____

_____

_____

_____

_____

Review: Using the social problem-solving steps in Figure 11.11, distinguish effective from ineffective social problem solvers. (p. 471)

_____

_____

_____

_____

_____

Connect: Does improved perspective taking contribute to gains in social problem solving from early to middle childhood? Explain. (p. 471)

_____

_____

_____

_____

_____

SUGGESTED STUDENT READINGS

Berk, L. E. (Ed.). (1999). *Landscapes of development: An anthology of readings.* Belmont, CA: Wadsworth. A collection of current reviews of research and essays by internationally recognized scholars and expert practitioners, each of which discusses applications to children's lives. An especially strong section on early childhood emotional and social development includes such topics as intersubjectivity in caregiver–child communication, young children's understanding of everyday emotions, discipline, bicultural development, and parent involvement in child protection programs.

Burack, J. A., Charman, T., Yirmiya, N., et al. (Eds.). (2001). *The development of autism: Perspectives from theory and research.* Mahwah, NJ: Lawrence Erlbaum Associates. Intended for students, researchers, and professionals interested in psychology and related fields, this book explores the development of children with autism by describing the following domains: family and genetic influences; perception and attention; cognition, theory of mind, and executive functioning; and social development and adaptive behaviors.

Kroger, J. (1999). *Identity development: Adolescence through adulthood.* Thousand Oaks, CA: Sage Publications. Presents the course of identity development throughout the lifespan by drawing on current theory and research. In addition, the author highlights the interactions between biological, social, and cultural forces that contribute to the identity process.

Rochat, P. (1999). *Early social cognition.* Mahwah, NJ: Erlbaum. Edited volume discussing current conceptualizations and research on the developmental origins of social cognition.

PUZZLE 11.1

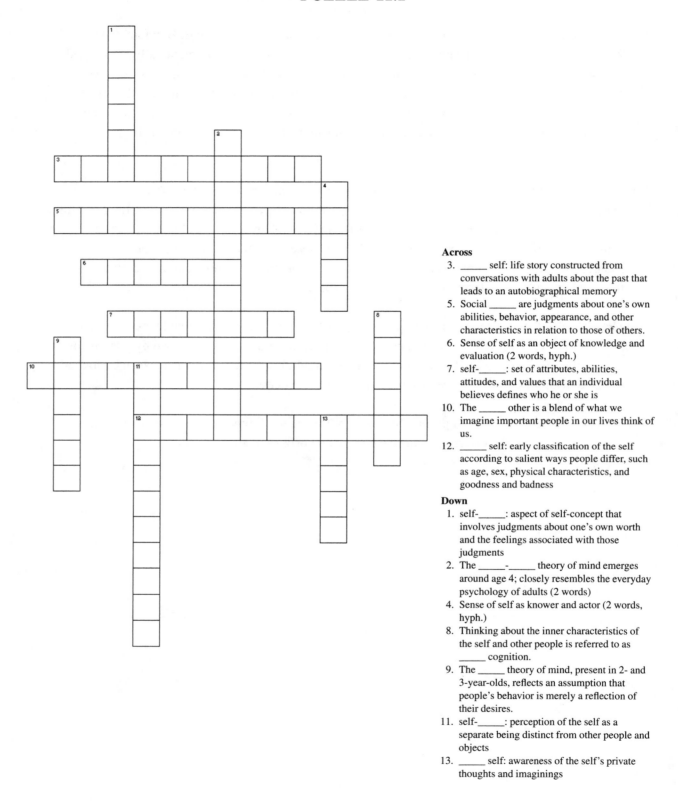

Across

3. _____ self: life story constructed from conversations with adults about the past that leads to an autobiographical memory
5. Social _____ are judgments about one's own abilities, behavior, appearance, and other characteristics in relation to those of others.
6. Sense of self as an object of knowledge and evaluation (2 words, hyph.)
7. self-_____: set of attributes, abilities, attitudes, and values that an individual believes defines who he or she is
10. The _____ other is a blend of what we imagine important people in our lives think of us.
12. _____ self: early classification of the self according to salient ways people differ, such as age, sex, physical characteristics, and goodness and badness

Down

1. self-_____: aspect of self-concept that involves judgments about one's own worth and the feelings associated with those judgments
2. The _____-_____ theory of mind emerges around age 4; closely resembles the everyday psychology of adults (2 words)
4. Sense of self as knower and actor (2 words, hyph.)
8. Thinking about the inner characteristics of the self and other people is referred to as _____ cognition.
9. The _____ theory of mind, present in 2- and 3-year-olds, reflects an assumption that people's behavior is merely a reflection of their desires.
11. self-_____: perception of the self as a separate being distinct from other people and objects
13. _____ self: awareness of the self's private thoughts and imaginings

PUZZLE 11.2

Across

4. The capacity to imagine what other people may be thinking and feeling is known as _____ taking.
5. Identity status of individuals who are exploring alternatives in an effort to find values and goals to guide their life
7. _____ problem solving: resolving conflicts in ways that are both acceptable to others and beneficial to the self
8. Those with an _____ view of ability regard ability as a fixed characteristic that cannot be improved through effort.
12. _____-_____ attributions credit success to high ability and failure to insufficient effort. (2 words)
15. A well-organized conception of the self made up of values, beliefs, and goals to which the individual is solidly committed
16. Achievement _____: tendency to persist at challenging tasks
17. _____ perception: the way individuals size up the attributes of people with whom they are familiar

Down

1. Identity _____: identity status of individuals who have explored and committed themselves to self-chosen values and goals
2. Learned _____ attributions credit success to external factors and failure to low ability.
3. _____ identity: identity constructed by adolescents who explore and adopt values from both their subculture and the dominant culture
6. Attribution _____ is an intervention that uses adult feedback to modify the attributions of learned-helpless children.
9. Those with an _____ view of ability believe that ability can be improved through effort.
10. Common, everyday explanations for the causes of behavior
11. Identity _____: identity status of individuals who have accepted ready-made values and goals that authority figures have chosen for them
13. Identity _____: identity status of individuals who do not have firm commitments to values and goals and are not actively trying to reach them
14. _____ thought: self-embedded form of perspective taking that involves thinking about what another person is thinking

353

PRACTICE TEST

1. Social cognition refers to: (p. 435)
   a. common everyday explanations for the causes of behavior.
   b. judgments of one's own abilities, appearance, and behavior in relation to those of others.
   c. resolving social conflicts in ways that are acceptable to others and beneficial to the self.
   d. thinking about the inner characteristics of the self and other people.

2. Which of the following terms refers to one's sense of self as an object of knowledge and evaluation? (p. 436)
   a. me-self
   b. I-self
   c. objective-self
   d. agentic-self

3. The beginnings of the I-self are grounded in: (p. 436)
   a. gains in perspective-taking.
   b. children's continually developing theory of mind.
   c. infants' recognition that their actions cause objects and people to react in predictable ways.
   d. infants' conscious awareness of the self's physical features.

4. By age 2, children have a well-developed sense of self-_____—perception of the self as a physically distinctive being. (p. 438)
   a. attribution
   b. concept
   c. recognition
   d. perception

5. When asked to describe himself, 2-year-old Josh says, "I am a big boy." What sense of self does this response represent? (p. 439)
   a. inner
   b. categorical
   c. remembered
   d. autonomous

6. Development of belief-desire reasoning is associated with gains in: (p. 440)
   a. perspective-taking.
   b. academic performance.
   c. social skills.
   d. self-esteem.

7. One factor that contributes to the development of the young child's theory of mind is: (p. 442)
   a. make-believe play.
   b. brain development.
   c. temperament.
   d. self-esteem.

8. Preschoolers' self-concepts are: (p. 444)
   a. concrete, typically focused on observable characteristics
   b. abstract, usually centered on their unique psychological characteristics
   c. internalized, since they cannot yet talk about their own subjective experiences
   d. based on stable personality traits

9. Compared to school-age children, adolescents place more emphasis on _____ in their self-descriptions. (p. 445)
   a. physical appearance
   b. favorite activities
   c. social virtues
   d. school performance

10. Based on George Herbert Mead's conception of the self, the ability to _____ is critical to the development of self-concept based on personality traits. (p. 445)
    a. become introspective
    b. compare one's own abilities and behaviors to those of others
    c. imagine what important people in our lives think of us
    d. resolve the Oedipal and Elektra conflicts

11. During middle childhood: (p. 448)
    a. children form at least four separate self-esteems.
    b. self-evaluations across multiple domains contribute equally to general self-esteem.
    c. children's overall sense of self-esteem is replaced by their separate self-evaluations regarding academic, social, and athletic competence and physical appearance.
    d. most children experience a steady increase in self-esteem.

12. Which of the following is true? (p. 450)
    a. Self-esteem is typically high across early and middle childhood and shows a dramatic drop in adolescence
    b. In adolescence, boys score lower than girls in overall sense of self-worth.
    c. African-American children and adolescents tend to have higher self-esteem than Caucasian-American children and adolescents.
    d. Adolescents exhibit higher self-esteem when parental support is conditional.

13. Preschoolers: (p. 452)
    a. hold negative expectancies of success on learning tasks.
    b. tend to rate their own ability as very high.
    c. often overestimate task difficulty.
    d. explain successes and failures based on both effort and ability.

14. Children who develop learned helplessness: (p. 453)
    a. have an incremental view of ability; that is, they think that ability can be altered through effort.
    b. tend to attribute their failures, but not their successes, to ability.
    c. often persevere on difficult tasks in an effort to gain a sense of mastery and competence.
    d. focus on learning goals rather than performance goals.

15. Attribution retraining: (p. 454)
    a. works best when begun in late childhood or early adolescence.
    b. provides children with easy tasks in order to prevent failure and negative attributions.
    c. teaches low-effort children to focus less on learning and more on grades.
    d. encourages children to view their successes as due to both ability and effort rather than chance factors.

16. Research on identity construction indicates that: (p. 457)
    a. most adolescents experience a serious identity crisis.
    b. adolescents typically retain the same identity status across adolescence and early adulthood.
    c. girls often postpone the task of identity development to focus instead on intimacy development.
    d. adolescents who go to work after high school settle on an identity status earlier than do college-bound youths.

17. Kieran has followed the religious path of his family without exploring alternatives and tends to be defensive when his teenage friends bring up the subject. Kieran is: (p. 457)
    a. identity foreclosed.
    b. identity diffused.
    c. in moratorium.
    d. identity achieved.

18. Adolescents who lack confidence in the prospect of ever knowing anything with certainty and who report low levels of warm, open communication in the home are likely to have which identity status? (p. 457)
    a. identity achievement
    b. moratorium
    c. identity foreclosure
    d. identity diffusion

19. At what age do children become sensitive to behavioral cues that help them tell if another person is acting intentionally? (p. 462)
    a. 14- to 18-months
    b. 2½ to 3 years
    c. 4 years
    d. between 5 and 9 years

20. Which of the following is true with regard to children's understanding of ethnicity and social class? (p. 464)
    a. Children form basic concepts of race and ethnicity between 12- and 18-months.
    b. Children understand the concept social class before they understand the concepts of race and ethnicity.
    c. Children begin to absorb prevailing societal attitudes toward social groups during early adolescence.
    d. Prejudice declines in middle childhood.

21. Children are more likely to hold prejudicial attitudes if: (p. 464)
    a. they have very high self-esteem.
    b. they view personality as changeable.
    c. adults highlight similarities between groups.
    d. they are members of an out-group.

22. The capacity to imagine what other people may be thinking and feeling is known as: (p. 465)
    a. social comparison.
    b. person perception.
    c. perspective taking.
    d. attributional perception.

23. During which of Selman's stages of perspective taking can children "step into another person's shoes" and view their feelings and behavior from the other person's perspective? (p. 466)
    a. self-reflective perspective taking
    b. third-party perspective taking
    c. societal perspective taking
    d. undifferentiated perspective taking

24. Perspective taking tasks for older children and adolescents focus on _____—thinking about what another person is thinking. (p. 467)
    a. metacognition
    b. recursive thought
    c. reflective thought
    d. empathic thought

25. During the early school years, social problem solving: (p. 470)
   a. is deficient in most children.
   b. is directed exclusively toward the child's own needs rather than the mutual needs of the self and others.
   c. is unrelated to socially competent behavior.
   d. profoundly affects peer relations.

CHAPTER 12
MORAL DEVELOPMENT

BRIEF CHAPTER SUMMARY

Accompanying the emergence of self-awareness and new representational capacities in the second year is another crowning achievement: The child becomes a moral being. What accounts for the early emergence of morality and children's expanding appreciation of standards of conduct with age? According to the biological perspective, morality is grounded in our genetic heritage through prewired emotional reactions. Although psychoanalytic and social learning theories offer different accounts of moral development, both emphasize internalization—the adoption of societal standards for right action as one's own.

Contrary to predictions from Freudian theory, emphasizing power assertion or love withdrawal does not promote conscience formation. Instead, induction, against a backdrop of nurturance, is far more effective. Social learning theorists have shown that modeling combined with reinforcement is effective in encouraging prosocial acts. In contrast, harsh punishment promotes only temporary compliance, not lasting changes in children's behavior. Overall, the most effective forms of discipline encourage good conduct.

The cognitive-developmental perspective regards construction—actively thinking about multiple aspects of situations in which social conflicts arise and deriving new moral insights—as central to moral development. Piaget's work was the original inspiration for this perspective. However, although Piaget's theory describes the general direction of moral development, it underestimates the moral capacities of young children.

According to Kohlberg, moral reasoning advances through three levels, each of which contains new stages. Moral reasoning is influenced by the young person's personality and a wide range of social experiences, such as peer interaction, child-rearing practices, schooling, and aspects of culture. In addition, emotions, temperament, personality and history of morally relevant experience contribute to the maturity of moral reasoning. The emergence of self-control is supported by self-awareness and representational and memory capacities.

Aggression, which first appears in late infancy, takes the form of either instrumental or hostile aggression. While boys tend to express overt aggression, girls display relational aggression. The incidence of delinquent acts rises in the teenage years, but few adolescents become recurrent offenders. Conduct problems that began in childhood are far more likely to persist than are those that first appear in adolescence. Although impulsive, overactive children are at risk for high aggression, whether they become so depends on child-rearing conditions. Among interventions designed to reduce aggression, procedures based on social learning theory and on social-cognitive theory are beneficial.

LEARNING OBJECTIVES

After reading this chapter, you should be able to:

12.1 Describe and evaluate the biological perspective of morality. (pp. 476–477)

12.2 Compare and evaluate psychoanalytic and social learning perspectives of moral development. (pp. 477–484)

12.3 Describe Piaget's theory of moral development and Kohlberg's extension of it, noting research that evaluates the accuracy of each. (pp. 484–492)

12.4 Discuss sex differences in moral reasoning, with particular attention to Gilligan's argument. (pp. 492–493)

12.5 Summarize influences on moral development, including personality, peer interaction, child-rearing practices, schooling, and culture. (pp. 493–495)

12.6 Explain how children distinguish moral imperatives from social conventions and matters of personal choice and trace changes in their understanding from childhood into adolescence. (pp. 498–501)

12.7 Discuss changes in children's concept of distributive justice over early and middle childhood. (pp. 501–502)

12.8 Trace the development of self-control from early childhood into adolescence, noting findings from Mischel's longitudinal research on individual differences in development of self-control. (pp. 502–506)

12.9 Trace the development of aggression from early childhood into adolescence, noting familial, community, and cultural influences. (pp. 507–512)

12.10 Describe successful interventions for helping children and parents control aggression. (pp. 512–515)

STUDY QUESTIONS

1. Summarize the three components of morality. (p. 476)

    A. _____

    _____

360

B. _____

_____

C. _____

_____

2. True or False: Research reveals that the three components of morality represent separate, unrelated facets. (p. 476)

Morality as Rooted in Human Nature

1. True or False: Researchers have identified a region of the brain which is vital for emotional responsiveness to the suffering of others and to one's own misdeeds. (p. 477)

2. Mortality (can / cannot) be fully explained by its biological foundations. Elaborate on your response. (p. 477)

_____

_____

_____

Morality as the Adoption of Societal Norms

1. Both psychoanalytic and social learning theories regard moral development as a matter of _____—adopting societal standards for right action as one's own. (p. 477)

2. List four factors that jointly affect the child's willingness to adopt societal standards. (p. 477)

A. _____

B. _____

C. _____

D. _____

Psychoanalytic Theory

1. Summarize Freud's psychoanalytic theory of moral development. (p. 478)

_____

_____

2. True or False: Most researchers agree with Freud's assertion that fear of punishment and loss of parental love motivate children to behave morally. (p. 478)

3. A special type of discipline called _____ supports conscience development by pointing out the effects of the child's misbehavior on others. Cite three ways in which it does so. (p. 478)

    A. _____

    _____

    B. _____

    _____

    C. _____

    _____

4. Why is discipline that relies too heavily on threats of punishment less effective than induction? (p. 479)

    _____

5. True or False: Recent research shows that Freud was incorrect in his assertion that guilt is an important motivator of moral action. (p. 479)

6. Recent psychoanalytic theories underscore the importance of a positive parent-child relationship, emphasizing _____ as a vital foundation for acquiring moral standards. (p. 479)

7. True or False: Current psychoanalytic theorists believe that positive guidelines, or "do's," are just as likely as prohibitions, or "don'ts," to influence children's superego development. (p. 479)

From Research to Practice: Temperament and Moral Internalization in Young Children

1. Contrast parenting practices that best promote responsibility and concern for others among temperamentally inhibited children and fearless, impulsive children. (p. 480)

    Inhibited children: _____

    _____

Fearless, impulsive children: _____

_____

2. Explain why secure attachment is predictive of conscience development in non-anxious children. (p. 480)

_____

_____

_____

Social Learning Theory

1. Why is operant conditioning insufficient for children to acquire moral responses? (p. 481)

_____

_____

2. Social learning theorists believe that children learn to behave morally largely through _____—observing and imitating adults who demonstrate appropriate behavior. (p. 481)

3. List three characteristics of models that affect children's willingness to imitate them. (p. 481)

   A. _____

   B. _____

   C. _____

4. Models exert their strongest influence during the (preschool / elementary school) years. (p. 481)

5. True or False: Punishment promotes immediate compliance but does not produce long-lasting changes in children's behavior. (p. 481)

6. List three undesirable side effects of harsh punishment. (p. 482)

   A. _____

   B. _____

   C. _____

7. Describe two alternatives to harsh punishment. (p. 482)

   A. _____

   _____

   B. _____

   _____

8. Describe three ways that parents can increase the effectiveness of punishment when they do decide to use it. (p. 483)

   A. _____

   _____

   B. _____

   _____

   C. _____

   _____

9. Explain *positive discipline*, noting how it reduces the need for punishment. (p. 483)

   _____

   _____

   _____

Limitations of "Morality as the Adoption of Societal Norms" Perspective

1. Cite one criticism of the psychoanalytic and social learning theories' view of moral development as a process of internalizing societal norms. (p. 484)

   _____

   _____

   _____

2. According to cognitive-developmental theorists, individuals develop morality through _____—the process in which children actively attend to and interrelate multiple aspects of situations in which social conflicts arise and derive new moral understandings. Elaborate on how this process takes place. (p. 484)

_____

_____

_____

Morality as Social Understanding

Piaget's Theory of Moral Development

1. Describe the main characteristics of Piaget's heteronomous and autonomous stages of moral development, noting the age at which children display each type of moral understanding. (p. 485)

   Heteronomous: _____

   _____

   Age: _____

   Autonomous: _____

   _____

   Age: _____

2. According to Piaget, what two factors limit children's moral understanding during the period of heteronomous morality? (p. 485)

   A. _____

   B. _____

3. During the period of heteronomous morality, children's moral understanding is characterized by _____—that is, they regard rules as external features of reality rather than as cooperative principles that can be modified at will. (p. 485)

4. Children gradually start to use a standard of fairness called _____, in which they express the same concern for the welfare of others as they do for themselves. (p. 485)

5. Explain the concept of *ideal reciprocity*, the advanced view of reciprocity developed by older children and adolescents. (p. 485)

   _____

   _____

Evaluation of Piaget's Theory

1. True or False: Piaget's theory accurately describes the general direction of change in moral judgment. (p. 485)

2. Piaget (underestimated / overestimated) young children's ability to make moral judgments. (p. 486)

3. True or False: Research supports Piaget's contention that young children regard adults with unquestioning authority. (p. 486)

4. When questioned about moral issues in a way that makes a person's intent stand out as strongly as the harm they do, preschool and early school-age children (are / are not) capable of judging ill-intentioned people as naughtier than well-intentioned ones. (p. 486)

Kohlberg's Extension of Piaget's Theory

1. Explain how Kohlberg's approach to the study of moral development differed from that of Piaget. (p. 487)

    _____

    _____

    _____

2. In Kohlberg's _____ *Interview*, individuals resolve dilemmas that present conflicts between two moral values. (p. 487)

3. True or False: Kohlberg emphasized that it is the *way an individual reasons* about a dilemma, not the *content of the response*, which determines moral maturity. (p. 487)

4. Name the most recently developed questionnaire instrument for assessing moral reasoning. (p. 488)

    _____

5. Describe the benefits of using the SRM-SF instead of the Moral Judgment Interview. (p. 488)

    _____

    _____

    _____

6. Cite three generalizations that Kohlberg made in relation to the sequence of his six stages of moral development. (p. 488)

    A. _____

    _____

B. _____

_____

C. _____

_____

7. List two factors that Kohlberg believed to promote moral understanding. (p. 488)

A. _____

B. _____

8. Explain the basic characteristics of moral reasoning at each of Kohlberg's three levels: (pp. 488–490)

Preconventional: _____

_____

Conventional: _____

_____

Postconventional: _____

_____

9. Match each of the following moral orientations with the appropriate description. (pp. 488–490)

_____ Laws must be obeyed under all circumstances; rules must be enforced in the same even-handed manner for everyone, and each member of society has a personal duty to uphold them

_____ Right action is defined by self-chosen ethical principles of conscience that are valid for all humanity, regardless of law and social agreement

_____ Ignore people's intentions and focus on fear of authority and avoidance of punishment as reasons for behaving morally

_____ Desire to obey rules because they promote social harmony

_____ Regard laws and rules as flexible and emphasize fair procedures for interpreting and changing the law in order to protect individual rights and the interests of the majority

_____ View right action as flowing from self-interest; reciprocity is understood as equal exchange of favors

1. Punishment and obedience orientation
2. Instrumental purpose orientation
3. "Good boy-good girl" orientation
4. Social-order-maintaining orientation
5. Social contract orientation
6. Universal ethical principle orientation

Research on Kohlberg's Stages

1. True or False: Longitudinal research suggests that individuals do not move through the stages of moral development in the order in which Kohlberg suggested. (p. 490)

2. True or False: The development of moral understanding is very slow and gradual. (p. 490)

3. Moral reasoning for real-life problems tends to fall at a (lower / higher) stage than does reasoning related to hypothetical dilemmas. Explain why this is the case. (p. 491)

_____

_____

_____

4. True or False: Kohlberg's stages develop in a neat, stepwise fashion. (p. 491)

5. True or False: Moral maturity is positively correlated with IQ, cognitive capacities, and perspective-taking skills. (p. 491)

6. Kohlberg argued that cognitive and perspective-taking capacities (are / are not) sufficient to ensure moral advances. (p. 491)

7. Match each of Kohlberg's moral stages with its parallel cognitive and perspective-taking stages. (p. 492)

KOHLBERG'S MORAL STAGE	PIAGET'S COGNITIVE STAGE	SELMAN'S PERSPECTIVE-TAKING STAGE
1. Punishment and obedience	___ Formal operational	___ Societal
2. Instrumental purpose	___ Concrete operational	___ Self-reflective
3. "Good boy-good girl"	___ Early formal operational	___ Third-party
4. Social-order maintaining	___ Preoperational, early	___ Social-informational
5. Social-contract	concrete operational	
6. Universal ethical principle		

Are There Sex-Related Differences in Moral Reasoning?

1. Carol Gilligan believes that feminine morality emphasizes an _____ *of* _____ that is devalued in Kohlberg's model. Explain what she meant by this. (p. 492)

_____

_____

_____

2. True or False: Research shows that when given a moral dilemma, females fall behind males in moral development according to Kohlberg's scheme, thus supporting Gilligan's claims. (p. 492)

3. Current evidence indicates that justice and caring (are / are not) gender-specific moralities. (p. 493)

Influences on Moral Reasoning

1. What characteristics of personality are associated with gains in moral reasoning? (p. 493)

_____

_____

2. Explain how peer conflict contributes to gains in moral reasoning. (p. 493)

_____

_____

_____

3. Cite two aspects of peer discussion that stimulate moral development. (p. 494)

A. _____

B. _____

4. Describe child-rearing practices that promote gains in moral development. (p. 494)

_____

_____

_____

5. True or False: Years of schooling is one of the most powerful predictors of moral maturity. (p. 494)

6. True or False: Cross-cultural research shows that individuals in technologically advanced, urban cultures move through Kohlberg's stages more quickly and advance to higher levels of moral reasoning than do individuals in village societies. Based on your response, provide some possible explanations. (pp. 494–495)

_____

_____

_____

_____

Moral Reasoning and Behavior

1. There is a (weak / moderate / strong) relationship between moral thought and action. (p. 496)

2. What is *moral self-relevance*? (p. 496)

_____

_____

Social Issues: Education—Development of Civic Responsibility

1. Civic responsibility involves _____ of political issues and the means through which citizens can resolve differing views fairly; _____ of attachment to the community, of wanting to make a difference in its welfare, and of trust in others' fairness and helpfulness; and _____ for achieving civic goals. (pp. 496–497)

2. Summarize family, school, and community influences that contribute to adolescents' civic responsibility. (pp. 496–497)

Family: _____

_____

School: _____

_____

Community: _____

_____

3. Cite two aspects of involvement in extracurricular activities and youth organizations that account for their lasting impact. (pp. 496–497)

A. _____

B. _____

Further Questions About Kohlberg's Theory

1. A key controversy regarding Kohlberg's theory has to do with his belief that moral maturity is not achieved until the _____ level. (p. 497)

2. Kohlberg's theory tells us little about moral understanding in (early and middle childhood / adolescence and adulthood). (p. 498)

Distinguishing Moral, Social-Conventional, and Personal Domains

1. Preschoolers are able to distinguish _____ *imperatives*, which protect people's rights and welfare, from two other forms of action: _____ *conventions*, or customs determined solely by consensus, such as table manners and dress style, and *matters of* _____, which do not violate rights or harm others, are not socially regulated, and therefore are up to the individual. (pp. 498–499)

2. Explain how young children learn to make distinctions between moral and social-conventional transgressions. (p. 499)

   _____

   _____

   _____

3. Cite four changes in the understanding of moral imperatives and social conventions that take place during early and middle childhood. (p. 499)

   A. _____

   B. _____

   C. _____

   D. _____

4. Justice considerations (do / do not) appear to be a universal feature of moral thought. (p. 499–501)

5. A unique domain of personal matters emerges with self-awareness in the (preschool / elementary school) years. (p. 501)

6. True or False: When children and adolescents challenge adult authority, they typically do so within the personal domain. (p. 501)

Social Issues: Education—Children's Environmental Moral Reasoning

1. True or False: In a study by Peter Kahn, Houston children from poverty-stricken African-American neighborhoods reported that animals, plants, and open spaces were not important to their lives. (p. 500)

2. True or False: Children from American, Brazilian, and Portuguese cultures all regard polluting the environment as a moral violation. (p. 500)

3. List and describe three forms of environmental moral reasoning. (p. 500)

   A. _____
      _____

   B. _____
      _____

   C. _____
      _____

4. Anthropocentric and biocentric reasoning (decrease / increase) with age. (p. 500)

5. True or False: Environmental moral reasoning differs greatly from culture to culture due to wide variations in people's experiences. (p. 500)

Distributive Justice

1. Define *distributive justice*. (p. 501)

   _____
   _____

2. Preschoolers recognize the importance of sharing, but their reasons often seem _____. (p. 501)

3. Trace the development of children's conception of distributive justice during middle childhood. (p. 501)

   A. _____

   B. _____

   C. _____

4. True or False: Peer interaction is particularly important in the development of standards of justice. (p. 502)

Beginnings of Self-Control

1. Define *self-control*, and list three developmental milestones which are essential for the development of this capacity. (pp. 502–503)

   A. _____

   B. _____

   C. _____

2. The first glimmerings of self-control appear in the form of _____—voluntary obedience to requests and commands. At what age does this occur? _____ (p. 503)

3. Researchers typically study self-control using *delay of* _____ tasks which require the child to wait for an appropriate time and place to engage in a tempting act or to obtain a desired object. (p. 504)

4. What type of parenting facilitates children's development of self-control? (p. 504)

   _____

   _____

Development of Self-Control in Childhood and Adolescence

1. Discuss Mischel's research on the development of self-control strategies in preschool children. (p. 504)

   _____

   _____

   _____

   _____

2. By the elementary school years, self-control has been transformed into a flexible capacity for _____—the ability to monitor one's own conduct, constantly adjusting it as circumstances present opportunities to violate inner standards. (pp. 504–505)

3. Summarize changes in children's knowledge of self-regulation strategies from middle to late childhood. (p. 505)

_____

_____

_____

_____

4. True or False: Longitudinal research shows modest stability in children's capacity to manage their behavior in a morally relevant fashion. (p. 505)

5. Distinguish the characteristics of Metcalfe and Mischel's Hot and Cool Processing Systems, which govern the development of self-control. (pp. 505–506)

Hot: _____

_____

_____

Cool: _____

_____

_____

6. True or False: With age, the hot and cool systems become increasingly segregated. Elaborate on your response. (p. 506)

_____

_____

_____

The Other Side of Self-Control: Development of Aggression

Emergence of Aggression

1. By the end of the preschool years, two general types of aggression emerge. The most common is _____ aggression, aimed at obtaining an object, privilege, or space with no deliberate intent to harm. The other type is _____ aggression, which is intended to hurt another person. (p. 507)

374

2. Distinguish between *overt aggression* and *relational aggression*. (p. 507)

Overt: _____

_____

Relational: _____

_____

Aggression in Early and Middle Childhood

1. Physical aggression is gradually replaced by _____ aggression after age 2. What developmental capacity contributes to this change? (p. 507)

_____

2. For most preschoolers, instrumental aggression (declines / increases) with age. Why is this the case? (p. 507)

_____

_____

3. Hostile outbursts (decline / increase) over early and middle childhood. Why is this the case? (p. 507)

_____

_____

4. Summarize sex differences in aggression, noting factors that contribute to these differences. (pp. 507–508)

_____

_____

_____

_____

Aggression and Delinquency in Adolescence

1. Young people under the age of 21 account for _____ percent of police arrests in the United States. (p. 508)

2. Explain why delinquency rises during early adolescence, remains high in middle adolescence, and then declines into young adulthood. (p. 508)

_____

_____

_____

Stability of Aggression

1. Describe the stability of aggression from kindergarten into adolescence, noting what group of children is most likely to become involved in violent delinquency in adolescence. (p. 508)

    _____

    _____

    _____

    _____

2. Conduct problems are more likely to persist when they emerge in (childhood / adolescence). (p. 509)

Biology and Environment: Two Routes to Adolescent Delinquency

1. Persistent adolescent delinquency follows two paths of development, one with an onset of _____ problems in childhood, the second with an onset in _____. Longitudinal research reveals that the (early / late) onset type is far more likely to lead to a life course pattern of aggression and criminality. (pp. 510–511)

2. True or False: Adolescent-onset delinquent youth show significantly higher levels of serious offenses, involvement with deviant peers, substance abuse, unsafe sex, dangerous driving, and time spent in correctional facilities than do childhood-onset delinquent youth. (pp. 510–511)

3. Describe characteristics that distinguish early-onset from late-onset delinquent youth. (pp. 510–511)

    Early-onset: _____

    _____

    Late-onset: _____

    _____

The Family as Training Ground for Aggressive Behavior

1. Describe child-rearing practices associated with antisocial behavior from early childhood through adolescence. (pp. 509–510)

    _____

    _____

    _____

2. (Boys / Girls) are more likely to be targets of angry, inconsistent discipline. (p. 510)

3. Explain how parents sometimes encourage aggression indirectly. (p. 511)

_____

_____

_____

Social-Cognitive Deficits and Distortions

1. Aggressive children often see _____ intent where it does not exist—in situations where a peer's intentions are unclear, where harm is accidental, and even where a peer is trying to be helpful. (p. 511)

2. True or False: Compared to their non-aggressive agemates, aggressive children are convinced that there are more benefits and fewer costs for engaging in hostile acts. Explain your response. (pp. 511–512)

_____

_____

_____

3. Many aggressive children have (low / high) self-esteem. (p. 512)

4. Explain how sex differences in social cognition may contribute to girls' lower rates of antisocial activity. (p. 512)

_____

_____

_____

Community and Cultural Influences

1. Discuss the link between neighborhood conditions and development of aggression. (p. 512)

_____

_____

_____

Cultural Influences: Impact of Ethnic and Political Violence on Children

1. Discuss children's adjustment to ethnic and political violence, noting differences between situations involving temporary crises and those involving chronic danger. (p. 513)

    _____

    _____

    _____

    _____

2. What is the best safeguard against lasting problems? (p. 513)

    _____

3. Discuss some interventions used to help children from Public School 31 in Brooklyn, New York in the wake of the September 11 attack on the World Trade Center. (p. 513)

    _____

    _____

    _____

    _____

Helping Children and Parents Control Aggression

1. Summarize the components of parent and child intervention programs for controlling aggression that are based on the principles of social learning theory. (pp. 512–514)

    _____

    _____

    _____

2. Social-cognitive treatments focus on improving _____ in antisocial youths. (p. 514)

3. Cite four components of a comprehensive treatment approach for helping antisocial children and adolescents. (p. 514)

    A. _____

    B. _____

    C. _____

    D. _____

4. In a program called EQUIP, _____—an adult-guided but youth-conducted small-group approach designed to create a climate in which prosocial acts replace antisocial behavior—served as a basis for treatment. What other techniques were used to supplement the program? (p. 514)

_____

_____

_____

ASK YOURSELF. . .

Review: Describe evidence suggesting that many morally relevant behaviors have roots in our evolutionary history. (p. 484)

_____

_____

_____

_____

_____

Review: Summarize the main features of the psychoanalytic and social learning perspectives on moral development. Why has each been criticized? (p. 484)

_____

_____

_____

_____

_____

Apply: Alice and Wayne want their two young children to develop a strong, internalized conscience and to become generous, caring individuals. Recommend parenting practices that would promote these goals, explaining why each is effective. (p. 484)

_____

_____

_____

_____

_____

Connect: What social-cognitive capacities discussed in Chapter 11 are probably fostered by inductive discipline? Explain. (p. 484)

_____

_____

_____

_____

_____

Review: Compare and contrast the moral development theories of Piaget and Kohlberg. Cite major criticisms of each. (p. 498)

_____

_____

_____

_____

_____

Review: How does an understanding of *ideal reciprocity* contribute to moral development? Why might Kohlberg's Stages 3 and 4 be morally mature constructions? At which stage is Leisl's reasoning about the elderly woman to be evicted from her home, presented in the introduction of the chapter? Explain. (p. 498)

_____

_____

_____

_____

_____

Apply: Tam grew up in a small village culture, Lydia in a large industrial city. At age 15, Tam reasons at Kohlberg's Stage 2, Lydia at Stage 4. What factors probably account for the differences? Is Lydia's reasoning morally mature? Explain. (p. 498)

_____

_____

_____

_____

_____

Connect: What experiences that promote mature moral reasoning are also likely to foster identity development? Explain. (See Chapter 11, page 460). (p. 498)

_____

_____

_____

_____

_____

Review: What experiences help children differentiate moral imperatives, social conventions, and matters of personal choice? How does children's understanding change from early to middle childhood? (p. 506)

_____

_____

_____

_____

_____

Apply: Parker Elementary School will give a cash reward to the classroom that sells the most raffle tickets for the school fundraiser. Children in the winning classroom will decide how to divide the award fairly. How are first through third graders likely to differ in their decision making? (p. 506)

_____

_____

_____

_____

_____

Connect: Explain how school-age children's understanding of moral imperatives, social conventions, and distributive justice takes into account an increasing number of variables. What cognitive and social-cognitive changes, discussed in Chapters 6 and 11, probably support these advances? (p. 506)

_____

_____

_____

_____

_____

Review: Cite factors that contribute to an improved ability to delay gratification from early to middle childhood, and explain why each makes a difference. (p. 515)

_____

_____

_____

_____

_____

Review: What temperamental, child-rearing, and social-cognitive factors are associated with persistence of high-level childhood aggression into adolescence? (p. 515)

_____

_____

_____

_____

_____

Apply: Zeke had been a well-behaved child in elementary school, but around age 13, he started spending time with the "wrong crowd." At age 16, he was arrested for property damage. Is Zeke likely to become a long-term offender? Why or why not? (p. 515)

_____

_____

_____

_____

_____

Connect: Reread the section on adolescent parenthood in Chapter 5 (pages 208–212) and the section on adolescent suicide in Chapter 11 (pages 458–459). How would you explain the findings that teenagers who experience one of these difficulties are likely to display others? (p. 515)

_____

_____

_____

_____

_____

SUGGESTED STUDENT READINGS

Bohart, A. C., & Stipek, D. J. (Eds.). (2001). *Constructive and destructive behavior: Implications for family, school, and society.* Washington: The American Psychological Association. An interdisciplinary collection of research, this book explores the influence of constructive and prosocial behavior on destructive and antisocial tendencies. Other topics include the effects of media violence on real-life violence, how self-control in childhood predicts adult behavior, how age and sex influence bullying, and whether early intervention can successfully prevent delinquency.

Hoffman, M. L. (2000). *Empathy and moral development: Implications for caring and justice.* New York: Cambridge University Press. Presents a comprehensive approach to studying and understanding moral development in young children. The author also examines the psychological processes involved in the development of empathy and altruism in a variety of situations.

Reed, D. R. C. (1998). *Following Kohlberg: Liberalism and the practice of democratic community.* Notre Dame, IN: University of Notre Dame Press. Describes Kohlberg's psychological studies and data, his philosophical and theoretical conceptions of morality, and the educational interventions in prisons and schools that he developed to put this theory into practice.

Straus, M. A. (2001). *Beating the devil out of them: Corporal punishment in American families and its effects on children.* Written primarily for parents, teachers, social workers, and other professionals who work with children, this book presents the negative effects of physical punishment on child development.

PUZZLE 12.1

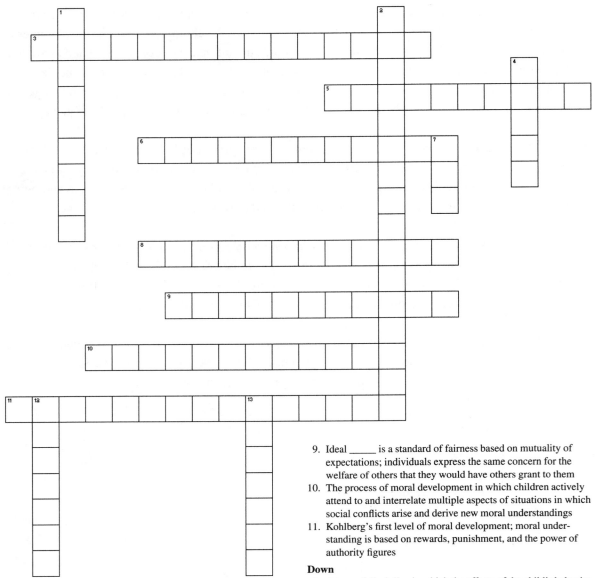

Across

3. The process of adopting societal standards for right action as one's own
5. _____ morality: Piaget's second stage of moral development in which children view rules as flexible, socially-agreed-on principles that can be revised to suit the will of the majority
6. _____ morality: Piaget's first stage of moral development in which children view rules as permanent and unchangeable
8. Kohlberg's second level of moral development; moral understanding is based on conforming to social rules to ensure positive relationships and societal order
9. Ideal _____ is a standard of fairness based on mutuality of expectations; individuals express the same concern for the welfare of others that they would have others grant to them
10. The process of moral development in which children actively attend to and interrelate multiple aspects of situations in which social conflicts arise and derive new moral understandings
11. Kohlberg's first level of moral development; moral understanding is based on rewards, punishment, and the power of authority figures

Down

1. A type of discipline in which the effects of the child's behavior on others are communicated to the child
2. Kohlberg's highest level of moral development; individuals define morality in terms of abstract principles and values that apply to all situations and societies
4. _____ dilemma: conflict situation presented to research participants, who are asked to decide what the actor should do and why
7. _____-SF: questionnaire for assessing moral understanding (abbr.)
12. View of rules as external features of reality rather than cooperative principles that can be modified at will
13. Form of mild punishment in which children are removed from the immediate setting until they are ready to act appropriately (2 words)

Across

1. Matters of _____ choice: concerns that do not violate rights or harm others, are not socially regulated, and are therefore up to the individual

6. Distributive _____: beliefs about how to divide resources fairly

7. Delay of _____: waiting for a more appropriate time and place to engage in a tempting act or obtain a desired object

11. Self-_____: inhibiting an impulse to engage in behavior that violates a moral standard

12. _____ aggression is intended to harm another person.

13. Moral self-_____: degree to which morality is central to self-concept

Down

2. _____ aggression is a form of hostile aggression that harms others through physical injury or the threat of such injury.

3. _____ aggression is a form of hostile aggression that damages another's peer relationships.

4. Moral self-_____: the ability to monitor one's own conduct, constantly adjusting it as circumstances present opportunities to violate inner standards

5. Social _____: customs determined solely by consensus, such as table manners, dress style, and rituals of social interaction

8. Moral _____: standards that protect people's rights and welfare

9. Voluntary obedience to requests and commands

10. _____ aggression is aimed at obtaining an object, privilege, or space with no deliberate intent to harm another person.

PRACTICE TEST

1. Which of the following is true? (p. 477)
   a. Biological theories stress the internalization of moral standards.
   b. Biological perspectives emphasize the adaptive significance of morality.
   c. Research shows that morality can be fully explained by its biological foundations.
   d. Animals, unlike humans, do not conform to moral-like rules, suggesting that morality is not rooted in our evolutionary history.

2. Both psychoanalytic and social learning theories regard moral development as a matter of: (p. 477)
   a. construction.
   b. realism.
   c. internalization.
   d. reciprocity.

3. According to Freud's psychoanalytic theory of moral development: (p. 478)
   a. conscience development results from the Oedipal and Elektra conflicts, wherein the child identifies with the same-sex parent and adopts his/her moral standards.
   b. humans are biologically predisposed to behave in a moral fashion by limiting disruptive acts and demonstrating concern for others.
   c. children acquire moral behavior through classical conditioning.
   d. children acquire moral behavior through modeling.

4. A form of discipline known as _____ supports conscience formation by pointing out the effects of the child's misbehavior on others. (p. 478)
   a. positive discipline
   b. induction
   c. punishment
   d. time out

5. Recent psychoanalytic theorists emphasize _____ as a vital foundation for acquiring moral standards. (p. 479)
   a. peer relations
   b. use of harsh discipline
   c. entry into school
   d. parent-child attachment

6. Modeling of prosocial behavior: (p. 481)
   a. is less effective than reinforcement in helping children acquire moral responses.
   b. has no long-term effects on children's behavior.
   c. exerts the greatest influence on children's behavior during the preschool years.
   d. is equally effective regardless of the model's characteristics.

7. Harsh discipline, such as yelling at, slapping, or spanking children for misbehavior: (p. 482)
   a. is never justified.
   b. promotes lasting changes in children's behavior.
   c. has been linked with increases in adaptive behavior and academic performance.
   d. often has undesirable side effects, including modeling of aggressive behavior.

8. The most effective form of discipline is: (p. 483)
   a. withdrawal of privileges.
   b. time out.
   c. rewarding good conduct.
   d. punishment.

9. The cognitive-developmental approach assumes that children learn to behave morally through
   _____—actively attending to and interrelating multiple perspectives on
   situations in which social conflicts arise and deriving new moral understandings. (p. 484)
   a. induction
   b. internalization
   c. construction
   d. assimilation

10. In Piaget's heteronomous stage: (p. 485)
    a. the wrongness of an act is judged on the basis of intent to do harm.
    b. moral rules are viewed as permanent, unchangeable features of the external world.
    c. rules are regarded as socially-agreed-upon principles that can be revised.
    d. a standard of fairness called reciprocity is used in making moral judgments.

11. Research evaluating the accuracy of Piaget's theory shows that: (p. 486)
    a. Piaget underestimated young children's moral capacities.
    b. Piaget was inaccurate in his description of the general direction of change in moral judgment.
    c. Piaget placed unwarranted emphasis on the role of cognitive development and peer interaction in the development of moral understanding.
    d. Piaget accurately described the age-dependent, stepwise sequence in which children develop moral reasoning capacities.

12. According to Kohlberg, which is more important in determining the maturity of responses to moral dilemmas? (p. 487)
    a. reasoning rather than content
    b. content rather than reasoning
    c. reasoning rather than emotion
    d. emotion rather than reasoning

13. During Kohlberg's _____ level of moral development, moral understanding is based on conforming to social rules to ensure positive human relationships and societal order. (p. 489)
    a. heteronomous
    b. preconventional
    c. conventional
    d. postconventional

14. When an individual's moral reasoning stems from self-interest, which stage of Kohlberg's theory would best characterize his or her level of moral understanding? (p. 489)
    a. Stage 2: The instrumental purpose orientation
    b. Stage 3: The "good boy-good girl" orientation
    c. Stage 4: The social-order-maintaining orientation
    d. Stage 6: The universal ethical principle orientation

15. Research on Kohlberg's stages indicates that: (p. 490)
    a. progress through the stages is not related to age.
    b. individuals rarely move through the six stages in the predicted order.
    c. most individuals move through all six stages by early adulthood.
    d. development of moral reasoning is slow and gradual.

16. When individuals are faced with real-life, as opposed to hypothetical, moral dilemmas, their moral reasoning tends to: (p. 491)
    a. become more mature.
    b. become less mature.
    c. remain at the same level of maturity.
    d. follow no predictable pattern.

17. Research shows that: (pp. 492–493)
    a. females show less mature moral reasoning than do males.
    b. females show more mature moral reasoning than do males.
    c. females and males reason about moral issues differently, with females tending to emphasize an "ethic of care", while males tend to emphasize justice or to use justice and care equally.
    d. males and females do not differ in the level or content of their moral reasoning.

18. Which of the following is true with regard to the influences on moral reasoning? (p. 493)
    a. A rigid, closed-minded approach to new information and experiences is linked to gains in moral reasoning.
    b. Peer conflict facilitates moral reasoning by making children aware of others' perspectives.
    c. Strict, authoritarian parenting is associated with more mature moral reasoning.
    d. Movement through Kohlberg's stages is the same in all cultures throughout the world.

19. Customs determined solely by consensus, such as table manners, dress styles, and rituals of social interaction are known as: (p. 498)
    a. moral dilemmas.
    b. moral imperatives.
    c. social conventions.
    d. matters of personal choice.

20. By around age 8, children view morality in terms of _____. They recognize that special consideration should be given to those at a disadvantage, such as the needy or the disabled. (p. 501)
    a. equality
    b. merit
    c. benevolence
    d. empathy

21. The first glimmerings of self-control appear in the form of: (p. 503)
    a. compliance.
    b. delay of gratification.
    c. moral self-regulation.
    d. social perspective taking.

22. _____ aggression, aimed at obtaining an object, privilege, or space with no deliberate intent to harm another person, is the most common form of aggression exhibited during the preschool years. (p. 507)
    a. Hostile
    b. Overt
    c. Instrumental
    d. Relational

23. During the preschool years: (pp. 507–508)
    a. boys and girls display the same type and amount of aggression.
    b. girls are less aggressive than are boys.
    c. boys are more overtly aggressive, whereas girls are more relationally aggressive.
    d. aggressive behavior is highly atypical and is cause for great concern.

24. Youth crime: (p. 508)
    a. has declined over the past decade.
    b. accounts for a minimal proportion of police arrests—less than 5 percent.
    c. is most often serious in nature.
    d. forecasts a long-term pattern of antisocial behavior for the majority of adolescents.

25. Research on the link between aggressive behavior and the family shows that: (p. 509)
    a. parenting has very little influence on children's development of aggression.
    b. peers are far more influential than are family members in children's development of aggressive behavior.
    c. physical punishment and inconsistent discipline are linked to antisocial behavior from early childhood through adolescence, in children of both sexes.
    d. punitive parenting promotes aggression at home but such aggressive behavior is rarely carried over to school and other social environments.

CHAPTER 13
DEVELOPMENT OF SEX DIFFERENCES
AND GENDER ROLES

BRIEF CHAPTER SUMMARY

Perhaps more than any other area of child development, the study of gender typing has responded to societal change. Largely because of progress in women's rights, the adoption of gender-typed beliefs and behavior is no longer regarded as essential for healthy psychological development. However, despite progress in women's rights, gender stereotypes have remained essentially the same. Social learning theory, with its emphasis on modeling and reinforcement, and cognitive-developmental theory, with its focus on children as active learners about their social world, are major current approaches to gender typing. An information-processing view, gender schema theory, combines elements of both theories to explain how children acquire gender-typed knowledge and behavior.

According to Maccoby, early on, hormones affect play styles, leading to rough, noisy movements among boys and calm, gentle actions among girls. Then, as children begin to interact with peers, they choose partners whose interests and behaviors are compatible with their own. During the preschool years, children acquire a wide variety of gender stereotypes about activities, behaviors, and occupations. Stereotypes involving personality traits and achievement areas are added in middle childhood. At the same time, a more flexible view of what males and females can do emerges.

Cross-cultural similarities in gender typing are not consistent enough to support a strong role for biology. Powerful environmental influences on gender typing exist. Beginning in infancy, adults view boys and girls differently and create different environments for them. In addition, teachers, peers, and siblings influence gender stereotyping and gender-role adoption. According to social learning theory, behavior precedes self-perceptions in the development of gender identity. In contrast, cognitive-developmental theory assumes that self-perceptions come before behavior. In fact, gender-typed behavior is present so early in development that modeling and reinforcement must account for its initial appearance, as social learning theory suggests.

Biological, social, and cognitive factors combine to make early adolescence a period of gender intensification. Girls are advanced in early language development and in reading achievement and are more emotionally sensitive, compliant, and dependent. Boys do better at spatial and mathematical skills and are more aggressive.

The developmental challenges of adolescence combined with gender-typed coping styles seem to be responsible for the higher rate of depression among adolescent girls. Parents and teachers can counteract young children's readiness to absorb gender-linked associations by delaying access to gender stereotypes and pointing out exceptions as well as the arbitrariness of many gender inequalities in society.

LEARNING OBJECTIVES

After reading this chapter, you should be able to:

13.1 Explain how the study of gender typing has responded to societal change, noting the development of new theories and the use of new terms. (pp. 520–522)

13.2 Discuss the development of gender stereotypes across childhood and adolescence, and summarize individual and group differences in gender stereotyping. (pp. 522–526)

13.3 Discuss the role of biology in gender stereotyping and gender-role adoption, including cross-cultural similarities in gender stereotypes and gender-role adoption and hormonal influences on gender-role behavior. (pp. 526–530)

13.4 Summarize environmental influences on gender stereotyping and gender-role adoption, including perceptions and expectations of adults, treatment by parents and teachers, observational learning, and peer and sibling relations. (pp. 530–537)

13.5 Trace the development of gender identity from early childhood into adolescence. (pp. 537–540)

13.6 Explain how gender schema theory accounts for the emergence of and maintenance of masculine and feminine orientations. (pp. 540–543)

13.7 Describe sex differences in mental abilities and personality attributes, noting factors that contribute to these differences. (pp. 544–552)

13.8 Cite ways to reduce gender stereotyping in children. (pp. 552–553)

STUDY QUESTIONS

1. Explain how psychologists' view of sex differences has changed over the past 30 years. (p. 520)

_____

_____

_____

2. What two theoretical approaches currently predominate the study of gender typing? (p. 520)

A. _____

B. _____

3. Match each of the following terms with the appropriate definition. (p. 520)

_____ The process of developing gender-linked beliefs, gender roles, and a gender-role identity

_____ The reflection of gender stereotypes in everyday behavior

_____ The perception of oneself as relatively masculine or feminine in characteristics

_____ Widely held beliefs about characteristics deemed appropriate for males and females

1. Gender stereotypes
2. Gender roles
3. Gender identity
4. Gender typing

Gender Stereotypes and Gender Roles

1. Distinguish between instrumental and expressive traits, citing examples of each. (p. 521)

Instrumental: _____

_____

Expressive: _____

_____

2. True or False: Stereotypes linked to the instrumental-expressive dichotomy are largely confined to the United States and are not evident in other regions of the world. (p. 521)

Gender Stereotyping in Early Childhood

1. Discuss research evidence suggesting that children stereotype their play world even before they can consistently label their own sex. (p. 522)

_____

_____

_____

2. Preschoolers' gender stereotypes are (flexible / rigid). (p. 522)

3. True or False: Most preschoolers believe that the characteristics associated with each sex (for example, clothes, hairstyles, and occupation) determine whether a person is male or female. (p. 523)

Gender Stereotyping in Middle Childhood and Adolescence

1. By age _____, gender stereotyping of activities and occupations is well established. (p. 523)

2. Cross-cultural research shows that stereotyping of personality traits (declines/increases) in middle childhood. (p. 523)

3. Describe the pattern of children's trait learning and stereotyping. (p. 523)

   _____

   _____

   _____

4. Differentiate academic subjects and skill areas that children regard as either masculine or feminine. (p. 523)

   Masculine: _____

   _____

   Feminine: _____

   _____

5. True or False: Research reveals that girls tend to adopt a general stereotype of males as smarter than females. (p. 523)

6. Define *gender-stereotype flexibility*. (pp. 523–524)

   _____

   _____

7. True or False: School-age children adopt a biological perspective of gender typing, and consequently, regard gender as a certain predictor of personality traits, activities, and behaviors. (p. 524)

8. As children's gender stereotypes become more flexible, they show a greater tendency to view gender differences as (biologically/socially) influenced. (p. 524)

9. Both children and adults judge (girls'/boys') violations of gender roles more harshly. (p. 524)

Individual and Group Differences in Gender Stereotyping

1. True or False: Since the components of gender stereotyping (i.e., activities, behaviors, occupations, personality traits) are highly correlated, children typically show equivalent levels of knowledge across all areas. (p. 524)

2. (Girls / Boys) hold more rigid gender-stereotyped views throughout childhood. (p. 524)

3. True or False: A few recent studies indicate that boys' views of gender roles may be becoming more flexible. (p. 524)

4. Black children hold (more/less) stereotyped views of females than do white children. What factor may account for this difference? (pp. 524–525)

   _____

5. In adolescence and adulthood, (higher- / lower-) SES individuals hold more flexible gender-stereotyped views. (p. 525)

Gender Stereotyping and Gender-Role Adoption

1. Cite three reasons why children's gender-stereotyped thinking may *not* be highly predictive of their gender-role adoption. (p. 525)

   A. _____

   _____

   B. _____

   _____

   C. _____

   _____

2. Explain how stereotype flexibility is related to children's gender-role adoption in middle childhood. (p. 525)

   _____

   _____

   _____

The Case for Biology

1. What two sources of evidence support the role of biological influences on gender typing? (p. 526)

    A. _____

    B. _____

2. Most societies promote (instrumental/expressive) traits in males and (instrumental/expressive) traits in females, but great diversity exists in the magnitude of this difference. (p. 526)

3. Why is there less of a dichotomy in the personality traits and behaviors of male and female children in Nyansongo than in other tribal and village cultures? (p. 527)

    _____

    _____

    _____

4. Cross-cultural research indicates that experience (does/does not) have an impact on gender typing. (p. 527)

5. Discuss Eleanor Maccoby's argument that hormonal differences between males and females have important consequences for gender typing, including play styles evidenced in early childhood. (p. 528)

    _____

    _____

    _____

6. What is *Congenital Adrenal Hyperplasia (CAH)*? (p. 529)

    _____

    _____

    _____

7. (Boys/Girls) with CAH show abnormal physical development. (p. 529)

8. Describe the play behavior of girls with CAH. (p. 529)

    _____

    _____

    _____

9. True or False: As CAH girls get older and have more opportunities for adults to influence them, they show increasingly feminized behaviors, often selecting "feminine" activities and careers. (p. 529)

10. True or False: When biological makeup and sex of rearing are at odds, children experience serious problems with sexual identity development and psychological adjustment. (p. 529)

Cultural Influences: Sweden's Commitment to Gender Equality

1. Explain Sweden's "equal roles family model." (p. 527)

_____

_____

_____

2. Cite policy changes that have been implemented in Swedish society to help support the goal of gender equality. (p. 527)

_____

_____

_____

3. Sweden's family model (is/is not) successful. Elaborate on your response. (p. 527)

_____

_____

_____

4. Explain how Sweden's progressive gender policy has affected the gender beliefs and behaviors of its youth. (p. 527)

_____

_____

_____

Biology and Environment: David—A Boy Reared as a Girl

1. Explain how David Reimer's personal experience confirms the impact of genetic sex and prenatal hormones on a person's sense of self as male or female, as well as highlighting the importance of social experience. (pp. 530–531)

Genetic sex and prenatal hormones: _____

_____

_____

_____

Social Experience: _____

_____

_____

_____

The Case for Environment

1. What happens when adults are asked to observe a neutrally dressed infant who is labeled as either a boy or a girl? (p. 530)

    _____

2. True or False: Parents continue to interpret children's behavior in a stereotyped fashion throughout childhood and adolescence. Briefly explain your response. (p. 531)

    _____

    _____

    _____

3. Parents of preschoolers respond more negatively to the idea of "cross-gender" (girls/boys). (p. 531)

4. Describe ways in which parents encourage gender-stereotyped beliefs and behavior in their children through play materials and social interactions during infancy and early childhood. (p. 532)

    _____

    _____

    _____

5. Explain how parents interact differently with sons and daughters in teaching situations. (p. 532)

    Sons: _____

    _____

    _____

Daughters: _____

_____

_____

6. True or False: Research shows that parents rate sons and daughters as being equally competent in school subjects such as English and math. (p. 532)

7. Explain how parents' differential treatment of sons and daughters extends to freedom granting behavior in everyday life. (pp. 532–533)

_____

_____

_____

8. True or False: Research overwhelmingly suggests that children benefit from assignment of "cross-gender" tasks. Elaborate on your response. (p. 533)

_____

_____

_____

9. (Mothers/Fathers) show more differential treatment of sons and daughters and are more likely to encourage "gender-appropriate" behavior. (pp. 533–534)

10. Discuss the "feminine bias" seen in most preschool and elementary school classrooms, noting its impact on students. (p. 534)

"Feminine bias": _____

_____

_____

Impact: _____

_____

_____

11. In what ways do teachers maintain or extend gender roles taught at home? (p. 534)

_____

_____

12. How can teachers promote gender equality? (p. 534)

_____

_____

13. True or False: Portrayals of gender roles in children's television programs and video games have changed dramatically in recent years, such that very few now display traditional gender stereotypes. (p. 534)

14. True or False: Children who often see their parents engaging in behavior that crosses traditional gender lines are less likely to endorse gender stereotypes. (p. 535)

15. Cite several benefits afforded to girls' with career-oriented mothers. (p. 535)

   A. _____

   B. _____

   C. _____

16. Boys in father-absent homes and girls in mother-absent homes are (more/less) gender-typed than children in two-parent homes. (p. 535)

17. By age _____, children positively reinforce one another for "gender-appropriate" play by praising, approving, imitating, or joining in. (p. 535)

18. Peer rejection is greater for (girls/boys) who frequently engage in "cross-gender" behavior. (p. 535)

19. Discuss the different styles of social influence promoted within gender-segregated peer groups. (p. 535)

   Boys: _____

   _____

   _____

   Girls: _____

   _____

   _____

20. Sibling effects on gender typing depend on what two factors? (p. 536)

   A. _____   B. _____

21. True or False: Whereas younger siblings have little impact on older siblings' gender typing, older siblings serve as powerful models for younger siblings. (p. 536)

22. Explain why some studies have found that children with same-sex siblings are more gender-stereotyped, whereas other studies have found the opposite effect. (p. 536)

_____

_____

_____

23. In what ways do families in which siblings are all of the same sex provide special opportunities for children to step out of traditional gender roles? (pp. 536–537)

_____

_____

_____

Gender Identity

1. Define *gender identity* and indicate how it is measured. (p. 537)

_____

_____

2. _____ refers to a type of gender identity in which the person scores highly on both masculine and feminine personality characteristics. (p. 537)

3. How is gender identity related to psychological adjustment? (p. 537)

_____

_____

_____

4. The (masculine/feminine) component of androgyny is largely responsible for the superior psychological health of androgynous women. (p. 537)

Emergence of Gender Identity

1. Contrast social learning and cognitive-developmental accounts of the emergence of gender identity. (p. 538)

   Social Learning: _____

   _____

   _____

   Cognitive-Developmental: _____

   _____

   _____

2. *Gender* _____ refers to the understanding that sex is biologically-based and remains the same even if clothing, hairstyles, and play activities change. (p. 538)

3. Lawrence Kohlberg proposed that before age _____ or _____, children cannot maintain the constancy of their gender. (p. 538)

4. Name and describe the three stages of gender constancy development proposed by Kohlberg. (pp. 538–539)

   A. _____

   B. _____

   C. _____

5. What Piagetian task is associated with the mastery of gender constancy? (pp. 538–539)

   _____

6. Cite evidence supporting the notion that cognitive immaturity, not social experience, is largely responsible for preschoolers' difficulty grasping the permanence of sex. (p. 539)

   _____

   _____

   _____

7. Is gender constancy responsible for children's gender-typed behavior? Why or why not? (p. 539)

_____

_____

_____

8. True or False: As soon as children understand basic gender categories, they use them for acquiring gender-relevant information and modifying their own behavior. (p. 539)

9. Overall, research indicates that gender constancy (does/does not) have a large impact on gender typing. (p. 539)

Gender Identity During Middle Childhood

1. Contrast the gender identity development of girls and boys during middle childhood, and note implications for behavior. (p. 539)

Girls: _____

_____

_____

Boys: _____

_____

_____

2. (Boys/Girls) are clearly the more androgynous of the two sexes during middle childhood. (p. 539)

3. True or False: Children of both sexes rate "masculine" occupations as having higher status than "feminine" occupations. (p. 539)

4. Explain how messages from adults and agemates are influential in children's development of gender identity. (p. 540)

Adults: _____

_____

_____

Agemates: _____

_____

_____

Gender Identity During Adolescence

1. What is *gender intensification*? (p. 540)

    _____

    _____

2. Although it occurs in both sexes, gender intensification is stronger for (boys/girls). (p. 540)

3. Discuss biological, social, and cognitive factors associated with gender intensification. (p. 540)

    Biological: _____

    _____

    _____

    Social: _____

    _____

    _____

    Cognitive: _____

    _____

    _____

4. As young people move toward a more mature personal identity and become less concerned with others' opinions of them, stereotypic self-perceptions (decline/increase). (p. 540)

Gender Schema Theory

1. Explain *gender schema theory*. (pp. 540–541)

    _____

    _____

    _____

2. What are *gender schemas*? (p. 541)

    _____

    _____

3. Using the principles of gender schema theory, explain why gender stereotypes and gender-role preferences are self-perpetuating and explain how they come to restrict children's alternatives. (p. 541)

_____

_____

_____

From Research to Practice: Reducing Gender Schematic Thinking with Cognitive Interventions

1. Summarize findings from Rebecca Bigler's research on the effects of "gender classrooms" versus "control classrooms." (p. 542)

Gender classrooms: _____

_____

_____

Control classrooms: _____

_____

_____

2. The impact of "gender classrooms" was largely limited to _____ thinkers—children who had trouble understanding that a person can belong to more than one social category at once. (p. 542)

3. According to gender schema theory, how are environmental influences on gender typing sustained by cognitive forces? (p. 542)

_____

_____

_____

4. Discuss the use of *classification training* to promote gender-equitable beliefs in children. (p. 542)

_____

_____

_____

To What Extent Do Boys and Girls *Really* Differ in Gender-Stereotyped Attributes?

1. Sex differences account for _____ to _____ percent of individual differences in mental abilities and personality traits. (p. 544)

2. Over the past several decades, the gender gap has (widened/narrowed) in all areas of mental ability for which differences have been identified. (p. 545)

Mental Abilities

1. True or False: Boys and girls do not differ in general intelligence, but they do vary in specific mental abilities. (p. 545)

2. True or False: Girls show an advantage over boys in language skills from early childhood into the school years. (p. 545)

3. Discuss biological and social factors that may contribute to girls' superior language and reading performance. (p. 545)

   Biological: _____

   _____

   _____

   Social: _____

   _____

   _____

4. Summarize research findings related to sex differences in mathematical ability. (pp. 545–546)

   _____

   _____

   _____

5. Evidence suggests that sex differences in mathematical ability are rooted in boys' biologically-based superior _____ reasoning. (p. 546)

6. Explain how the gender gap in mathematics is related to student attitudes and self-esteem. (pp. 546–547)

   _____

   _____

   _____

7. Sex differences in mathematical reasoning have (decreased/increased) over the past several decades. (p. 547)

8. True or False: Boys and girls reach advanced levels of high school math and science study in equal proportions. (p. 547)

9. Cite ways in which parents and teachers can promote girls' interest in and confidence at math and science. (p. 548)

_____

_____

_____

Biology and Environment: Sex Differences in Spatial Abilities

1. Describe two spatial tasks for which the gender gap favors males. (pp. 546–547)

   A. _____

   _____

   B. _____

   _____

2. Sex differences on _____ tasks, involving analysis of complex visual forms, are weak or nonexistent. (pp. 546–547)

3. True or False: Sex differences in spatial abilities persist throughout the lifespan. (pp. 546–547)

4. Summarize biological and environmental factors that may contribute to sex differences in spatial abilities. (pp. 546–547)

   Biological: _____

   _____

   _____

   Environmental: _____

   _____

   _____

Personality Traits

1. Summarize sex differences in emotional sensitivity. (p. 548)

    _____

    _____

    _____

2. True or False: Research supports the conclusion that girls are genetically prewired to be more emotionally sensitive as a way of preparing them for the caregiving role. (p. 548)

3. Sex differences in emotional sensitivity (are/are not) present in adulthood when parents interact with their babies. (p. 548)

4. Discuss the role of cultural expectations in accounting for the gender gap in emotional sensitivity. (p. 548)

    _____

    _____

    _____

5. (Boys/Girls) show greater compliance and dependency. Explain how activity patterns may contribute to this pattern. (p. 549)

    _____

    _____

    _____

6. About _____ to _____ percent of American teenagers have experienced one or more depressive episodes, and _____ to _____ percent are chronically depressed. (p. 549)

7. True or False: Depressive symptoms increase sharply around the time of puberty. (p. 549)

8. Depression is more common in adolescent (boys/girls). (p. 549)

9. Kinship studies of identical and fraternal twins reveal that heredity (does/does not) play an important role in depression. (p. 549)

10. Explain how experience combines with biology to activate depression in youths. (p. 549)

    _____

    _____

    _____

11. Biological changes associated with puberty (can/cannot) account for sex differences in depression. Elaborate on your response. (p. 549)

_____

_____

_____

12. Describe how stressful life events and gender-typed coping styles account for girls' higher rates of depression. (p. 550)

_____

_____

_____

13. Explain why adolescent depressive symptoms tend to be overlooked by parents and teachers. (p. 550)

_____

_____

14. Why does research tend to underestimate girls' aggressiveness? (p. 550)

_____

_____

15. Why do almost all researchers agree that biology must be involved in male aggression? (p. 551)

_____

16. Androgen exposure has a (direct/indirect) effect on aggressive behavior. Cite two possible ways in which androgens may exert such effects. (p. 551)

A. _____

_____

B. _____

_____

17. Explain how coercive child-rearing practices and strife-ridden family interactions promote aggressive behavior in boys. (p. 551)

_____

_____

_____

1. How and why does Sandra Bem suggest that parents and teachers make a special effort to delay young children's learning of gender stereotyped messages? (p. 552)

    How: _____

    _____

    _____

    Why: _____

    _____

ASK YOURSELF . . .

Review: Explain how gender stereotyping in the environment and young children's cognitive limitations contribute to rigid gender stereotypes in early childhood. (p. 526)

_____

_____

_____

_____

_____

Review: What factors allow for greater gender-stereotype flexibility in middle childhood and adolescence? How is gender-stereotyped flexibility related to gender-typed preferences and behavior? (p. 526)

_____

_____

_____

_____

_____

Apply: Dennis is the only boy in his seventh-grade home-economics cooking class. His friends Tom and Bill tease him relentlessly. Cite evidence that explains this negative reaction to Dennis's "cross-gender" behavior. (p. 526)

_____

_____

_____

_____

Connect: Cite parallels between the development of gender stereotyping and children's understanding of ethnicity and social class (See Chapter 11, pages 463–465). (p. 526)

_____

_____

_____

_____

Review: Cite research indicating that biology influences gender-role adoption. (p. 537)

_____

_____

_____

_____

Review: Summarize parent, peer, and sibling influences on gender-role adoption. Why are sibling influences more complex than parent and peer influences? (p. 537)

_____

_____

_____

_____

Apply: Pat and Chris had to do a science project. Pat's mother said, "You can go to the library tonight to choose your topic." Chris's mother said, "You'd better get started right away. We have some books on whales, so you can do it on that." Is Pat more likely to be a boy or a girl? How about Chris? Explain, using research findings. (p. 537)

_____

_____

_____

_____

_____

Connect: Girls are more susceptible than boys to learned helplessness in achievement situations. Explain why this is so, using research in this chapter (see page 532) and in Chapter 11 (see pages 453–454). (p. 537)

_____

_____

_____

_____

_____

Review: Define androgyny. Which of the two sexes is more androgynous in middle childhood, and why? (p. 543)

_____

_____

_____

_____

_____

Review: Describe the general path of gender identity development, from early childhood through adolescence. (p. 543)

_____

_____

_____

_____

_____

Apply: When 4-year-old Roger was in the hospital, he was cared for by a male nurse named Jared. After Roger recovered, he told his friends about Dr. Jared. Using gender schema theory, explain why Roger remembered Jared as a doctor, not a nurse. (p. 543)

_____

_____

_____

_____

_____

Connect: Discuss gains in perspective taking that lead young teenagers to be very concerned with what others think, thereby contributing to gender intensification.

_____

_____

_____

_____

_____

Review: Cite evidence indicating that both biological and environmental factors contribute to girls' early advantage in verbal abilities and boys' superior performance in mathematical reasoning. (p. 553)

_____

_____

_____

_____

_____

Review: Explain the *indirect* link between androgen hormones and boys' greater overt aggression, noting the influence of both family and peer-group experiences. (p. 553)

_____

_____

_____

_____

_____

Apply: Thirteen-year-old Donna reached puberty early and feels negatively about her physical appearance. She also has a feminine gender identity. Explain why Donna is at risk for depression. (p. 553)

_____

_____

_____

_____

_____

Connect: Using Brofenbrenner's ecological systems theory (See Chapter 1, page 28), describe steps that can be taken in each level of the environment to reduce gender stereotyping in children.

_____

_____

_____

_____

_____

SUGGESTED STUDENT READINGS

Brannon, L. (1998). _Gender: Psychological perspectives._ Boston, MA: Allyn & Bacon. Summarizes the literature on gender differences and includes personal narrative accounts of gender-relevant real-life experiences. Topics include the brain, health and fitness, gender stereotypes, discrimination, sexual harassment, and emotion.

Kinder, M. (Ed.). (2000). _Kid's media culture._ Durham, NC: Duke University Press. Explores the effects of children's media on development. Also compares the books, cartoons, and television shows of the 1950s and 1960s with today's mass media. Finally, this book addresses concerns with television in schools and how various forms of mass media communicate messages about gender and socialization.

Moeller, T. G. (2001). _Youth aggression and violence: A psychological approach._ Mahwah, NJ: Lawrence Erlbaum Associates, Inc. A collection of chapters highlighting theory and research in the study of adolescent aggression and violence. Other topics include genetic and environmental contributions to the development of aggression, media violence, firearm accessibility, and the relationship between self-esteem and aggression.

PUZZLE 13

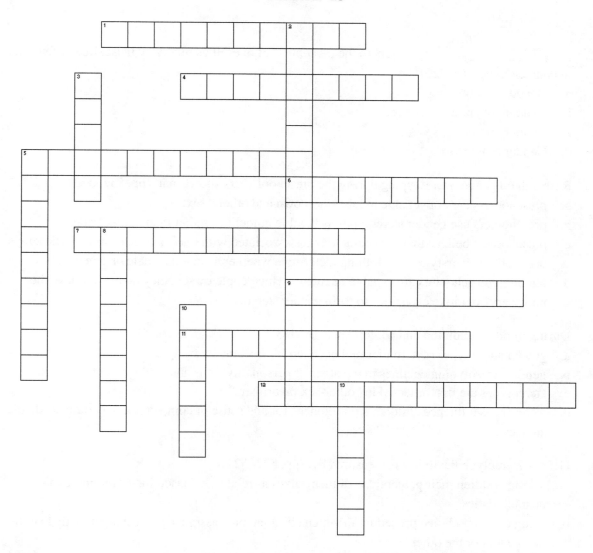

Across

1. _____ traits: feminine-stereotyped personality traits that reflect warmth, caring, and sensitivity

4. Gender _____: understanding that sex is biologically-based and remains the same even if clothing. hairstyle, and play activities change

5. Gender _____: widely held beliefs about characteristics deemed appropriate for males and females

6. Gender _____: the perception of oneself as relatively masculine or feminine in characteristics

7. The belief that both genders can display a gender-stereotyped personality trait or activity is known as gender-stereotype _____.

9. Type of gender identity in which the person scores high on both masculine and feminine personality characteristics

11. Gender _____: Kohlberg's final stage of gender understanding in which children master gender constancy

12. _____ traits: masculine-stereotyped traits that reflect competence, rationality, and assertiveness

Down

2. Gender _____: increased stereotyping of attitudes and behavior, movement toward a more traditional gender identity

3. Gender _____: the reflection of gender stereotypes in everyday behavior

5. Gender _____: Kohlberg's second stage of gender understanding; preschoolers have a partial understanding of the permanence of sex

8. Gender _____: Kohlberg's first stage of gender understanding; preschoolers can label their own gender and that of others

10. Gender _____ theory is an information processing approach to gender typing that combines social learning and cognitive-developmental features.

13. Gender _____: the process of developing gender-linked beliefs, gender roles, and a gender-role identity

PRACTICE TEST

1. _____ refers to the perception of oneself as relatively masculine or feminine in characteristics. (p. 520)
   a. Gender stereotyping
   b. Gender-role intensification
   c. Gender identity
   d. Gender typing

2. Research on gender stereotyping during the preschool years shows that: (pp. 552–523)
   a. preschoolers are not yet able to label their own and others' sex.
   b. preschoolers use gender stereotypes as flexible guidelines rather than blanket rules.
   c. preschoolers believe that the characteristics associated with one's sex, such as activities, toys, occupations, hairstyle, and clothing, determine whether a person is male or female.
   d. although preschoolers are capable of categorizing people by sex, they do not yet have the necessary cognitive capacities to form gender stereotypes.

3. During middle childhood and adolescence: (p. 523)
   a. gender stereotypes of activities and occupations become more rigid.
   b. gender stereotyping declines in the areas of personality traits and achievement.
   c. stereotypes are first reflected in "other-sex favoritism."
   d. stereotypes influence children's preferences for and sense of competence at certain academic subjects.

4. Gender-stereotype flexibility is measured by: (pp. 523–524)
   a. asking children their perceptions of themselves as relatively masculine or feminine in characteristics.
   b. using a forced-choice procedure in which children must assign a given characteristic to either one gender or the other.
   c. asking children whether both genders can display a personality trait or activity.
   d. assessing children's personal sense of androgyny.

5. Research on individual and group differences in gender stereotyping shows that: (p. 524)
   a. since the components of gender stereotyping (e.g., activities, behaviors, occupations, personality traits) are highly correlated, children typically show equivalent levels of knowledge across all areas.
   b. girls hold more rigid gender-stereotyped views than do boys throughout childhood and adolescence.
   c. lower-SES individuals tend to hold more flexible gender-stereotyped views than their higher-SES counterparts.
   d. black children hold less stereotyped views of females than do white children.

6. Eleanor Maccoby's research on hormonal influences on play indicates that: (p. 528)
   a. preferences for same-sex playmates is rarely found in cultures outside of the United States, suggesting that hormones exert little influence on play behavior.
   b. hormonal differences lead boys to prefer rough, noisy play while girls prefer calm, gentle actions.
   c. preference for same-sex playmates declines during the preschool years.
   d. hormonal differences lead girls to prefer large group activities, while boys prefer to play in pairs.

7. Females with congenital adrenal hyperplasia (CAH), a disorder in which a genetic defect causes the adrenal system to produce unusually high levels of androgens from the prenatal period onward: (p. 529)
   a. are more "masculine" in toy and playmate preferences in childhood and activity and career preferences in adulthood.
   b. are more "feminine" in toy and playmate preferences in childhood and activity and career preferences in adulthood.
   c. are more "masculine" in toys and playmate preferences in childhood but become more "feminine" in activity and career preferences in adulthood.
   d. are more "feminine" in toys and playmate preferences in childhood but become more "masculine" in activity and career preferences in adulthood.

8. Research on environmental influences on children's gender-role development indicates that: (p. 531)
   a. during childhood and adolescence, parents come to hold similar perceptions and expectations of their sons and daughters.
   b. parents espouse similar child-rearing values for sons and daughters, describing achievement, competition, and emotional control as equally important for children of both sexes.
   c. parents hold more negative attitudes of "cross-gender" behavior in boys than in girls.
   d. older children receive more direct training in gender roles than do younger children.

9. In teaching situations with their school-age children, parents: (p. 532)
   a. demand greater independence from girls than boys.
   b. more often ignore or refuse to respond to a son's request for help, while offering help to a daughter right away.
   c. behave in a more mastery-oriented fashion with daughters, setting higher standards and pointing out important features of the task.
   d. use more directive speech with boys than with girls.

10. In the classroom setting, teachers: (p. 534)
    a. often act in ways that contradict gender roles taught in the home.
    b. praise girls for their knowledge and boys for their obedience.
    c. discourage aggressive behavior more frequently and forcefully in girls than in boys.
    d. reinforce children of both sexes for "feminine" rather than "masculine" behavior.

11. Which of the following is true? (p. 535)
    a. Portrayal of gender roles in children's television programs, video games, and storybooks has changed dramatically in recent years to provide a more gender equitable picture.
    b. Even when children are exposed to nonstereotyped role models, they still tend to maintain highly stereotypic beliefs and behaviors.
    c. Among children of divorced parents, boys in father-absent homes and girls in mother-absent homes are less gender stereotyped.
    d. Children from single-parent homes are less likely to have other-sex friends than are agemates from two-parent homes.

12. Which of the following is true with regard to siblings' influence on children's gender typing? (p. 536)
    a. Younger siblings have a powerful impact on older siblings' gender typing.
    b. Children from two-child families with a same-sex sibling tend to be more gender typed than children with no siblings.
    c. Children from large families who have all same-sex siblings are more gender-stereotyped in their interests and personality traits than are those children from mixed-sex families.
    d. Parents usually increase pressures toward gender typing when their children are all of the same sex.

13. Individuals who are androgynous: (p. 537)
    a. display highly gender-stereotyped behavior.
    b. demonstrate mostly cross-gender behaviors.
    c. score highly on both masculine and feminine personality characteristics.
    d. have a poorly developed gender identity.

14. Anne knows that boys grow up to be men and girls grow up to be women. Nevertheless, she also thinks that if a boy has long hair, he becomes a girl. She is in the _____ stage of gender constancy development. (p. 538)
    a. gender labeling
    b. gender permanence
    c. gender stability
    d. gender consistency

15. Research on gender constancy shows that: (p. 539)
    a. providing children with information about genital differences between males and females significantly improves their understanding of gender constancy.
    b. gender constancy is responsible for children's gender-typed behavior.
    c. understanding of gender constancy leads to a reduction in gender-stereotyped behaviors.
    d. cognitive immaturity, not social experience, is largely responsible for preschoolers' difficulty grasping the permanence of sex.

16. During middle childhood: (p. 539)
    a. boys' identification with the "masculine" role declines.
    b. girls' identification with the "feminine" role increases.
    c. girls are more androgynous than are boys.
    d. parents are less tolerant when daughters, as opposed to sons, cross gender lines.

17. During early adolescence, gender intensification is: (p. 540)
    a. stronger for boys.
    b. stronger for girls.
    c. the same for boys and girls.
    d. not yet an important issue.

18. Gender schema theory: (pp. 540–541)
    a. stresses genetic influences on gender typing.
    b. emphasizes development of gender-stereotyped beliefs through identification with the same-sex parent.
    c. focuses on the role of modeling and reinforcement in gender identity development.
    d. emphasizes how environmental pressures and children's cognitions work together to shape gender-role development.

19. In relation to verbal abilities: (p. 545)
    a. boys are ahead of girls in language progress early in development.
    b. girls attain higher scores on reading and written achievement tests throughout the school years.
    c. boys show an advantage over girls in general verbal ability during adolescence.
    d. girls retain a highly significant advantage over boys in verbal ability throughout the lifespan.

20. Research on sex differences in mathematical ability among academically talented students shows that boys' advantage is primarily limited to: (p. 545)
    a. complex word problems and geometry.
    b. basic math knowledge.
    c. computational skills.
    d. areas of advanced mathematics, such as trigonometry and calculus.

21. Which of the following is true with regard to sex differences in mathematical ability? (p. 547)
    a. Boys regard mathematics as less useful for their future lives than do girls.
    b. Girls are more likely than boys to consider math- or science-related careers.
    c. Sex differences in mathematics reasoning have continued to increase over the past several decades.
    d. At present, boys and girls reach advanced levels of high school math and science study in equal proportions.

22. Research on sex differences in personality traits shows that: (p. 548)
    a. girls are genetically prewired to be more nurturant and emotionally sensitive as a means of preparing them for the caregiving role.
    b. sex differences in emotional sensitivity remain noticeable into adulthood as parents interact with their babies.
    c. cultural expectations for behavior, rather than biological influences, are largely responsible for the gender gap in emotional sensitivity.
    d. boys and girls show equivalent levels of emotional sensitivity throughout the lifespan.

23. Adolescent depression: (p. 549)
    a. occurs more often in boys than in girls.
    b. is usually recognized quickly by parents and teachers.
    c. can be entirely attributed to biological causes, namely hormonal changes during puberty.
    d. can seriously impair social, academic, and vocational functioning if allowed to persist.

24. Research examining why girls are more prone to depression than are boys shows that: (p. 550)
    a. the biological changes associated with puberty are primarily responsible for the gender gap.
    b. rates of depression for males and females are similar in all developing and industrialized countries around the world.
    c. stressful life events and gender-typed coping styles account for girls' higher rates of depression.
    d. girls with an androgynous or masculine gender identity are as likely as girls with a strong feminine identity to show signs of depression.

25. Research on aggression shows that: (p. 551)
    a. biological differences do not contribute to males' greater overt aggression.
    b. males inherit a predisposition for aggression as a result of prenatal exposure to the androgen hormone.
    c. exposure to androgens is a direct cause of aggression, regardless of environmental influences.
    d. environmental influences have a far greater impact on boys' aggression than do biological influences.

CHAPTER 14
THE FAMILY

BRIEF CHAPTER SUMMARY

The family is the child's first, and longest lasting, context for development. Although other contexts also mold children's development, in power and breadth of influence, none equals the family. The human family in its most common form can be traced to our hunting-and-gathering ancestors, for whom it was uniquely suited to promote survival. Important functions of the modern family include reproduction, socialization, and emotional support.

According to the social systems perspective, the family consists of a complex network of bidirectional relationships that continually readjust as family members change over time. The quality of these relationships, and therefore children's development, depends in part on links established with formal and informal social supports in the surrounding community.

Three features differentiate major child-rearing styles: acceptance and involvement, control, and autonomy granting. When combined, these characteristics yield four parenting styles: authoritative, authoritarian, permissive, and uninvolved. Consistent SES differences in child rearing exist, and ethnic variations in child rearing can be understood in terms of cultural values and the context in which families live.

Familes in industrialized nations have become more diverse. The recent trend toward a smaller family size is associated with more favorable child development. Most children grow up with at least one sibling and sibling interactions promote many aspects of social competence. Only children are just as well adjusted and socially competent as other children and advantaged in some respects. Adopted children and adolescents have more learning and emotional difficulties than do their nonadopted agemates, but by adulthood this difference disappears. Transracially and transculturally adopted young people typically develop identities that are healthy blends of their birth and rearing backgrounds. Although limited and based on small samples, research on gay and lesbian parents indicates that they are as committed to and effective at child rearing as are heterosexuals.

Children of never-married mothers show slightly better academic performance and emotional adjustment than do children of divorced or remarried mothers but not as good as children in first-marriage families. Large numbers of American children experience the divorce of their parents. Although divorce is painful for children, evidence shows that remaining in a high-conflict intact family is much worse than making the transition to a low conflict, single-parent household. Effective parenting is the most important factor in helping children adapt to life in a single-parent or a blended family.

Maternal employment is related to positive outcomes in children, although these vary depending on the children's sex and SES, the demands of the mother's job, and the father's participation in child rearing. High-quality child care fosters cognitive, language, and social development. Unfortunately, much child care in the United States is substandard and poses serious risks to children's development.

Self-care children who have a history of authoritative child rearing, and who are monitored from a distance by telephone calls, and have regular after-school chores, appear responsible and well adjusted.

Child maltreatment is related to factors within the family, community, and larger culture, and efforts to prevent it must be directed at each of these levels. Child and parent characteristics often feed on one another to produce abusive behavior. A society that approves of force and violence as an appropriate means for solving problems promotes child abuse.

LEARNING OBJECTIVES

After reading this chapter, you should be able to:

14.1   Discuss the evolutionary origins of the family unit. (pp. 558–559)

14.2   Describe the functions of the family, noting changes in these functions from the time of our evolutionary ancestors to the present. (p. 559)

14.3   Describe the social systems perspective of family functioning, including its view of family interaction and the influence of surrounding social contexts. (pp. 559–563)

14.4   Describe the four styles of child-rearing, indicating which is most effective, and explain how the use of adaptable parenting practices in middle childhood and adolescence helps to support children's development. (pp. 563–569)

14.5   Summarize socioeconomic and ethnic variations in child-rearing, with attention to the impact of poverty on parenting behavior. (pp. 569–573)

14.6   Explain how family size impacts child-rearing. (pp. 573–574)

14.7   Trace the changes in sibling relationships from infancy to adolescence, and compare the experiences and developmental outcomes of only children with those of children who have siblings. (pp. 574–576)

14.8   Discuss the adjustment and developmental outcomes of children reared in a variety of family types, including adoptive families, gay and lesbian families, and never-married single-parent families. (pp. 576–578)

14.9   Discuss factors that influence children's adjustment to divorce and blended families. (pp. 578–583)

14.10 Discuss the impact of maternal employment and dual-earner families on children's development. (pp. 583–584)

14.11 Discuss issues related to child care, including the impact of child care quality on children's development, the status of child care in the United States compared to that of other industrialized nations, and the impact of self-care on school-age children's adjustment. (pp. 584–586)

14.12 Describe the five forms of child maltreatment, and note factors associated with child maltreatment, consequences of child maltreatment, and strategies for the prevention of child maltreatment. (pp. 587–592)

STUDY QUESTIONS

Evolutionary Origins

1. True or False: Almost all species of animals organize into family-like units. (p. 558)

2. Why do anthropologists believe that bipedalism-the ability to walk upright on two legs-was an important evolutionary step in the formation of the human family unit? (p. 558)

_____

_____

_____

Functions of the Family

1. In our evolutionary past, what five functions did the family unit serve for society? (p. 559)

    A. _____

    B. _____

    C. _____

    D. _____

    E. _____

2. Of the five functions listed above, list the three that remain the primary province of the family. (p. 559)

    A. _____

B. _____

C. _____

3. For the two functions that no longer remain the primary province of the family, discuss how societal institutions have assumed responsibility for these services. (p. 559)

A. _____
_____

B. _____
_____

4. Summarize the *social systems perspective* of family functioning. (p. 559)

_____
_____
_____

The Family as a Social System

Direct and Indirect Influences

1. Distinguish between direct and indirect familial influences. (p. 560)

Direct: _____
_____
_____

Indirect: _____
_____
_____

From Research to Practice: The Transition to Parenthood

1. Discuss several changes in the family system following the birth of a new baby. (p. 561)

_____
_____
_____

2. True or False: For most new parents, the arrival of a baby causes significant marital strain. (p. 561)

3. In what ways does postponing childbearing until the late twenties or thirties ease the transition to parenthood? (p. 561)

_____

_____

_____

4. Discuss the ways in which interventions for parents who are not at risk differ from interventions for high-risk parents. (p. 561)

Not at risk: _____

_____

_____

High risk: _____

_____

_____

Adapting to Change

1. Discuss some of the ways in which the family system must adapt over time. (p. 562)

_____

_____

_____

The Family System in Context

1. Discuss three ways that familial ties to the neighborhood and community help to reduce stress and foster child development. (p. 562)

A. _____

_____

B. _____

_____

C. _____

_____

2. Neighborhood resources have a greater impact on children growing up in (disadvantaged / well-to-do) areas. Why is this so? (p. 563)

_____

_____

Socialization Within the Family

Styles of Child Rearing

1. Based on the research findings of Baumrind and others, cite three features that consistently differentiate a competent, authoritative parenting style from less effective authoritarian and permissive styles. (pp. 563–564)

A. _____

B. _____

C. _____

2. Describe the four styles of child-rearing, noting where each stands in relation to the characteristics listed above. (pp. 564)

Authoritative: _____

_____

_____

Authoritarian: _____

_____

_____

Permissive: _____

_____

_____

Uninvolved: _____

_____

_____

3. Summarize child outcomes associated with each of the following styles of parenting: (pp. 564–566)

Authoritative: _____

_____

_____

Authoritarian: _____

_____

_____

Permissive: _____

_____

_____

Uninvolved: _____

_____

_____

4. What child-rearing approach is most effective? (p. 564)

_____

5. At its extreme, uninvolved parenting is a form of child maltreatment called
_____. (p. 565)

What Makes the Authoritative Style So Effective?

1. Discuss five reasons why authoritative parenting is especially effective for supporting children's competence and helping to bring intractable behavior under control. (pp. 566–567)

A. _____

_____

B. _____

_____

C. _____

_____

D. _____

_____

E. _____

_____

Biology and Environment: Do Parents Really Matter?

1. Judith Harris believes that parents play only a minor role in children's development. According to Harris, parents are overshadowed by children's _____ makeup and _____ culture. (p. 568)

2. Upon what evidence does Harris base her conclusions? (p. 568)

_____

_____

_____

3. Research shows that the relationship between authoritative parenting and children's development is (weak / substantial). (p. 568)

4. True or False: Child-rearing practices affect different children in different ways. (p. 568)

5. Summarize longitudinal research findings related to the impact of parenting on children's development. (p. 568)

_____

_____

_____

6. True or False: Research on parenting interventions shows that even when child-rearing improves, children fail to show appropriate developmental changes. (p. 568)

7. Parents (do / do not) influence children's peer relations. (p. 568)

8. Describe four strategies that parents can use to ensure the best outcomes for their children. (p. 568)

A. _____

_____

B. _____

_____

C. _____

_____

D _____

_____

Adapting Child Rearing to Children's Development

1. True or False: In middle childhood, the amount of time that children spend with their parents declines dramatically. (p. 567)

2. During the school years, child rearing becomes easier for those parents who established a(n) _____ parenting style during the early years. (p. 567)

3. What is *coregulation*? (p. 567)

_____

_____

4. During adolescence, _____—establishing oneself as a separate, self-governing individual—becomes a salient task. (p. 567)

5. Describe two components of autonomy. (p. 567)

A. _____

_____

B. _____

_____

6. Summarize changes within the adolescent that support the development of autonomy. (pp. 567–569)

_____

_____

_____

7. Discuss parenting practices that foster adolescent autonomy. (p. 569)

_____

_____

_____

8. Discuss the life transition that parents may be experiencing as their adolescent children are undergoing their own life transitions, and note how this impacts the parent-child relationship. (p. 569)

Parent transition: _____

_____

_____

Impact: _____

_____

_____

9. Explain how mild parent-child conflict is beneficial to adolescents and parents. (p. 569)

Adolescents: _____

_____

Parents: _____

_____

Socioeconomic and Ethnic Variations in Child Rearing

1. Compare child characteristics emphasized in lower-SES families with those emphasized in higher-SES families. (p. 570)

Lower-SES: _____

_____

Higher-SES: _____

_____

2. Describe the influence of SES on parenting practices and parent-child interaction. (p. 570)

_____

_____

_____

3. Describe how the constant stresses that accompany poverty gradually weaken the family system. (p. 570)

_____

_____

_____

4. Describe how the parenting practices of the following cultural groups often differ from those of Caucasian Americans. (p. 571)

Chinese: _____

_____

Hispanic and Asian Pacific Island: _____

_____

African-American: _____

_____

5. Low-SES African-American and Hispanic parents who use more controlling strategies tend to have children who are (more / less) cognitively and socially competent. (p. 571)

6. The African _____ household, in which one or more adult relatives live with the parent-child nuclear family unit, is a vital feature of black family life. (p. 572)

Cultural Influences: The African-American Extended Family

1. Describe some ways in which extended family relationships benefit African-American families. (p. 572)

_____

_____

_____

From Large to Small Families

1. Cite four reasons that family size has declined in industrialized nations. (p. 573)

   A. _____

   B. _____

   C. _____

   D. _____

2. Describe the benefits of growing up in a small family. (p. 573)

   _____

   _____

   _____

3. What factor likely contributes to the negative relationship between family size and children's well-being? (p. 574)

   _____

4. When a new baby arrives, how is a preschool-age sibling likely to respond? Include both positive and negative reactions in your answer. (p. 574)

   Positive: _____

   _____

   Negative: _____

   _____

5. Explain how parenting impacts sibling relationships. (p. 574)

   _____

   _____

   _____

6. During middle childhood, sibling rivalry tends to (increase / decrease). Why is this the case? (p. 575)

_____

_____

7. Cite two characteristics of sibling pairs that are associated with more frequent parental comparisons. (p. 575)

A. _____   B. _____

8. During adolescence, teenagers invest (more / less) time and energy in siblings. Why is this the case? (p. 575)

_____

_____

9. Sibling relationships become (more / less) intense during adolescence, in both positive and negative feelings. (p. 575)

10. True or False: Quality of sibling relationships is fairly stable over time. (p. 575)

One-Child Families

1. True or False: Research indicates that sibling relationships are essential for healthy development. (p. 575)

2. True or False: Research supports the commonly held belief that only children are spoiled and selfish. (p. 575)

3. Discuss the adjustment of children in one-child families. (p. 576)

_____

_____

_____

4. Discuss some of the pros and cons of living in a one-child family, including perspectives of parents as well as children. (p. 576)

Pros (children): _____

_____

Cons (children): _____

_____

Pros (parents): _____

_____

Cons (parents): _____

_____

Adoptive Families

1. Adopted children and adolescents have (fewer / more) learning and emotional difficulties than do other children. Cite four possible reasons for this trend. (p. 576)

   A. _____

   B. _____

   C. _____

   D. _____

2. True or False: Children with special needs usually benefit from adoption, even when they are adopted at older ages. (p. 577)

3. True or False: Most adoptees have serious, long-term adjustment problems that are evident well into adulthood. (p. 577)

Gay and Lesbian Families

1. True or False: Research shows that gay and lesbian parents are as committed to and effective at child-rearing as are heterosexual parents. (p. 577)

2. What does research indicate about the parenting behaviors of gay fathers in comparison to their heterosexual counterparts? (p. 577)

   _____

   _____

3. True or False: Children from homosexual families are as well-adjusted as other children. (p. 577)

4. The majority of children from gay and lesbian families are (heterosexual / homosexual). (p. 577)

Never-Married Single-Parent Families

1. About _____ percent of American children have parents who have never married. (p. 577)

2. What group constitutes the largest proportion of never-married parents? What factors may contribute to this trend? (p. 578)

   _____

   _____

3. Discuss outcomes associated with children of never-married mothers relative to children in low-income, first-married families. (p. 578)

   _____

   _____

Divorce

1. True or False: The United States has the highest divorce rate in the world. (p. 578)

2. About half of American marriages end in divorce; just over _____ percent of them involve children. (p. 578)

3. Summarize ways in which divorce has an immediate impact on the home environment. (pp. 578–579)

   _____

   _____

   _____

4. Discuss how children's ages affect their reactions to divorce, noting differences between younger and older children. (p. 579)

   _____

   _____

   _____

5. Summarize sex differences in children's reactions to divorce. (p. 580)

   Boys: _____

   _____

   _____

Girls: _____

_____

_____

6. In mother-custody families, (girls / boys) typically experience more serious adjustment problems. (p. 580)

7. True or False: Boys of divorcing parents receive more emotional support from mothers, teachers, and peers than do girls of divorcing parents. (p. 580)

8. Most children show improved adjustment by _____ years after their parents' divorce. (p. 580)

9. True or False: Children of divorced parents score lower than children with continually married parents in self-esteem and social competence. (p. 580)

10. (Boys / Girls) and children with _____ temperaments are especially likely to drop out of school and display antisocial behavior in adolescence following a parental divorce. (p. 580)

11. True or False: For both sexes, divorce is linked to problems with adolescent sexuality and development of intimate ties. (p. 580)

12. What is the overriding factor in children's positive adjustment following a parental divorce? (p. 580)

_____

13. Explain why a good father–child relationship is important for both boys and girls following divorce. (p. 580)

Girls: _____

_____

Boys: _____

_____

14. True or False: Making the transition to a low-conflict, single-parent household is better for children than staying in a high-conflict intact family. (pp. 580–581)

15. Describe *divorce mediation*, and explain why it is likely to have benefits for children. (p. 581)

_____

_____

_____

_____

16. In _____, the court grants the mother and father equal say in important decisions regarding the child's upbringing. Describe common living arrangements associated with this option, noting their impact on children's adjustment. (p. 581)

Living arrangements: _____

_____

_____

Impact: _____

_____

_____

Blended Families

1. When single parents remarry or cohabitate, the parent, stepparent, and children form a new family structure called a _____, or *reconstituted*, family. (p. 581)

2. List two reasons why blended families present adjustment difficulties for most children. (p. 581)

   A. _____

   _____

   B. _____

   _____

3. (Older / Younger) children and (girls / boys) have the hardest time adjusting to a parent's divorce. (p. 581)

4. The most frequent form of blended family is a (father-stepmother / mother-stepfather) arrangement. Contrast boys' and girls' adjustment in this type of family arrangement. (p. 581)

   Boys: _____

   _____

Girls: _____

_____

5. Explain why older children and adolescents of both sexes living in mother-stepfather families display more irresponsible, acting out, and antisocial behavior than do their agemates in nonstepfamilies. (p. 582)

_____

_____

_____

6. Remarriage of noncustodial fathers often leads to (reduced / increased) contact with children, particularly if they have daughters. (p. 582)

7. Cite two reasons why children tend to react negatively to the remarriage of custodial fathers. (p. 582)

A. _____

B. _____

8. (Girls / Boys) have an especially hard time getting along with stepmothers. Briefly explain your response. (p. 582)

_____

_____

_____

9. Explain how family life education and therapy can help parents and children in blended families adapt to the complexities of their new circumstances. (p. 583)

_____

_____

_____

Maternal Employment and Dual-Earner Families

1. True or False: Single mothers are far more likely than their married counterparts to enter the workforce. (p. 583)

2. For children of any age, _____ percent of their mothers are employed. (p. 583)

3. Describe potential benefits of maternal employment for school-age children, and note the circumstances under which such outcomes are achieved. (p. 583)

_____

_____

_____

4. True or False: Maternal employment results in more time with fathers, who take on greater responsibility with child care. (p. 583)

5. List four supports which help parents juggle the demands of work and child-rearing. (p. 584)

A. _____

B. _____

C. _____

D. _____

Child Care

1. True or False: Preschoolers exposed to poor-quality child care, regardless of family SES level, score lower on measures of cognitive and social skills. (p. 584)

2. List four characteristics of high quality child care. (pp. 584–585)

A. _____

B. _____

C. _____

D. _____

3. True or False: The United States has a national child care policy, and consequently, far surpasses other industrialized nations in supply, quality, and affordability of child care. (p. 585)

Self-Care

1. Differentiate self-care children who fare well from those who fare poorly. (p. 586)

   Children who fare well: _____

   _____

   _____

   Children who fare poorly: _____

   _____

   _____

2. Before age _____ or _____, children should not be left unsupervised because most are not yet competent to handle emergencies. (p. 586)

Vulnerable Families: Child Maltreatment

Incidence and Definitions

1. List and describe five forms of child maltreatment. (p. 587)

   A. _____

   _____

   B. _____

   _____

   C. _____

   _____

   D. _____

   _____

   E. _____

   _____

2. Which form of abuse may be the most common, since it accompanies most other types? (p. 587)

   _____

1. Sexual abuse is committed against children of both sexes, but more often against (girls / boys). (pp. 588–589)

2. Describe typical characteristics of sexual abusers. (pp. 588–589)

    _____

    _____

    _____

    _____

3. Abusers often pick out child victims who are _____

    _____. (pp. 588–589)

4. Discuss the adjustment problems of sexually abused children, noting differences between younger children and adolescents. (pp. 588–589)

    Younger children: _____

    _____

    _____

    Adolescents: _____

    _____

    _____

5. Describe common behavioral characteristics of sexually abused girls as they move into young adulthood. (pp. 588–589)

    _____

    _____

    _____

6. Why is it difficult to treat victims of child sexual abuse? (pp. 588–589)

    _____

    _____

    _____

7. Discuss the role of educational programs in preventing child sexual abuse. (pp. 588–589)

_____

_____

_____

Origins of Child Maltreatment

1. True or False: Researchers have identified a single "abusive" personality type. (pp. 587–588)

2. For help in understanding child maltreatment, researchers turned to the
_____ perspective of family functioning. (p. 588)

3. List parent, child, and general family environment characteristics associated with an increased likelihood of abuse. (pp. 589–591)

Parent: _____

_____

_____

Child: _____

_____

_____

Family Environment: _____

_____

_____

4. List two reasons that most abusive parents are isolated from supportive ties to their communities. (p. 590)

A. _____

_____

B. _____

_____

5. Societies that view violence as an appropriate way to solve problems set the stage for child abuse. These conditions (do / do not) exist in the United States. (pp. 590–591)

6. True or False: The majority of American parents report at least occasional use of slaps and spanking to discipline their children. (p. 591)

Consequences of Child Maltreatment

1. Summarize the consequences of child maltreatment for abused children. (p. 591)

_____

_____

_____

2. Cite one family characteristic strongly associated with child abuse. (p. 591)

_____

3. True or False: At school, maltreated children are serious adjustment problems. Elaborate on your response. (p. 591)

_____

_____

_____

4. Summarize psychophysiological changes that result from repeated abuse. (p. 591)

_____

_____

_____

Preventing Child Maltreatment

1. Discuss strategies for preventing child maltreatment. (pp. 591–592)

_____

_____

_____

2. Providing social supports to families (is / is not) effective in reducing child maltreatment. (p. 591)

3. List three reasons why judges hesitate to permanently remove maltreated children from the family. (p. 592)

A. _____

B. _____

C. _____

ASK YOURSELF . . .

Review: In our evolutionary history, why was the family adaptive? (p. 563)

_____

_____

_____

_____

_____

Review: Explain how, on the social systems perspective, the responses of all family members are interrelated. (p. 563)

_____

_____

_____

_____

_____

Apply: On a trip to a shopping center, you see a father getting angry with his young son. Using the social systems perspective, list as many factors as you can that might account for the father's behavior. (p. 563)

_____

_____

_____

_____

_____

Connect: How does the goodness-of-fit model, discussed in Chapter 10 (see page 416), illustrate central features of the social systems perspective on family functioning? (p. 563)

_____

_____

_____

_____

_____

Review: How do authoritative, authoritarian, and permissive child-rearing styles in acceptance and involvement, control, and autonomy granting? Why is authoritative parenting effective? (p. 573)

_____

_____

_____

_____

_____

Review: Why are lower-SES parents less likely to engage in authoritative child rearing? Is the authoritative style limited to Western middle-SES cultures? Explain. (p. 573)

_____

_____

_____

_____

_____

Apply: Prepare a short talk for a parent–teacher organization showing that parents matter greatly in children's lives. Support each of your points with research evidence. (p. 573)

_____

_____

_____

_____

_____

Connect: Explain how factors that support autonomy in adolescence also foster identity development. (p. 573)

_____

_____

_____

_____

_____

Review: Describe and explain changes in sibling relationships from early childhood to adolescence. How does parenting influence the quality of sibling ties? (p. 586)

_____

_____

_____

_____

_____

Review: Under what conditions do maternal employment and child care lead to benefits for preschool and school-age children? (p. 586)

_____

_____

_____

_____

_____

Apply: What advice would you give divorcing parents of two school-age sons about how to help their children to live in a single-parent family? (p. 586)

_____

_____

_____

_____

_____

Connect: Review research on resilient children in Chapter 1 (see page 10). Are factors that foster resiliency similar to those that promote favorable adjustment to divorce and remarriage? Explain. (p. 586)

_____

_____

_____

_____

_____

Review: How do personal and situational factors that contribute to child maltreatment illustrate the social systems perspective on family functioning? (p. 592)

_____

_____

_____

_____

_____

Review: Explain how the consequences of maltreatment for children's development can increase the chances of further maltreatment and lead to lasting adjustment problems. (p. 592)

_____

_____

_____

_____

_____

Apply: Claire told her 6-year-old daughter to be very careful to never talk to or take candy from strangers. Why will Claire's directive not protect her daughter from sexual abuse? (p. 592)

_____

_____

_____

_____

_____

Connect: After reviewing factors linked to adolescent parenthood (Chapter 5, pages 208–212), explain why it places children at risk for abuse and neglect. (p. 592)

_____

_____

_____

_____

_____

SUGGESTED STUDENT READINGS

Grych, J. H., & Fincham, G. D. (Eds.). (2001). *Interparental conflict and child development: Theory, research, and applications.* New York: Cambridge University Press. Drawing on research from developmental and family systems perspectives, this book highlights the impact of parental conflict on children's well-being. Topics include: the role of gender and ethnicity in parental conflict, the influence of family conflict on sibling and peer relations, family violence, clinical intervention, and public policy.

Hetherington, E. M. (Ed.). (1999). *Coping with divorce, single parenting, and remarriage: A risk and resiliency perspective.* Mahwah, NJ: Erlbaum. Examines family functioning and child adjustment in different kinds of families. Discusses interactions among individual, familial, and extra familial risk and protective factors associated with different kinds of experiences associated with marriage, divorce, single parenting, and remarriage.

Violato, C., & Oddone-Paolucci, E., Genius, M. (Eds.). (2000). *The changing family and child development.* Aldershot, England: Ashgate Publishing. An interdisciplinary approach to understanding the modern family, this book explores the causal impact of early childhood experiences, factors contributing to resiliency, the impact of family size, changing roles for girls and women, and the long-term consequences of nonmaternal care.

PUZZLE 14

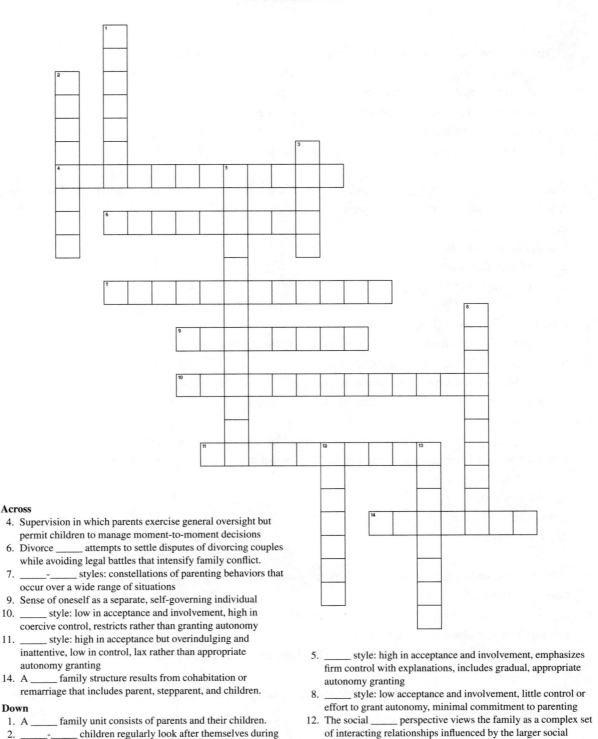

Across

4. Supervision in which parents exercise general oversight but permit children to manage moment-to-moment decisions
6. Divorce _____ attempts to settle disputes of divorcing couples while avoiding legal battles that intensify family conflict.
7. _____-_____ styles: constellations of parenting behaviors that occur over a wide range of situations
9. Sense of oneself as a separate, self-governing individual
10. _____ style: low in acceptance and involvement, high in coercive control, restricts rather than granting autonomy
11. _____ style: high in acceptance but overindulging and inattentive, low in control, lax rather than appropriate autonomy granting
14. A _____ family structure results from cohabitation or remarriage that includes parent, stepparent, and children.

Down

1. A _____ family unit consists of parents and their children.
2. _____-_____ children regularly look after themselves during after-school hours.
3. _____ custody: the court grants both parents equal say in important decisions about the child's upbringing
5. _____ style: high in acceptance and involvement, emphasizes firm control with explanations, includes gradual, appropriate autonomy granting
8. _____ style: low acceptance and involvement, little control or effort to grant autonomy, minimal commitment to parenting
12. The social _____ perspective views the family as a complex set of interacting relationships influenced by the larger social context.
13. In an _____-family household, the parent and child live with one or more adult relatives.

449

PRACTICE TEST

1. Of the five historical functions of the family, the three that remain the primary province of the family are: (p. 559)
    a. reproduction, economic services, and social order.
    b. economic services, social order, and socialization.
    c. social order, emotional support, and socialization.
    d. reproduction, socialization, and emotional support.

2. The _____ perspective views the family as a complex set of interacting relationships influenced by the larger social context. (p. 559)
    a. social systems
    b. dynamic systems
    c. ecological systems
    d. social dynamic

3. Researchers view the family as: (p. 559)
    a. a self-contained unit which is impervious to "third party" effects.
    b. a system of interdependent relationships.
    c. a stable system which is resistant to change.
    d. a network of unidirectional influences.

4. _____ child-rearing is marked by high acceptance and involvement, use of firm control with explanations, and gradual, appropriate autonomy granting. (p. 564)
    a. Authoritative
    b. Authoritarian
    c. Permissive
    d. Uninvolved

5. Which of the following outcomes are typically associated with children exposed to permissive parenting? (pp. 565–566)
    a. positive mood, high self-confidence and self-control, superior academic achievement
    b. anxiety, withdrawal, unhappiness
    c. poor impulse control, disobedience, rebelliousness, dependence on adults, low persistence on tasks
    d. poor emotional self-regulation, low academic self-esteem and school performance, frequent anti-social behavior.

6. A transitional form of supervision in which parents exercise general oversight while permitting children to be in charge of moment-by-moment decision making is called: (p. 567)
   a. permissive parenting.
   b. cooperative parenting.
   c. coregulation.
   d. self-regulation.

7. Which of the following is true of the parent-child relationship during adolescence? (p. 569)
   a. Parents and adolescents need to focus less on their attachment relationship and should begin to focus entirely on issues of separation.
   b. Adolescents tend to idealize their parents and are more compliant with parental authority than they were at earlier ages.
   c. Both adolescents and parents are undergoing major life transitions, and the pressures of each generation often oppose the other.
   d. Positive parent-child interaction declines from early adolescence into late adolescence as teenagers start to drive, hold part-time jobs, and stay out late.

8. Which of the following is true with regard to socioeconomic influences on child-rearing? (p. 570)
   a. Lower-SES fathers tend to play a more supportive role in child-rearing, while higher-SES fathers focus more on their provider role.
   b. Lower-SES parents tend to emphasize external characteristics, such as obedience, neatness, and cleanliness, whereas higher-SES parents emphasize psychological traits, such as curiosity, happiness, and self-direction.
   c. Lower-SES families use more warmth, explanations, inductive discipline, and verbal praise, while higher-SES parents use more commands, criticism, and physical punishment.
   d. Education has little impact on SES differences in parenting.

9. Research on the child-rearing beliefs and practices of particular ethnic groups indicates that: (p. 571)
   a. Chinese parents tend to emphasize control.
   b. Hispanic fathers show little parental warmth and low commitment to parenting.
   c. African-American mothers tend to be permissive.
   d. there are no distinct ethnic child-rearing practices and beliefs.

10. The unfavorable outcomes associated with large family size are eliminated when: (p. 574)
   a. parents are economically advantaged and provide a stimulating environment for their children.
   b. parents are more punitive in disciplining their children.
   c. siblings are spaced close together in age.
   d. parents have their children at a young age so that they are more energetic and better able to keep up with the demands of a large family.

11. During middle childhood, sibling rivalry: (p. 575)
    a. tends to decrease.
    b. tends to increase.
    c. is very rare.
    d. is more common when siblings are far apart in age.

12. During adolescence, siblings: (p. 575)
    a. have a more unequal relationship, with younger siblings showing greater willingness to accept direction from older siblings.
    b. devote more time to each other.
    c. have less intense interactions.
    d. experience a decline in the quality of their relationship.

13. Only children: (p. 575)
    a. are typically spoiled and selfish.
    b. tend to exhibit higher self-esteem and achievement motivation.
    c. have more distant relationships with parents.
    d. are less socially competent than children with siblings.

14. Which of the following is true? (p. 576)
    a. Adopted children have more learning and emotional difficulties than do other children.
    b. Children with special needs rarely benefit from adoption, especially when they are adopted at older ages.
    c. Most adoptees are poorly adjusted as adults.
    d. Children adopted from foreign countries often struggle with identity development despite parental attempts to help them blend their birth and rearing backgrounds.

15. Gay and lesbian families: (p. 577)
    a. often experience strain due to the ineffective parenting skills adopted by many homosexual parents.
    b. are often characterized by poor parent–child relationships.
    c. often produce children with long-term adjustment difficulties.
    d. are very similar to heterosexual families in terms of parenting commitment and effectiveness.

16. The disorganized family situation often seen immediately following a divorce is called: (p. 579)
    a. optimal parenting.
    b. minimal parenting.
    c. reconstruction.
    d. divorce mediation.

17. Which of the following is true with regard to age and sex differences in children's adjustment to divorce? (p. 580)
    a. Preschool and early school-age children are too cognitively immature to understand the circumstances of parental divorce, and consequently, they show few, if any, adverse effects.
    b. School-age children and adolescents are more likely than are preschool children to fantasize that their parents will get back together.
    c. In mother-custody families, girls experience more serious adjustment problems than do boys.
    d. Boys of divorcing parents receive less emotional support from mothers, teachers, and peers than do girls.

18. The overriding factor in positive adjustment following divorce is: (p. 580)
    a. child temperament.
    b. child age at the time of the divorce.
    c. effective parenting.
    d. economic stability.

19. Research suggests that, in the long run, divorce: (p. 580)
    a. is better for children than is remaining in a high-conflict intact family.
    b. has no impact on children's behavior and adjustment.
    c. is often associated with serious difficulties which persist into adulthood.
    d. is linked with more detrimental effects for girls than for boys.

20. Which of the following is true of blended families? (p. 582)
    a. Girls are especially likely to experience positive adjustment in mother–stepfather families.
    b. Older school-age children and adolescents of both sexes display more irresponsible and antisocial behavior than do their agemates in nonblended families.
    c. Remarriage of a noncustodial father often leads to increased contact with children.
    d. Both boys and girls react more positively to the remarriage of a custodial father than a custodial mother.

21. Maternal employment: (p. 583)
    a. is linked with more positive outcomes for sons than for daughters.
    b. results in a decline in the amount of time that children spend on homework and household chores.
    c. results in a decline in the amount of time that fathers devote to child care and household duties.
    d. is associated with positive adjustment for children as long as the mother remains committed to her role as a parent.

22. Which of the following is true? (p. 584)
    a. The number of young children in child care has decreased steadily over the last 30 years.
    b. Most American child care centers meet NAEYC standards for developmentally appropriate practice.
    c. Because the United States has a national child care policy, it exceeds other industrialized nations in supply, quality, and affordability to child care.
    d. Preschoolers in poor-quality care, regardless of their family's SES level, score lower on measures of cognitive and social skills.

23. Childhood self-care: (p. 586)
    a. is consistently linked with adjustment problems, including low self-esteem, anti-social behavior, and poor academic achievement.
    b. is associated with worse outcomes for older children than for younger children.
    c. is inappropriate for children under the age of 9.
    d. is associated with positive outcomes for children who have a history of permissive parenting.

24. Which form of abuse is likely to be the most common, since it also accompanies most other types? (p. 587)
    a. physical abuse
    b. psychological abuse
    c. emotional neglect
    d. physical neglect

25. Child maltreatment: (p. 591)
    a. is rare in large, industrialized nations and has declined in recent years.
    b. is rooted in adult psychological disturbance, and therefore, abusers demonstrate an easily identifiable abusive personality type.
    c. is best understood from a social learning perspective.
    d. is associated with peer difficulties, academic failure, depression, substance abuse, and delinquency.

CHAPTER 15
PEERS, MEDIA, AND SCHOOLING

BRIEF CHAPTER SUMMARY

Beginning at an early age, socialization in the family is supplemented by experiences in the wider world of peers, media, and school. In all human societies, children spend many hours in one another's company. Experiments with rhesus monkeys reveal that peer interaction is a vital source of social competence.

Peer sociability begins in infancy with social acts that are gradually replaced by coordinated exchanges in the second year of life. During the preschool years, interactive play with peers increases. In middle childhood and adolescence, gains in communication skills and a greater awareness of social norms contribute to advances in peer interaction. Parents influence children's peer sociability both directly, through attempts to influence their children's peer relations, and indirectly, through their child-rearing practices and play behaviors. Secure attachment, authoritative child rearing, inductive discipline, and emotionally positive and cooperative parent–child play also foster positive peer relations.

Preschool and young children view friendship as a concrete relationship based on shared activities and material goods. During middle childhood, children come to understand friendship as a mutual relationship based on trust. Adolescents stress intimacy and loyalty as the basis of friendship. Warm, gratifying friendships foster a variety of social and cognitive skills.

Peer acceptance is a powerful predictor of long-term psychological adjustment. Children's social behavior is a major determinant of peer acceptance. A particularly destructive form of interaction that emerges during middle childhood is peer victimization. By the end of middle childhood, peer groups form, through which children and adolescents learn about the functioning of social organizations. Children socialize one another through reinforcement, modeling, and direct pressures to conform to peer expectations.

American children spend more time watching TV than they do in any other waking activity. Heavy TV viewing promotes aggressive behavior, indifference to real-life violence, a fearful view of the world, ethnic and gender stereotypes, and a naive belief in the truthfulness of advertising. However, television can foster prosocial behavior as long as it is free of violent content.

Computers have become increasingly common in the lives of children. Computer-assisted instruction, word processing, programming, and electronic communications each offer unique educational benefits. Although speed-and-action videogames foster attentional and spatial skills, violent videogames promote aggression and desensitize children to violence. The Internet may enhance an understanding of other cultures, but excessive home use negatively affects emotional and social adjustment.

Schools are powerful forces in children's development. Pupils in traditional classrooms are slightly advantaged in achievement; those in open classrooms are more independent, tolerant of individual differences, and excited about learning. Teachers who are effective classroom managers and who provide cognitively stimulating activities enhance children's involvement and academic performance. Educational self-fulfilling prophecies are likely to occur when teachers emphasize competition and comparisons between pupils, have difficulty controlling the class, and engage in ability grouping. To be effective, mainstreaming must be carefully tailored to meet the academic and social needs of children with learning disabilities. Largely due to pressure from parents, some schools have extended mainstreaming to full inclusion.

Regardless of students' abilities, parent involvement in education is crucial for children's optimum learning. Cross-national comparisons of mathematics and science achievement reveal that students in Asian nations are consistently among the top performers, whereas Americans score no better than average and often below it; these differences become greater with increasing grades. American adolescents have no widespread vocational training system to assist them in preparing for challenging, well-paid careers.

LEARNING OBJECTIVES

After reading this chapter, you should be able to:

15.1 Discuss evidence indicating that both parental and peer relationships are vital for children's development. (pp. 598–599)

15.2 Discuss the emergence of peer sociability during infancy and toddlerhood, noting how early peer interactions are influenced by the child-caregiver bond. (p. 599)

15.3 Describe advances in peer sociability over the preschool years, with particular attention to the types of play outlined by Mildred Parten. (pp. 599–600)

15.4 Summarize changes in peer interaction during middle childhood and adolescence. (pp. 600–601)

15.5 Describe factors that influence peer sociability, including parental guidance and encouragement, child-rearing practices, play behavior, age mix of children, and cultural values. (pp. 601–604)

15.6 Describe the three stages of friendship outlined by William Damon, noting the corresponding age range for each stage. (pp. 604–605)

15.7 Summarize characteristics of children's friendships, including stability, resemblance, and interaction. (pp. 605–607)

15.8 Explain the relationship between childhood and adolescent friendships and adjustment in early adulthood. (p. 608)

15.9 Describe the four categories of peer acceptance, noting how each is related to social behavior, and discuss ways to help rejected children. (pp. 609–612)

15.10 Describe peer group formation in middle childhood and adolescence, including factors that influence group norms and social structures. (pp. 613–615)

15.11 Describe the techniques that children use to socialize one another, including reinforcement, modeling, and direct pressure to conform. (pp. 615–619)

15.12 Explain how television influences children's attitudes and behaviors, particularly in relation to aggression, ethnic and gender stereotypes, consumerism, prosocial behavior, academic learning, and imagination. (pp. 619–623)

15.13 Explain the influence of computer use on children's academic and social learning. (pp. 624–626)

15.14 Discuss the impact of class size, educational philosophy, school transitions, teacher-student interaction, and grouping practices on student motivation and academic achievement. (pp. 626–634)

15.15 Explain issues surrounding the educational placement of students with learning disabilities, and discuss the effectiveness of mainstreaming and full inclusion. (pp. 634–635)

15.16 Cite ways that schools can increase parental involvement. (p. 635)

15.17 Compare the American cultural climate for academic achievement with that of Asian nations. (pp. 636–638)

15.18 Discuss the problems faced by non-college bound youths in making the transition from school to work. (pp. 638–639)

STUDY QUESTIONS

The Importance of Peer Relations

1. Researchers studying non-human primates have found that peer relationships (are / are not) vital for social competence. (p. 598)

2. How do parent and peer associations complement one another? (p. 598)

_____

_____

3. Describe the research findings of Freud and Dann, who studied the development of six young German-Jewish orphans who lived together in a concentration camp for several years without close ties to adults. (p. 598)

_____

_____

_____

Development of Peer Sociability

Infant and Toddler Beginnings

1. What types of social acts occur between infants during the first year? (p. 599)

_____

_____

2. Between one and two years of age, _____ interaction occurs more often, largely in the form of mutual imitation involving jumping, chasing, or banging a toy. (p. 599)

3. Around age _____, toddlers begin to use words to talk about and influence a peer's behavior. (p. 599)

4. Explain how the caregiver-child bond fosters peer sociability during the first two years. (p. 599)

_____

_____

_____

The Preschool Years

1. Describe Parten's three-step sequence of social development. (p. 599)

A. _____

_____

B. _____

_____

C. 1. _____

_____

C. 2. _____

_____

2. True or False: Longitudinal research shows that Parten's play types emerge in a developmental sequence, with later-appearing ones replacing earlier ones. (p. 599)

3. It is the _____, rather than the *amount*, of solitary and parallel play that changes during early childhood. (p. 600)

4. Provide a description of the following categories of cognitive play: (p. 600)

Functional play: _____

_____

Constructive play: _____

_____

Make-believe play: _____

_____

Games with rules: _____

_____

5. True or False: High rates of nonsocial activity during the preschool years is a sign of maladjustment. (p. 600)

6. List three ways in which sociodramatic play contributes to cognitive and social development. (p. 600)

A. _____

B. _____

C. _____

Middle Childhood and Adolescence

1. As children enter middle childhood, _____ and _____ *play*, a form of peer interaction involving friendly chasing and play-fighting, becomes more common. (p. 601)

2. In our evolutionary past, rough-and-tumble play may have been important for the development of _____ skill. Another possibility is that rough-and-tumble play assists children in establishing a _____, a stable ordering of group members that predicts who will win when conflict arises. (p. 601)

3. True or False: By midadolescence, children spend more time with peers than with any other social partners. (p. 601)

Influences on Peer Sociability

Direct Parental Influences

1. List three ways in which parents influence their children's peer relationships. (p. 602)

   A. _____

   B. _____

   C. _____

Indirect Parental Influences

1. Explain how parent-child attachment and parent-child play can promote children's peer-interaction skills. (p. 602)

   Attachment: _____

   _____

   _____

   Play: _____

   _____

   _____

Age Mix of Children

1. Contrast the theories of Piaget and Vygotsky regarding the benefits of same- versus mixed-age peer interaction. (p. 603)

   Piaget: _____

   _____

Vygotsky: _____

_____

2. The play of younger children is more cognitively and socially mature in (same-age / mixed-age) classrooms. (p. 603)

3. Summarize the benefits that children derive from interacting with both younger and older children. (p. 603)

Younger: _____

_____

Older: _____

_____

Cultural Values

1. Explain how peer sociability in collectivist cultures differs from that in Western individualistic cultures. (p. 603)

_____

_____

_____

2. True or False: Peer contact increases during adolescence in all societies. (p. 604)

Friendship

Thinking About Friendship

1. Name and describe each of the stages outlined in Damon's three-stage sequence of friendship development, noting the corresponding age range for each stage. (pp. 604–605)

A. _____

_____

_____

B. _____

_____

_____

C. _____

_____

_____

Characteristics of Friendship

1. Friendship stability (increases / decreases) with age. Elaborate on your response. (p. 606)

_____

_____

_____

2. True or False: Friendships are highly stable during preschool and childhood. (p. 606)

3. More mature understanding of friendship (does / does not) lead to greater prosocial behavior between friends. (p. 606)

4. True or False: Friends are more likely to disagree and compete with each other than are nonfriends. Briefly explain your response. (p. 606)

_____

_____

_____

5. Explain how children's individual characteristics influence the impact of their friendships on development. (p. 606)

_____

_____

_____

6. Summarize the ways in which friends are likely to resemble each other during childhood and adolescence. (p. 607)

_____

_____

_____

7. Explain why adolescents are more likely than are younger children to befriend an individual who differs from themselves. (p. 607)

_____

_____

_____

8. Summarize sex differences in children's friendships during middle childhood, noting how these differences are related to boys' and girls' different social needs. (p. 607)

_____

_____

_____

9. True or False: Androgynous boys are just as likely as girls to form intimate same-sex ties, whereas boys who identify strongly with the traditional masculine role are less likely to do so. (p. 607)

10. (Boys / Girls) are more likely to have other-sex friends. (p. 607)

11. Cite four reasons why gratifying childhood and adolescent friendships are related to psychological health and competence during early adulthood. (p. 608)

A. _____

_____

B. _____

_____

C. _____

_____

D. _____

_____

12. Describe two circumstances in which friendship is linked to poor adjustment. (p. 608)

A. _____

_____

B. _____

_____

Peer Acceptance

1. Define *peer acceptance*, noting how it is different from friendship. (p. 609)

   _____

   _____

   _____

2. Researchers usually assess peer acceptance with self-report measures called
   _____ *techniques*. (p. 609)

3. Name and describe four categories of peer acceptance. (p. 609)

   A. _____

   B. _____

   C. _____

   D. _____

4. True or False: All school-age children fit into one of the four categories of peer acceptance described above in Question 3. (p. 609)

5. Discuss emotional and social outcomes associated with peer rejection. (p. 609)

   _____

   _____

   _____

Origins of Acceptance in the Peer Situation

1. Identify and describe two subtypes of popular children. (pp. 609–610)

   A. _____

   _____

   _____

   B. _____

   _____

   _____

2. Describe the social behavior of rejected-aggressive and rejected-withdrawn children. (p. 610)

Aggressive: _____

_____

Withdrawn: _____

_____

3. True or False: Controversial children are hostile and disruptive but also engage in high rates of positive, prosocial behavior. (p. 610)

4. True or False: Controversial children have as many friends as do popular children. (p. 610)

5. True or False: Neglected children are more poorly adjusted and display less socially competent behavior than do their "average" counterparts. (pp. 610–612)

Helping Rejected Children

1. Describe three interventions designed to help rejected children. (p. 612)

A. _____

_____

B. _____

_____

C. _____

_____

Biology and Environment: Peer Victimization

1. What is *peer victimization*? (p. 611)

_____

_____

2. Describe biological and familial characteristics common to victimized children. (p. 611)

Biological: _____

_____

_____

Familial: _____

_____

_____

3. List adjustment difficulties associated with victimization by peers. (p. 611)

_____

_____

_____

4. True or False: Passive victims of bullying are more despised by peers than are aggressive bully / victims. (p. 611)

5. Discuss individual and school-based interventions for peer victimization. (p. 611)

_____

_____

_____

Peer Groups

1. What are the characteristics of a peer group? (p. 613)

_____

_____

First Peer Groups

1. Describe the positive functions of children's peer groups. (p. 613)

_____

_____

_____

_____

2. How do school-age boys and girls express hostility toward the "outgroup" differently? (p. 613)

Boys: _____

_____

Girls: _____

_____

Cliques and Crowds

1. Differentiate between cliques and crowds, noting the characteristics of each. (p. 614)

Cliques: _____

_____

_____

Crowds: _____

_____

_____

2. True or False: Membership in a clique predicts girls' academic and social competence, but not boys'. (p. 614)

3. Provide some examples of typical high school crowds. (p. 614)

_____

_____

4. True or False: Peer group values are often an extension of values learned in the home. Elaborate on your response. (p. 614)

_____

_____

_____

5. Describe the function of mixed-sex cliques in early adolescence. (pp. 614–615)

_____

_____

_____

6. True or False: Crowds increase in importance from early to late adolescence. (p. 615)

Peer Reinforcement and Modeling

1. Children's responses to one another serve as _____, modifying the extent to which they display certain behaviors. (p. 615)

2. Children (are / are not) as receptive to peer reinforcement for antisocial behavior as they are for prosocial behavior. (p. 615)

3. Explain how peer reinforcement and modeling can be used as agents of behavioral change. (p. 615)

    _____

    _____

    _____

Peer Conformity

1. True or False: Conformity to peer pressure is greater during adolescence than during childhood or young adulthood. (p. 615)

2. Describe the differing spheres of influence of parents and peers during the adolescent years. (pp. 616–617)

    Parents: _____

    _____

    Peers: _____

    _____

3. Summarize the link between parenting behavior and adolescents' conformity to peer pressure. (pp. 617–618)

    _____

    _____

    _____

From Research to Practice: Adolescent Substance Use and Abuse

1. Discuss the impact of culture on adolescent substance use. (pp. 616–617)

    _____

    _____

    _____

2. True or False: Teenagers who experiment with alcohol, tobacco, and marijuana tend to be seriously maladjusted. (pp. 616–617)

3. Distinguish the characteristics of adolescents who experiment with drugs from those of adolescents who are drug abusers. (pp. 616–617)

Experimenters: _____

_____

_____

Abusers: _____

_____

_____

4. Discuss the long-term adjustment of adolescent substance abusers. (pp. 616–617)

_____

_____

_____

5. Cite intervention strategies that help reduce adolescent drug experimentation and help to prevent drug users from endangering themselves and others. (pp. 616–617)

_____

_____

_____

6. Discuss prevention and treatment strategies for adolescent drug abuse. (pp. 616–617)

Prevention: _____

_____

_____

Treatment: _____

_____

_____

1. True or False: Children in the United States spend far more time watching television than do children in other industrialized nations. (p. 619)

2. Summarize child outcome results from the investigation in which researchers studied residents of a small Canadian town just before TV reception became available in their community and then two years later. (p. 619)

   _____

   _____

   _____

How Much Television Do Children View?

1. True or False: Television viewing rises from early childhood into middle childhood and then declines in adolescence. (p. 619)

2. The average American school-age child watches _____ hours of TV per week. (p. 619)

3. List the three groups of children who tend to watch the most TV. (p. 619)

   A. _____

   B. _____

   C. _____

Development of Television Literacy

1. What is *television literacy*? (p. 619)

   _____

   _____

2. Describe the two interrelated parts of television literacy. (p. 620)

   A. _____

   B. _____

3. At what age do children fully grasp the unreality of TV fiction? (p. 620) _____

4. Discuss the consequences of young children's difficulty connecting separate scenes into a meaningful story line. (p. 620)

_____

_____

_____

Television and Social Learning

1. True or False: Violent content is depicted at above average rates in children's television programming, and cartoons are the most violent. (p. 620)

2. Why are preschool and school-age children more likely to imitate TV violence? (p. 620)

_____

3. Discuss the impact of TV violence on aggressive children. (p. 621)

_____

_____

_____

4. True or False: TV violence hardens children to aggression, making them more willing to tolerate it in others. (p. 621)

5. True or False: Research shows that the correlation between media violence and aggression is weak, and consequently, only a few heavy TV viewers are negatively affected by exposure to violent programming. (p. 621)

6. Discuss the portrayal of ethnic and gender stereotypes in children's television programming. (p. 621)

_____

_____

_____

7. Although younger children can distinguish a TV program from a commercial, it is not until age _____ that children grasp the selling purpose of an ad. (p. 622)

8. True or False: Prosocial TV has positive effects only when it is free of violent content. (p. 622)

Television, Academic Learning, and Imagination

1. True or False: The more often children watch *Sesame Street*, the higher they score on tests designed to measure the program's learning goals. (p. 622)

2. Discuss the impact of television viewing on children's cognitive development. (p. 623)

    _____

    _____

    _____

Regulating Children's Television

1. Why is the federal government reluctant to place limits on television content? (p. 623)

    _____

    _____

    _____

2. Government regulation requires broadcasters to provide at least _____ hours per week of educational programming. (p. 623)

3. Why are television ratings and the use of V Chips incomplete solutions for regulating children's television? (p. 623)

    _____

    _____

    _____

4. List several strategies that parents can use to monitor and control children's television viewing. (p. 623)

    A. _____

    B. _____

    C. _____

Computers

Computers and Academic Learning

1. Explain how the use of word processing programs can be beneficial to children as they learn to read and write. (p. 624)

   _____

   _____

   _____

2. Summarize the competencies gained by children who learn computer-programming skills. (p. 624)

   _____

   _____

   _____

Computers and Social Learning

1. Speed-and-action computer games foster _____ and
   _____ skills in both boys and girls. (p. 625)

2. True or False: Playing violent videogames promotes hostility and aggression, while at the same time reducing prosocial behavior. (p. 625)

3. Discuss evidence that heavy internet use negatively affects emotional and social adjustment. (pp. 625–626)

   _____

   _____

   _____

Schooling

Class and Student Body Size

1. Discuss the benefits of small class size. (p. 626)

   _____

   _____

   _____

2. Explain how small student body size is beneficial to secondary students, including those at risk for school dropout. (pp. 626–627)

_____

_____

_____

Educational Philosophies

1. Distinguish between traditional and open classrooms. (p. 627)

   Traditional: _____

   _____

   _____

   Open: _____

   _____

   _____

2. Older students in (open / traditional) classrooms have a slight edge in academic achievement. (p. 627)

3. Cite several benefits of open classrooms. (p. 627)

   _____

   _____

   _____

4. True or False: Traditional-classroom kindergartners, particularly those from low-SES homes, show better study habits and increased grade-school achievement compared to children in open kindergarten classrooms. (p. 627)

5. List and describe three educational themes that were inspired by Vygotsky's emphasis on the social origins of learning. (pp. 628–629)

   A. _____

   _____

   B. _____

   _____

C. _____

_____

6. Describe the main features of the *Kamehameha Elementary Education Program (KEEP)*, and state whether or not research supports the effectiveness of this model. (p. 629)

_____

_____

_____

_____

_____

Social Issues: Education—When Are Children Ready For School? Academic Redshirting and Early Retention

1. Define *academic redshirting*, and discuss research evaluating the effectiveness of this practice. (p. 628)

_____

_____

_____

2. True or False: Children retained in kindergarten show many learning benefits, as well as other positive consequences in motivation, self-esteem, and attitudes toward school. (p. 628)

3. _____ classes, or way stations between kindergarten and first grade, are a form of homogeneous grouping and have the same implications for teacher–student interactions as other "low-ability" groups. (p. 628)

School Transitions

1. Contrast the characteristics of children who show positive adjustment to kindergarten with those of children who have adjustment difficulties. (pp. 629–630)

Positive adjustment: _____

_____

_____

Adjustment difficulties: _____

_____

_____

2. With each school transition, adolescents' course grades (improve / decline). Cite four reasons for this occurrence. (p. 630)

   A. _____

   B. _____

   C. _____

   D. _____

3. Contrast adolescents' adjustment to school transitions in districts having a 6-3-3 grade organization with those having an 8-4 grade organization. (p. 631)

   6-3-3: _____

   _____

   _____

   8-4: _____

   _____

   _____

4. Overall, findings show that the (earlier / later) the school transition occurs, the more dramatic and long-lasting its impact on psychological well-being, especially for (boys / girls). Explain why this is the case. (p. 631)

   _____

   _____

   _____

5. List three ways of helping adolescents adjust to school transitions. (pp. 631–632)

   A. _____

   B. _____

   C. _____

Teacher-Student Interaction

1. Research suggests that students are more attentive when teachers encourage _____-*level thinking*, such as analyzing, synthesizing, and applying ideas and concepts, rather than rote, repetitive drill. (p. 632)

2. Describe how teachers interact differently with high-achieving students versus low-achieving, disruptive students. (p. 632)

    High-achieving students: _____

    _____

    Low-achieving students: _____

    _____

3. What is an *educational self-fulfilling prophecy*, and how does it affect students' motivation and performance? (p. 632)

    _____

    _____

    _____

Grouping Practices

1. Homogeneous ability grouping (widens / narrows) the gap between high- and low-achieving students. Explain why this is the case. (p. 633)

    _____

    _____

    _____

2. True or False: Self-esteem and attitudes toward school are more positive in multi-grade classrooms than in single-grade classrooms. (p. 633)

3. True or False: When teachers provide assistance, heterogeneous classes are desirable into junior high school. (p. 633)

4. True or False: A good student from a disadvantaged family is just as likely to be placed in an academically-oriented, college-bound track as a student of equal ability from a middle-SES background. What affect does this have on student achievement? (p. 634)

    _____

    _____

    _____

5. True or False: High school students are separated into academic and vocational tracks in virtually all industrialized nations. (p. 634)

6. Explain how the system of educational placement in the United States differs from that in Japan, China, and many Western European nations, and note the impact of these differences on student outcomes. (p. 634)

_____

_____

_____

_____

_____

Teaching Students with Special Needs

1. Distinguish between *mainstreaming* and *full inclusion*. (p. 634)

   Mainstreaming: _____

   _____

   Full inclusion: _____

   _____

2. Describe characteristics of a *learning disability*. (p. 634)

   _____

   _____

   _____

3. Discuss findings on the effectiveness of mainstreaming and full inclusion in relation to student academic experiences and integrated participation in classroom life. (pp. 634–635)

   _____

   _____

   _____

4. Special-needs children placed in regular classrooms often do best when they receive instruction in a _____ room for part of the day and in the regular classroom for the remainder of the day. Describe this approach to instruction. (p. 635)

_____

_____

_____

5. Describe three ways in which teachers can promote peer acceptance of mainstreamed children. (p. 635)

A. _____

B. _____

C. _____

Parent-School Partnerships

1. Summarize the benefits of parental involvement in education. (p. 635)

_____

_____

_____

2. List five ways in which schools can increase parental involvement. (p. 635)

A. _____

B. _____

C. _____

D. _____

E. _____

Cross-Cultural Research on Academic Achievement

1. Describe the findings of international studies comparing the achievement of American children with that of children in other industrialized nations. (pp. 636–637)

   _____

   _____

   _____

2. True or False: Research shows that Asian children are high achievers because they are smarter, and they start school with cognitive advantages over their American peers. (p. 637)

3. True or False: The achievement of U. S. elementary and secondary school students has improved over the past decade in reading, science, and mathematics. (p. 638)

Cultural Influences: Education in Japan, Taiwan, and the United States

1. Describe five cultural conditions in Japan and Taiwan that support high academic achievement, noting how this compares to conditions in the United States. (pp. 636–637)

   A. _____

   _____

   _____

   B. _____

   _____

   _____

   C. _____

   _____

   _____

   D. _____

   _____

   _____

E. _____

_____

_____

Making the Transition from School to Work

1. Approximately _____ percent of American adolescents graduate from high school without plans to go to college. (p. 638)

2. Describe the nature of most jobs held by adolescents, and discuss the impact of heavy job commitment on adolescents' attitudes and behaviors. (p. 639)

_____

_____

_____

3. List four benefits of participation in work-study programs. (p. 639)

A. _____

B. _____

C. _____

D. _____

4. True or False: Like some European nations, the United States has a widespread training system designed to prepare youth for skilled business and industrial occupations and manual trades. (p. 639)

5. Cite the components of a youth apprenticeship program, and identify three major challenges to the implementation of a national apprenticeship program in the Unites States. (p. 639)

Components: _____

_____

_____

Challenges:

A. _____

_____

B. _____

_____

C. _____

_____

ASK YOURSELF. . .

Review: Cite major changes in children's peer sociability during early and middle childhood. Why do children engage in rough-and-tumble play? (p. 604)

_____

_____

_____

_____

_____

Review: How do parents contribute, both directly and indirectly, to children's peer sociability? (p. 604)

_____

_____

_____

_____

_____

Apply: Roger's mother is worried about his social development because he likes to play alone, working puzzles, painting, and looking at books. Is Roger likely to be deficient in social skills? Explain. (p. 604)

_____

_____

_____

_____

_____

Connect: What aspects of parent–child interaction probably contribute to the relationship between attachment and security and children's peer sociability? (See Chapter 10, pages 422–427). (p. 604)

_____

_____

_____

_____

_____

Review: Describe the unique qualities of interaction between close friends, and explain how they contribute to development. (p. 608)

_____

_____

_____

_____

_____

Review: Why are aggressive children's friendships likely to magnify their antisocial behavior? (p. 608)

_____

_____

_____

_____

_____

Apply: In his junior year of high school, Ralph, of Irish Catholic background, befriended Jonathan, a Chinese-American of the Buddhist faith. Both boys are from middle-SES homes and are good students. What might explain Ralph's desire for a friend both similar to and different from himself? (p. 608)

_____

_____

_____

_____

_____

Connect: Cite similarities in the development of self-concept and the concepts of friendship. (See Chapter 11, pages 444–445.) Explain how Stu's, Pete's, Denise's, and Mari's discussion in the introduction of the chapter reflect understandings that typically emerge at adolescence. (p. 608)

_____

_____

_____

_____

_____

Review: Why are rejected children at risk for maladjustment? What experiences with peers probably contribute to their serious, long-term adjustment problems? (p. 612)

_____

_____

_____

_____

_____

Review: What factors make some children susceptible to peer victimization? What consequences does victimization have for adjustment, and how can it be prevented? (p. 612)

_____

_____

_____

_____

_____

Connect: Cite parenting influence on children's social skills, and explain why interventions that focus only on the rejected child are unlikely to produce lasting changes in peer acceptance (See page 602). What changes in parent-child relationships are probably necessary?

_____

_____

_____

_____

_____

Review: What positive functions do group ties serve in young people's development? What factors lead some peer groups to have harmful consequences? (p. 619)

_____

_____

_____

_____

_____

Review: Do adolescents indiscriminately bend to peer pressures? Explain. (p. 619)

_____

_____

_____

_____

_____

Apply: Thirteen-year-old Mattie's parents are warm, firm in their expectations, and consistent in monitoring her peer activities. What type of crowd is Mattie likely to belong to, and why? (p. 619)

_____

_____

_____

_____

_____

Review: Why are preschool and young school-age children more likely than older children and adolescents to imitate TV violence? (p. 626)

_____

_____

_____

_____

_____

Review: Describe research that supports the academic and social benefits of educational television and computer use. (p. 626)

_____

_____

_____

_____

_____

Apply: Eleven-year-old Tommy spends hours each afternoon surfing the Net and playing computer games. Using research findings, explain why his parents should intervene in both activities. (p. 626)

_____

_____

_____

_____

_____

Connect: Which of the following children is more likely to be attracted to watching violent TV: Jane, a popular child; Mack, a rejected child; Tim, a neglected child? Explain. (p. 626)

_____

_____

_____

_____

_____

Review: List educational practices that promote children's satisfaction with school life and academic achievement, explaining why each is effective. (p. 639)

_____

_____

_____

_____

_____

Review: Why is homogenous grouping in elementary school likely to induce educational self-fulfilling prophecies? (p. 639)

_____

_____

_____

_____

Apply: Tom and Sandy want to do everything possible to ensure their 5-year-old son's favorable transition to kindergarten and high academic achievement in elementary school. Provide a list of suggestions. (p. 639)

_____

_____

_____

_____

Connect: What common factors contribute to the high academic achievement of children and adolescents in Asian nations and to the academic success of immigrant youths, discussed on pages 50–51 of Chapter 2? (p. 639)

_____

_____

_____

_____

_____

SUGGESTED STUDENT READINGS

Grant, S. G. (Ed.). (1998). *Reforming reading, writing, and mathematics: Teachers' responses and the prospects for systemic reform.* Mahwah, NJ: Erlbaum. Examines teachers' responses to educational reforms in reading, writing, and mathematics and analyses the current trend toward systemic reform in the United States.

Jacobson, M. J., & Kozma, R. B. (Eds.). (2000). *Innovations in science and mathematics education: Advanced designs for technologies of learning.* Mahwah, NJ: Lawrence Erlbaum Associates. For those interested in computers in the classroom, this book presents the use of educational technology for optimal learning experiences, particularly in the fields of math and science.

Nangle, D. W., & Erdley, C. A. (Eds.). (2001). *The role of friendship in psychological adjustment: New directions for child and adolescent development.* San Francisco, CA: Jossey-Bass. A collection of chapters exploring the role of children's peer relations in socioemotional development. Topics include popularity, peer acceptance, the complex interactions that take place between friends, and historical and conceptual issues that have contributed to our understanding of childhood friendship.

PUZZLE 15.1

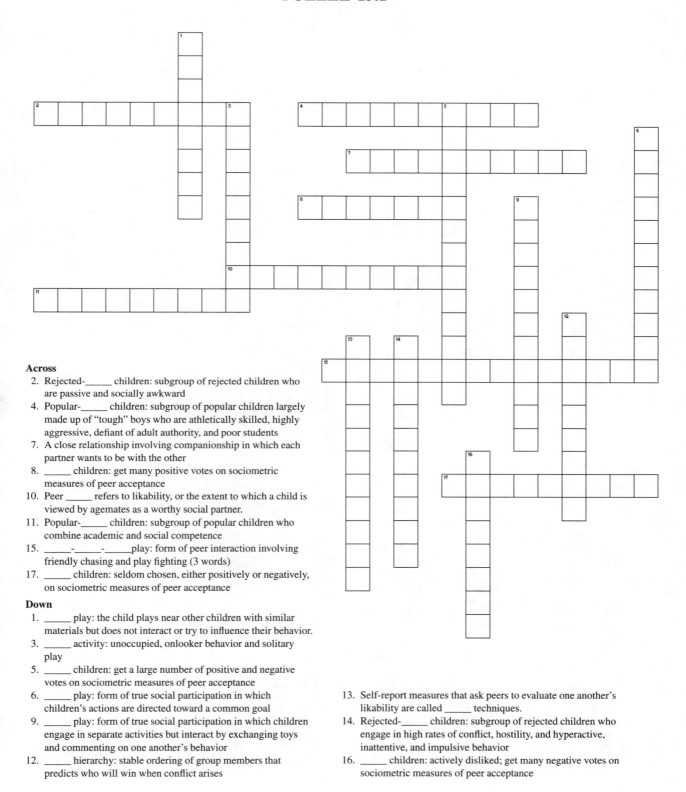

Across

2. Rejected-_____ children: subgroup of rejected children who are passive and socially awkward
4. Popular-_____ children: subgroup of popular children largely made up of "tough" boys who are athletically skilled, highly aggressive, defiant of adult authority, and poor students
7. A close relationship involving companionship in which each partner wants to be with the other
8. _____ children: get many positive votes on sociometric measures of peer acceptance
10. Peer _____ refers to likability, or the extent to which a child is viewed by agemates as a worthy social partner.
11. Popular-_____ children: subgroup of popular children who combine academic and social competence
15. _____-_____-_____play: form of peer interaction involving friendly chasing and play fighting (3 words)
17. _____ children: seldom chosen, either positively or negatively, on sociometric measures of peer acceptance

Down

1. _____ play: the child plays near other children with similar materials but does not interact or try to influence their behavior.
3. _____ activity: unoccupied, onlooker behavior and solitary play
5. _____ children: get a large number of positive and negative votes on sociometric measures of peer acceptance
6. _____ play: form of true social participation in which children's actions are directed toward a common goal
9. _____ play: form of true social participation in which children engage in separate activities but interact by exchanging toys and commenting on one another's behavior
12. _____ hierarchy: stable ordering of group members that predicts who will win when conflict arises
13. Self-report measures that ask peers to evaluate one another's likability are called _____ techniques.
14. Rejected-_____ children: subgroup of rejected children who engage in high rates of conflict, hostility, and hyperactive, inattentive, and impulsive behavior
16. _____ children: actively disliked; get many negative votes on sociometric measures of peer acceptance

PUZZLE 15.2

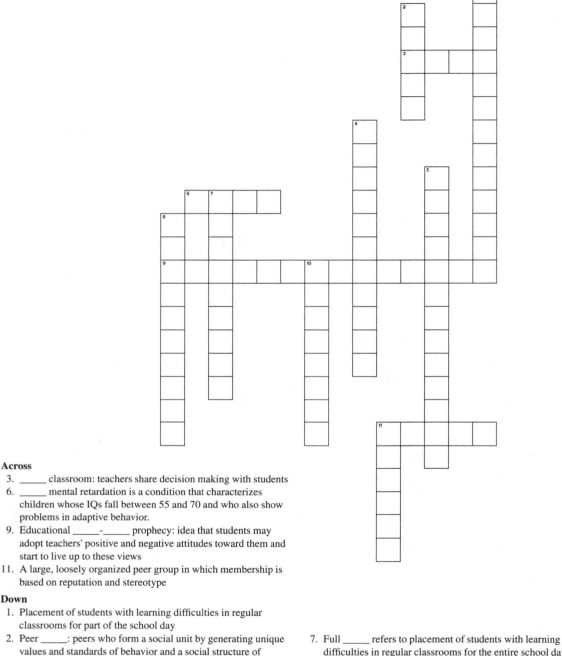

Across

3. _____ classroom: teachers share decision making with students
6. _____ mental retardation is a condition that characterizes children whose IQs fall between 55 and 70 and who also show problems in adaptive behavior.
9. Educational _____-_____ prophecy: idea that students may adopt teachers' positive and negative attitudes toward them and start to live up to these views
11. A large, loosely organized peer group in which membership is based on reputation and stereotype

Down

1. Placement of students with learning difficulties in regular classrooms for part of the school day
2. Peer _____: peers who form a social unit by generating unique values and standards of behavior and a social structure of leaders and followers
4. _____ classroom: children are regarded as passive learners who acquire information presented by teachers
5. Peer _____: destructive form of peer interaction in which certain children become frequent targets of verbal and physical attacks or other forms of abuse

7. Full _____ refers to placement of students with learning difficulties in regular classrooms for the entire school day.
8. Learning _____: great difficulty with one or more aspects of learning that results in poor school achievement, despite average to above average IQ
10. The task of learning television's specialized symbolic code of conveying information is known as television _____.
11. A small group of about five to seven peers who are friends

PRACTICE TEST

1. In _____ play, a child plays near another child, with similar materials, but they do not interact. (p. 599)
   a. nonsocial
   b. parallel
   c. associative
   d. cooperative

2. Recent research on peer interaction indicates that: (p. 600)
   a. it is the *type*, rather than the *amount*, of play that changes during early childhood.
   b. Parten's play types emerge in a developmental sequence, with later-appearing ones replacing earlier ones.
   c. nonsocial activity among preschoolers is a sign of maladjustment.
   d. sociodramatic play declines during the preschool years.

3. Rough-and-tumble play: (p. 601)
   a. cannot be distinguished from aggressive fighting.
   b. is characterized by friendly chasing and play fighting.
   c. takes the same form for both boys and girls.
   d. is an important indicator of social skills deficits.

4. During middle childhood: (p. 605)
   a. children view a friend as someone who likes you, with whom you spend a lot of time playing, and with whom you share toys.
   b. children regard trust as the defining feature of friendships.
   c. children stress intimacy and loyalty as the most significant features of friendship.
   d. children regard friendship as a consensual relationship involving companionship, sharing, understanding of thoughts and feelings, and caring for one another in times of need.

5. Research on the characteristics of children's friendships shows that: (p. 607)
   a. friendships are highly unstable in early and middle childhood.
   b. beginning in the preschool years, children become highly selective about their friendships.
   c. children are far less likely to disagree and compete with friends than with nonfriends.
   d. in selecting friends, young adolescents begin to focus less on similarity to oneself and more on superficial features such as popularity, physical attractiveness, and athletic skill.

6. Research on peer acceptance indicates that: (p. 610)
   a. all children fit into one of the four categories of peer acceptance—popular, rejected, neglected, or controversial.
   b. rejected children, in particular, are at risk for poor school performance, absenteeism, dropping out, and antisocial behavior.
   c. peer status during the school years is unrelated to later adjustment.
   d. controversial children have few friends and are typically unhappy with their peer relationships.

7. Research on social behavior indicates that: (p. 610)
   a. neglected children are usually well adjusted.
   b. rejected-withdrawn children display a blend of positive and negative social behaviors.
   c. controversial children are at high risk for social exclusion.
   d. popular-prosocial children are often "tough" boys who are athletically skilled but poor students.

8. Which of the following is true of children's first peer relationships? (p. 613)
   a. Peer groups are highly stable, even when children experience a change in classroom setting.
   b. Once children begin to form peer groups, relational and overt aggression toward "outgroup" members declines dramatically.
   c. Peer groups often direct their hostilities toward no-longer "respected" children within their own group.
   d. Formal group ties (e.g., scouting, 4-H) are ineffective for meeting school-age children's desire for group belonging.

9. Adolescent crowds: (p. 614)
   a. are more intimate than cliques.
   b. become increasingly important across adolescence.
   c. are typically small groups of about five to seven members who are close friends.
   d. are based on reputation and stereotype.

10. Peers would be most likely to influence one another's: (p. 616)
   a. religious values.
   b. choice of college.
   c. choice of clothes.
   d. career plans.

11. Research on children's television viewing shows that: (p. 620)
    a. during early childhood, children are inattentive to most TV shows because they have difficulty following the fast-paced character movement, special effects, loud music, and nonhuman speech.
    b. when involved in other activities, children rarely attend to the TV soundtrack in the background.
    c. not until age 7 do children fully grasp the unreality of TV fiction.
    d. by age 4, children can detect the motives and consequences of a TV character's behavior.

12. TV violence: (p. 621)
    a. hardens children to aggression, making them more willing to tolerate it in others.
    b. teaches children that violence is socially unacceptable and has harsh negative consequences.
    c. is unlikely to increase violent behavior, even among highly aggressive children.
    d. is uncommon in children's programming, particularly cartoons.

13. Research suggests that children who watch *Sesame Street*: (p. 622)
    a. score higher on tests designed to measure the program's learning objectives.
    b. experience only minimal, short-term gains in academic achievement.
    c. display less elaborate make-believe play.
    d. score significantly higher than other children on childhood intelligence tests.

14. Which of the following is true of computers in classrooms? (p. 624)
    a. Computers benefit children cognitively but hinder them socially since they result in less collaborative work between students.
    b. The use of computers for word-processing results in shorter, lower quality written products.
    c. It is recommended that word-processing replace other classroom writing experiences.
    d. Computer programming is associated with improved concept formation, problem solving, and creativity.

15. Children's computer games: (p. 625)
    a. are equally appealing to boys and girls.
    b. foster attentional and spatial skills in boys and girls alike when they emphasize speed and action.
    c. have less impact than does television violence in promoting hostility and aggression.
    d. rarely contain ethnic and gender stereotypes.

16. Research on the effects of class and student body size indicates that: (p. 626)
    a. small class size is associated with higher achievement in reading and math, particularly for minority students.
    b. regular-size classes are as effective as small classes when teacher's aides are placed in these classrooms.
    c. large high schools are more beneficial for students because they provide more social support and more opportunities for enrichment.
    d. "marginal" students are at less risk for high school dropout in large schools than in small schools.

17. In an open classroom: (p. 627)
    a. the teacher is the sole authority for knowledge, rules, and decision making.
    b. teachers share decision making with students and rate children's progress in relation to their own prior development.
    c. older students show a slight edge in academic achievement.
    d. students fail to learn appropriate study habits and report lower ratings of school liking compared to students in traditional classrooms.

18. Research on school transitions shows that: (p. 631)
    a. the earlier the transition occurs, the more dramatic and long-lasting its negative impact on psychological well-being, especially for girls.
    b. earlier transitions are associated with negative outcomes for boys, whereas later transitions are associated with negative outcomes for girls.
    c. the transition from junior high to high school is relatively problem-free for most adolescents and rarely has an affect on academic achievement.
    d. young people identified as "multiple problem" youths tend to show improved adjustment following the transition to high school.

19. Which of the following is an effective way to ease the strain of school transition in adolescence? (pp. 631–632)
    a. reorganizing schools into 6-3-3 arrangements rather than 8-4 arrangements
    b. making sure that academic expectations in junior high are tougher than those in elementary school
    c. assigning students to classes with several familiar peers or a constant group of new peers
    d. reducing the number of extracurricular activities available in high school so that students have more time to focus on academic work

20. The term *educational self-fulfilling prophecy* refers to the idea that: (p. 632)
    a. children may adopt teachers' positive or negative attitudes toward them and start to live up to these expectations.
    b. students' self-esteem and attitudes toward school are enhanced by placement in a multigrade classroom.
    c. high-achieving students typically experience more positive interactions with teachers than do low-achieving students.
    d. students with learning disabilities should be placed in regular classrooms for part of the day in order to better prepare them for participation in society.

21. Research on ability grouping shows that: (p. 633)
    a. students in low-ability groups evidence gains in academic achievement since instruction is adapted to meet their needs.
    b. mixed-ability classes are preferable, at least into the early years of secondary school.
    c. good students from low-SES families are just as likely to be placed in academically oriented, college-bound tracks as are students of equal ability from middle-SES homes.
    d. mixed-ability groups stifle high-achieving students and provide few, if any, intellectual or social benefits to low-achieving students.

22. Mainstreaming refers to: (p. 634)
    a. full-time placement of students with disabilities in regular classrooms.
    b. placement of students with disabilities in regular classrooms for part of the school day.
    c. homogeneous grouping of students with disabilities in a self-contained classroom.
    d. full-time placement of students with disabilities in a resource room, where they work with a special education teacher on an individual and small group basis.

23. Research on the educational placement of students with disabilities reveals that: (p. 635)
    a. mainstreaming and full inclusion provide all students with the greatest academic benefit.
    b. mainstreamed students are usually well-accepted by regular classroom peers.
    c. students with disabilities do best when placed in a resource room for part of the day and in a regular classroom for the remainder of the day.
    d. mainstreaming and full inclusion do not have any benefit for students with disabilities.

24. Cross-national research on academic achievement indicates that: (p. 638)
    a. the math and science performance of U. S. secondary school students far exceeds that of students in other industrialized nations.
    b. while Asian students show an advantage over American students in science and math, U. S. students score higher than their Asian counterparts on measures of reading achievement.
    c. Asian students are smarter and start school with cognitive advantages over their American peers.
    d. the achievement of U. S. elementary and secondary students has improved over the past decade in reading, math, and science, although not enough to enhance their standing internationally.

25. High school students who work more than 15 hours per week: (p. 639)
    a. develop a sense of responsibility which often leads to improved academic performance.
    b. develop many job skills that help them gain employment after high school.
    c. have poor school attendance and lower grades.
    d. develop positive attitudes about work life.

PUZZLE 1.1

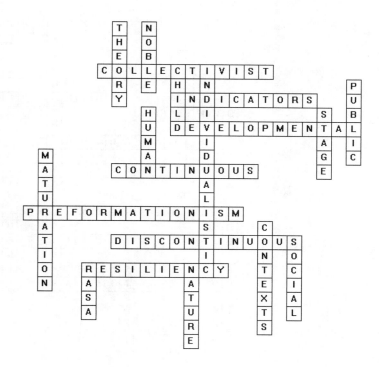

PUZZLE 1.2

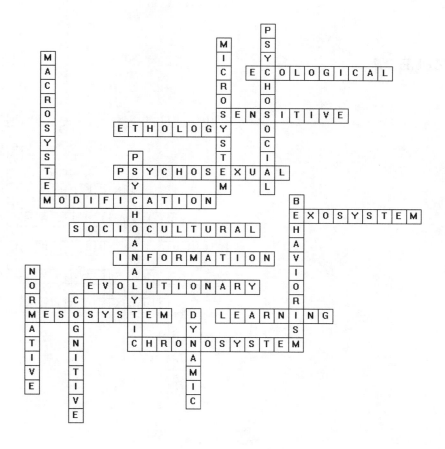

497

PUZZLE 2.1

PUZZLE 2.2

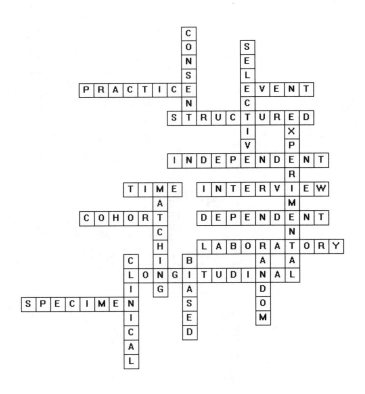

498

PUZZLE 3.1

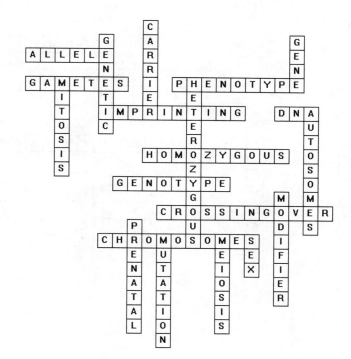

PUZZLE 3.2

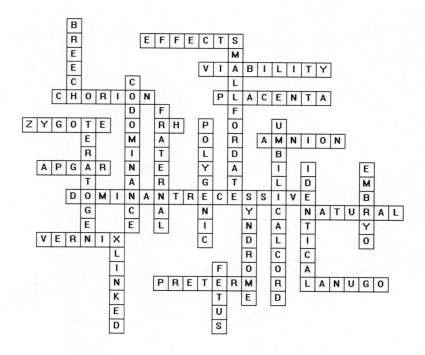

PUZZLE 3.3

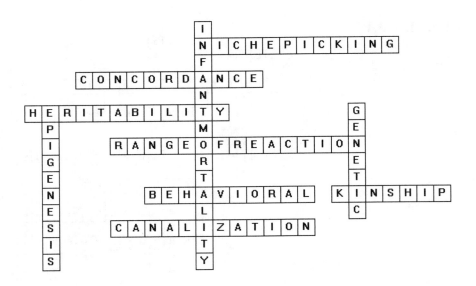

PUZZLE 4.1

500

PUZZLE 4.2

PUZZLE 5.1

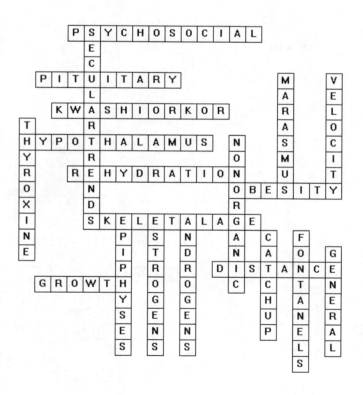

PUZZLE 5.2

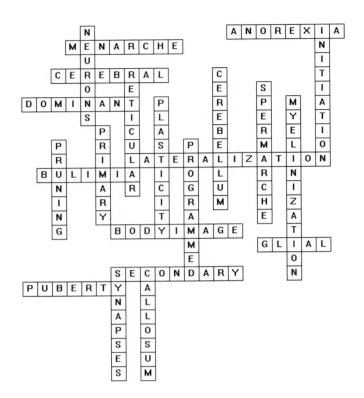

PUZZLE 6.1

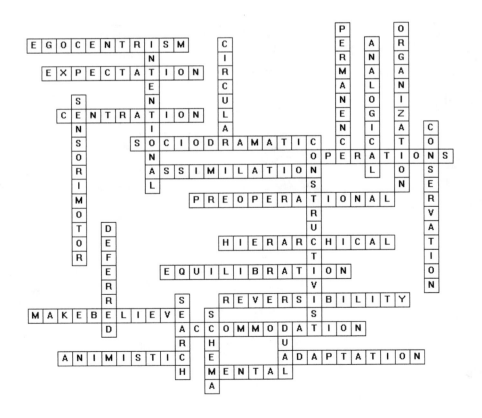

PUZZLE 6.2

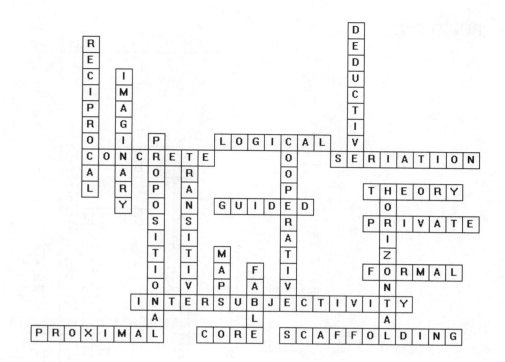

PUZZLE 7.1

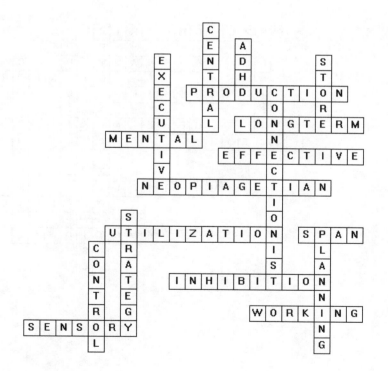

503

PUZZLE 7.2

PUZZLE 8.1

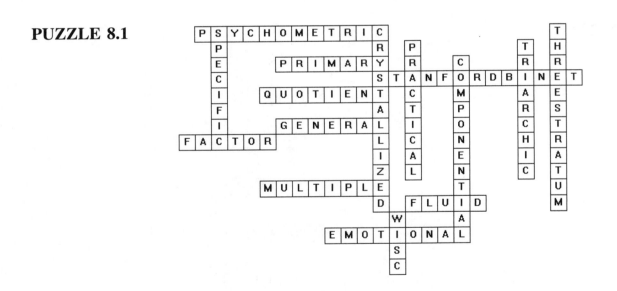

PUZZLE 8.2

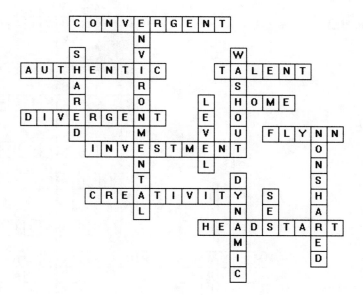

PUZZLE 9.1

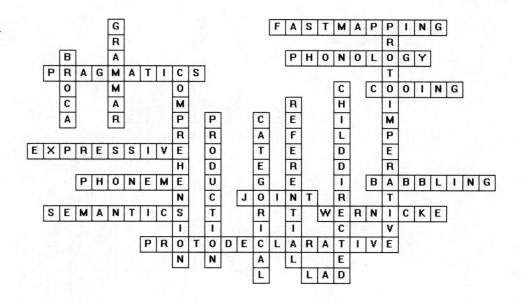

505

PUZZLE 9.2

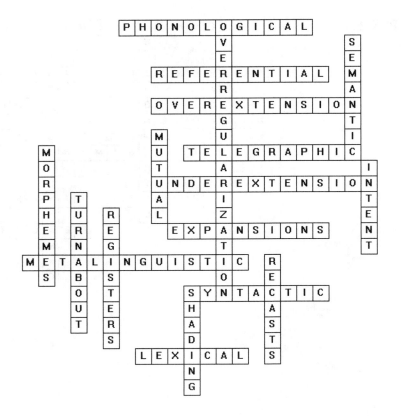

PUZZLE 10.1

PUZZLE 10.2

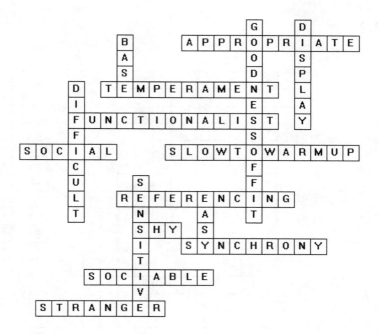

PUZZLE 11.1

PUZZLE 11.2

PUZZLE 12.1

508

PUZZLE 12.2

PUZZLE 13.1

PUZZLE 14

PUZZLE 15.1

PUZZLE 15.2

ANSWERS TO PRACTICE TESTS

CHAPTER 1

1. C	6. C	11. C	16. C	21. C
2. B	7. D	12. D	17. A	22. A
3. B	8. B	13. B	18. A	23. A
4. D	9. D	14. D	19. B	24. C
5. A	10. B	15. B	20. B	25. B

CHAPTER 2

1. A	6. A	11. C	16. A	21. C
2. B	7. C	12. B	17. B	22. A
3. D	8. B	13. B	18. D	23. C
4. B	9. D	14. C	19. C	24. C
5. B	10. A	15. A	20. B	25. A

CHAPTER 3

1. B	6. C	11. C	16. C	21. B
2. D	7. A	12. A	17. A	22. C
3. A	8. D	13. C	18. C	23. A
4. A	9. C	14. A	19. A	24. A
5. C	10. D	15. D	20. B	25. C

CHAPTER 4

1. A	6. B	11. C	16. A	21. A
2. D	7. A	12. B	17. C	22. B
3. B	8. C	13. C	18. B	23. A
4. A	9. D	14. B	19. C	24. B
5. C	10. A	15. C	20. D	25. C

CHAPTER 5

1. D	6. A	11. A	16. B	21. C
2. C	7. B	12. B	17. D	22. C
3. D	8. D	13. B	18. C	23. A
4. C	9. D	14. C	19. B	24. C
5. B	10. D	15. D	20. C	25. B

CHAPTER 6

1. A	6. C	11. B	16. C	21. A
2. B	7. B	12. C	17. A	22. A
3. C	8. A	13. B	18. D	23. D
4. D	9. A	14. C	19. B	24. D
5. A	10. D	15. A	20. B	25. B

CHAPTER 7

1. D	6. C	11. C	16. D	21. B
2. C	7. B	12. B	17. C	22. A
3. C	8. B	13. B	18. A	23. D
4. A	9. A	14. B	19. B	24. C
5. A	10. C	15. B	20. B	25. D

CHAPTER 8

1. D	6. C	11. A	16. A	21. B
2. A	7. B	12. B	17. C	22. A
3. C	8. D	13. C	18. B	23. B
4. B	9. C	14. C	19. A	24. B
5. B	10. C	15. C	20. B	25. A

CHAPTER 9

1. B	6. A	11. C	16. C	21. A
2. B	7. D	12. B	17. B	22. C
3. A	8. C	13. A	18. B	23. B
4. D	9. B	14. C	19. D	24. C
5. C	10. A	15. D	20. D	25. D

CHAPTER 10

1. A	6. D	11. B	16. C	21. D
2. C	7. B	12. D	17. C	22. A
3. D	8. A	13. B	18. D	23. C
4. B	9. B	14. D	19. C	24. A
5. B	10. C	15. B	20. B	25. A

CHAPTER 11

1. D	6. C	11. A	16. D	21. A
2. A	7. A	12. C	17. A	22. C
3. C	8. A	13. B	18. D	23. A
4. C	9. C	14. B	19. B	24. B
5. B	10. C	15. D	20. D	25. D

CHAPTER 12

1. B	6. C	11. A	16. B	21. A
2. C	7. D	12. A	17. C	22. C
3. A	8. C	13. C	18. B	23. C
4. B	9. C	14. A	19. C	24. A
5. D	10. B	15. D	20. C	25. C

CHAPTER 13

1. C	6. B	11. C	16. C	21. D
2. C	7. A	12. B	17. B	22. C
3. D	8. C	13. C	18. D	23. D
4. C	9. B	14. A	19. B	24. C
5. D	10. D	15. D	20. A	25. B

CHAPTER 14

1. D	6. C	11. B	16. B	21. D
2. A	7. C	12. C	17. D	22. D
3. B	8. B	13. B	18. A	23. C
4. A	9. A	14. A	19. C	24. B
5. C	10. A	15. D	20. B	25. D

CHAPTER 15

1. B	6. B	11. C	16. A	21. B
2. A	7. A	12. A	17. B	22. B
3. B	8. C	13. A	18. A	23. C
4. B	9. D	14. D	19. C	24. D
5. D	10. C	15. B	20. A	25. C

NOTES

NOTES

NOTES

NOTES

NOTES